From

JO

THE COMING CHURCH

A fierce invasion from Heaven is drawing near.

The Coming Church

Revised 2014

Cover design and layout by John Burton
www.burtonsites.com

ISBN-13: 978-1493599387

ISBN-10: 1493599380

Published by Significant Publishing

Printed in the United States of America

To pastors and church leaders, I honor you.
I am both humbled and excited about the opportunity to
run the race of revival with you.

is a church planter, conference speaker and author with a mandate to see the fire of God's presence invade cities and nations. He planted Revolution Church in Manitou Springs, Colorado and Revival Church in Detroit, Michigan.

John's ministry style could be described as wildly passionate, engaging, humorous and loaded with the flow and power of the Holy Spirit.

The prevailing theme of the ministry God has given John revolves around the topic of encountering God. Where God is, things happen. In His presence, the place where He is, is the fullness of joy. As we discover the wonderful mystery of walking in the Spirit, praying always and making aggressive strides in faith, life becomes incredible!

It truly is an experience in the invisible realm. As we tangibly experience God through deep and active prayer, we are interacting *in the Spirit.* As we walk by faith and understand how amazing a Holy Spirit driven life is, being a Christian believer quickly becomes the greatest adventure on earth!

John is currently focused on teaching, consulting, writing and ministering to churches.

If you would like to invite John to speak at your church, conference, camp or other event, please visit johnburton.net.

This book will rock your boat! John Burton isn't an ordinary church leader. He is one of the emerging, cutting edge and at times raw (cuts to the chase) ministries who are changing the face of the church. Some will be upset with this book. Those lovers of God, radical revelatory types will jump up and down. John's book will set them on fire. Read with care. This is the future.

Barbara J Yoder
Senior Pastor and Lead Apostle
Shekinah Regional Apostolic Center
Breakthrough Apostolic Ministries Network
www.shekinahchurch.org
www.barbaraYODERblog.com

Want to grow your church? Increase your success and influence in the community? Don't read this book! John Burton isn't going to give you the latest Church growth strategies or messages that will make your life easier. This book is a clarion call to the Church to quit selling her birthright and to accomplish all God has for her. Anyone can criticize the church, John tears down while building up and calling fourth the Coming Glorious Church!

Chris Ferguson
Internships
International House of Prayer Kansas City

The Coming Church is a must read for every Christian. This is a timely word and challenge to seriously get aligned with the Kingdom for such a time as this. It will ignite an urgency and fire in any reader who is willing to wrestle and respond.

Amy Smith
Director of Intercession
Revival Church

A praying remnant will birth a great awakening that will change the church as we know it today. John, in this publication, provides some spiritual snapshots of a coming profound transformation of the church.

Rick Warzywak
Transformation Michigan

The spirit of God has rested upon John Burton; the Lord has placed fire in his hands. That translates in the intercession-driven ministry that pours out of him. The power & revelation the Lord has released into John Burton is a breath of fresh air. It is so fresh that I have not seen the uniqueness he bears elsewhere.

This book carries fire on every page. That fire leaps out bringing awakening to the deep places within you as the Holy Spirit moves through the revelation of the coming church and our part in it. There's no denying it, and there's no hiding it as the revelatory words are laid out on the table. This book screams 'Ready or not, here I (the church) come!' Are we ready to receive the revelation? Better yet, are we willing to receive it?

Jill Janco
Experience Department Director
Revival Church

This is more than a book, it's a mandate from heaven! It is a culmination of the revelations from heaven we have been learning through Apostle John Burton. The coming church is volatile and ready to explode! There is much danger ahead as we come against systems, tradition, and everything that is held so dear to the hearts of those not willing to come to the mountain. This is a calling out to those who will see the vision and respond with brokenness, humility and boldness!

I believe many will respond to the call. Though it will be amazing and many will be set free, it will cost everything! Are you willing to respond or are you going to stay where it is safe? The structure that is seemingly safe now will be destroyed. Now is the time to take a stand on new, dangerous ground, the solid rock of The Coming Church!

Whatever city God has you planted is where you are needed to become the awakening and birth many more laborers through intercession, modeling Christ and revival (biblical normalcy). Allow God to do a new thing in you and your region! Many are called to take a city, how many will submit, respond and endure!?

Nick Carrier
Product of Jesus' Holy Spirit & theLab School of Fire
Intercessor at the Detroit Prayer Furnace

I just finished reading your book and it's excellent! The only way I would have enjoyed it more is if I had been sitting with a group of like-minded people while I read it and we could have gotten excited together! It was kind of like watching a football game by yourself where your team is trouncing the opposing team and you have no one to cheer with and shout, "YES!" I so wanted to do that!

Personally, I say, yay for the confrontation. It's time! It kind of reminds me of the confrontation in 1 Kings 18 with the Elijah and the prophets of Baal.

What you write in this book certainly resonates very deeply with me. At times I have written in our Community Healing Rooms email newsletters or made a post on Facebook with nearly identical sentiments.

I have always liked your fiery hot passion for the Lord, John! Please keep going! Don't stop! We need you; Detroit needs you.

Keep running with His torch!

Beverly Bubb
Healing Rooms
Michigan State Directors

From a vision of Hell, to Pikes Peak and Manitou Springs to Detroit! This riveting book details John's incredible journey and message that may shake, rattle and roll your current lifestyle and belief systems—just as John the Baptist's message did in his day!! This book is a wake up call to the sleeping Bride of Christ to take her place and be the church God has mandated—a House of Prayer for all Nations! This is our destiny. This is our call!

Leah Hanrahan
Children's Director
Revival Church

Are you a sold out, on fire, disciple of the Lord Jesus Christ, walking in the tremendous power and dominion God has ordained for His last days Church? If not, this book will show you how to become one. It will enable you to take your position in God's victorious end-time army and prevail against the forces of darkness that would steal your destiny. In it, John Burton exposes the snares of the enemy pervasive in the culture and the doctrines of demons that have invaded God's church. Get equipped, put on your battle armor, take your position and prepare to wage war with the enemies of The Cross. The eternal destinies of perhaps a billion souls are hanging in the balance. Will you receive, internalize and walk out the message of this book for King Jesus, the Glory of His Kingdom and the souls He has placed within your sphere of influence?

Ed Hull
Revival Church

The Coming Church will bring reformation to what religious systems have been teaching and of what they communicate church is "supposed" to be like. This book will bring awakening to anyone that reads it. It isn't a "feel good" message, it's one that will bring awakening through the truth and revelation that God has given to John Burton on what The Coming Church will be like.

David Gooding

CONTENTS

~ *Forward* ~

Brian Simmons

Stairway Ministries & The Passion Translation Project

There was a man sent from God whose name was John. The anointed Baptizer refused to yield to the status quo; the lethargy of those around him couldn't stick to him, for he was sent from God. The atmosphere of heaven's reality clothed him, and his words lit a fire. He was the greatest man who had ever lived in human history, up to his time. A burning and shining lamp for God. Everything he said and everything he did was to point people to the coming Messiah, the King who would seize the hearts of men.

The Lord is giving us another glimpse of that powerful grace in the lives of awakeners today. The anointing of John the Baptist is being restored to the Church! There is a desperation growing in the hearts of God's people, for desperate times will always demand that desperate men arise. I am thankful to see that anointing rise upon

God's men and women today who refuse to march to the incessant drumbeat of this culture. But instead, they will eat locusts and honey, wearing not the religious garments of pride and superiority but the humble garment of a camel's skin. There is a company of men and women who will turn the dark night into a bright light—daybreakers are rising to bring the dawning of awakening to the nations!

I'm thankful for men like John Burton who hear a sound coming out of heaven, a trumpet sound, calling this generation to something more than good meetings and life as usual. We need men and women who are more than echoes of the past, but voices who prophesy what is to come. I believe those men and women are being prepared to arise and take their place in human history. A message of The Coming Church is needed more than ever! The Holy Spirit has anointed this message, and it will roll on throughout the nations. The call of God is gripping hearts of awakeners to leave the predictability of the church and move into the reality of the ever-fresh kingdom of God!

God has in store a day, a day of glory, that will unveil Jesus Christ before our eyes. But we need to be awakened by the sound. I'm glad to hear that sound as I read through The Coming Church! I see the awakening in my soul, I hear the sound of the church migrating from our lax Laodicean ways and rushing into the dawning of a new day! Revival is in the air and The Coming Church will be alive and well, exporting the glory to the nations. You can be thankful that you live in this day. I am. I'm very thankful to be alive and serving God. I will tell my grandchildren that we lived for days of His manifest presence. Be encouraged as you read this book, written by another John, sent by God for our generation. I know you'll want to read it more than once and share it with your friends. Get ready for the fires of awakening, and keep your heart tender and pure, for the coming of the Lord draws near!

Brian Simmons
Stairway Ministries
The Passion Translation Project

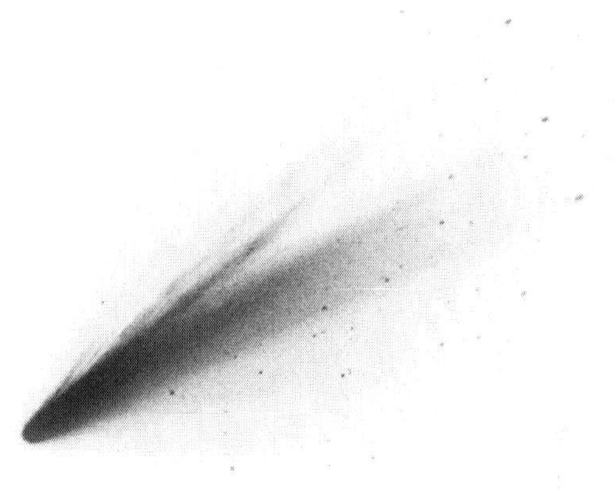

~ One ~
The Encounter

The Coming Church will be shocking.

Spiritual encounters, whether they are visions, dreams or visitations, can go a long way in preparing individuals, groups, and even nations for the otherworldly, dramatic and critical shifts that God is setting into motion. Of course, we know in Scripture that spiritual things must be discerned spiritually, and it's important to understand clearly what's being communicated. We also know that all dreams, for example, are not necessarily spiritual dreams. That must be discerned. I challenge you to stay up until 3AM and then consume a bucket of hot wings, a can of Mountain Dew and a half a gallon of ice cream and see what kind of crazy images dance around in your head when you finally fall asleep. Experiences like that won't shake nations. However, the encounter I had absolutely must.

I had a vision of the *soon coming Church*. For me, a spiritual revelation, a message delivered directly by the Creator of the world, is usually very easy to discern. It's rare that I have to go to someone seeking out an interpretation. The scene and the message are almost always extremely vivid and revealing. I immediately understand what the players, atmosphere and story line are attempting to communicate to me.

> America doesn't need another bed-and-breakfast church that comforts our flesh.
>
> Our nation needs a Church with a volatile atmosphere that explodes, burns human flesh and shocks our culture.

This particular encounter was no different—in fact, it was so striking, fearful, engulfing and overpowering that the imagery and message will keep me trembling in my spirit forever.

In order to appreciate the magnitude of the message that was communicated to me in the vision, it will be helpful to understand the context. Try to imagine, at least to an incredibly small degree, the picture of the true Church that God himself sees. It shouldn't be a stretch to realize the picture of the compromised Church that we see on the Earth today clearly cannot match up. Meaning, when God drew up the designs for the glorious Church, leading up to its launch in the book of Acts, the blueprint that was before him looks *little* like the Church we see today. God's Church looks *little* like the Church we have come to know.

> *When the Day of Pentecost had fully come, they were all with one accord in one place. And suddenly there came a sound from heaven, as of a rushing mighty wind, and it filled the*

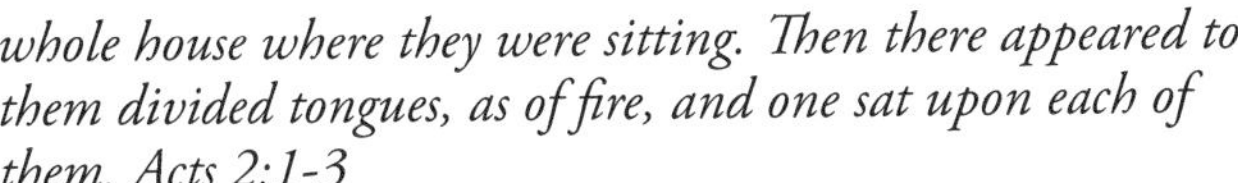

> *whole house where they were sitting. Then there appeared to them divided tongues, as of fire, and one sat upon each of them. Acts 2:1-3*

Do me a favor and read that passage in Acts chapter 2 one more time. I want those three verses to dive into your spirit and shake you up. When God started diagramming the Church, this is what he envisioned—this is where he started. When you compare this passage of Scripture with descriptions of the modern-day Church as we know it, it seems like we are comparing apples and oranges, or even the living and the dead.

I'd like to ask you to read the passage one more time. As I'm writing this, I feel the Spirit of the Lord starting to burn in my inner man. Let me pray for you right now just before you read it again:

> *Mighty God, I pray the burnings of your Spirit would be transmitted into your friend's heart. Give them a glimpse into the supernatural yet strikingly real realm of the Church. Give them the capacity to release old paradigms, structures, traditions, mind sets and cultures as they come alive to the reality of the Church as you see it. Amen.*

Okay, go ahead and read the passage in Acts chapter 2 one more time.

> *When the Day of Pentecost had fully come, they were all with one accord in one place. And suddenly there came a sound from heaven, as of a rushing mighty wind, and it filled the whole house where they were sitting. Then there appeared to them divided tongues, as of fire, and one sat upon each of them. Acts 2:1-3*

Is it becoming a little bit easier to understand just what the Church should look like? You see, as God designed and then launched the Church, it was literally blowing and burning and every

one of those in that upper room experienced it. As we begin to embrace the truth that passages like this are not science fiction, and that they communicate actual phenomena that are expected to be normal for us as believers, it will become easier to leave behind what we know and press toward the soon coming Church. We will suddenly find ourselves so deeply dissatisfied that any thought of maintenance becomes quite ridiculous.

America doesn't need another bed-and-breakfast church that comforts our flesh (our natural desires). Our nation needs a Church with a volatile atmosphere that explodes, burns human flesh and shocks our culture.

Now, keep in mind that this fiery Acts 2 reality was communicated to us by the Spirit through the Word. This passage is the Word of God, not simply a descriptive, historical report. So, God's plan is for the Church to be a supernatural raging furnace of Holy Spirit activity.

Mark 7:13 reveals how powerful tradition of man is. It actually makes the Word of God ineffective! The traditions of man overpower the greatest power in existence—Jesus Christ himself. Do you feel the weight of that? Is it possible that we need to embrace the fear of the Lord again? There is a holy tremble that will come as the fierceness of God is revealed to us at the same time the burning love of God does. The thought of allowing man-made concepts, structures or agendas to push aside and nullify God's plans seems nonsensical. Yet it happens with stunning regularity every day all over the world.

> *...making the word of God of no effect through your tradition which you have handed down... Mark 7:13*

Of course it's true that the definition of the Church cannot be limited to a perspective of one segment of the greater structure. It is certainly true, as is revealed later on in Acts chapter 2, that the healthy Church will include Kingdom-focused fellowship, breaking of bread, bold proclamation of the Gospel, discipleship, evangelism, prayer and other critical activities. However, what we see in the Church today is a lot of activity, even good activity, but usually without the tangible burning and blowing of God's Spirit.

The Crater

If you take a look at the cover of this book, you will see a futilely poor attempt at visually communicating what I experienced in my vision. In the vision, I found myself in a dramatic, apocalyptic scene. Everything seemed to be colorless, or at best a variety of dark blues, grays and greens. The ominous clouds matched up with the dark and wild landscape all around me.

Directly in front of me was the focal point of the vision, a tremendously massive crater. I can't begin to describe in human language the overwhelmingly weighty, urgent, and fearsome atmosphere that gripped me and demanded my complete attention. I was trembling as I looked at the edge of the crater in the distance. As I slowly walked toward the gigantic hole in the ground, I knew I could not approach it casually. The fear of the Lord surrounded me. I couldn't imagine what type of alien invasion could have created an impression this deep in such solid ground. The force had to have been greater than anything my human mind could comprehend.

As I was analyzing the drama that I was experiencing, God revealed to me that the crater I was drawing near to was not simply a hole in the ground. It was, in fact, the coming Church. The Church? My mind certainly couldn't even begin to analyze what that meant, but my spirit was raging. My mind presumed I should be looking at a small white church building with a steeple, but that was not at all what my spiritual eyes were seeing.

My spirit was provoked and alive, but I knew that those who were more logical than spiritual in their life experience would most probably resist what is just over the horizon.

But the natural man does not receive the things of the Spirit of God, for they are foolishness to him; nor can he know them, because they are spiritually discerned. 1 Corinthians 2:14

Note that this doesn't mean the unsaved; it means those who are naturally minded. That's a lot of Christians. Here's what Paul says next:

And I, brethren, could not speak to you as to spiritual people but as to carnal, as to babes in Christ. I fed you with milk and not with solid food; for until now you were not able to receive it, and even now you are still not able; 1 Corinthians 3:1-2

I continued to tremble as the increasingly intense, colorless atmosphere engulfed me, and as I ever so carefully, fearfully, yet with intense curiosity approached the edge of the coming Church, the crater.

Again, I realized I couldn't casually participate. This was a very clear message that I was receiving. The days of casually connecting in secular fellowship in the Church were over. The shaking and trembling rocked my whole being as I approached this invasion of Heaven on Earth.

Once at the edge, I was stunned and my senses were overwhelmed as I looked at what seemed to be alive. While everything else around me was grayscale, I saw vivid, bright and glowing, neon hues of orange, yellow and red and a prism of colors in between. The bright, colorful, burning lava was living and active. It was moving, coursing throughout the crater. My trembling intensified.

Holocaust?

I received an email from someone in theLab University, our ministry training center, here in the Detroit area. The message instantly received my attention when I saw the content contained the word holocaust. Of course, that's a provocative and sensitive word and it takes some care to handle it when applying it to current situations.

The email was sent to several of us at theLab in reference to a conference I was about to minister at. I'll share the complete, unedited email so you have a full glimpse of what was being communicated. Keep the vision of the crater in mind as you read.

> *Hey Fellow Fireball Launchers! I've been hit w/ this urgency thing to pray for John, his upcoming trip to Connecticut to speak at the conference w/ Brian Simmons & James Levesque, & well, the conference as a whole. I just feel like we need to rally around him & call down fire on this conference! I'm feelin that God is gonna break through in a crazy way during this, & John is carrying this crazy powerful message. As the Lord impressed it on my heart to pray, I heard 1 word... holocaust. At first, the only thing that came to mind was "the" holocaust of World War II. After my initial thoughts on the word subsided, I started to think about the word. As I was talking to the Lord, I kept asking "What do you mean?". He prompted me to look up the definition.*
>
> *Here it is:*
>
> *hol•o•caust noun*
>
> 1. *a great or complete devastation or destruction, especially by fire.*
> 2. *a sacrifice completely consumed by fire; burnt offering (Dictionary.com Unabridged. Retrieved October 23, 2013, from Dictionary.com website: http://dictionary.reference.com/browse/HOLOCAUST)*
>
> *Hah! How crazy is that? I'm not even sure what else to say right now, but whoah! It feels like the meaning He's relaying is not negative. It feels powerful! Still grasping the full context of what's going on here, but I do know that God is bringin down the house with this one!!*

This word was given right after I shared the vision of the crater with the students and staff at theLab. What is coming to the Church is not an enhancement or an adjustment. The destruction (or we could use the word deconstruction) will be so comprehensive and total that it will not only remove current structures, but also the faulty foundations (anything other than the foundation of Christ) they were built on. The coming Church will look nothing like the Church we now know.

Instead of hoping for God to manifest in our natural realm alone we will begin manifesting in God's supernatural realm!

This transformation will take us well beyond our human ability to understand. I believe God intentionally overwhelmed me with such a vivid vision while also leaving almost every question unanswered. This plan for reformation won't easily translate into a formulaic church growth process. The only way we can apply it to our own situation is by falling on our faces, being consumed by another world and submitting ourselves to the risky, vulnerable and shocking process of transformation.

> *Trust in the LORD with all your heart, And lean not on your own understanding; In all your ways acknowledge Him, And He shall direct your paths. Do not be wise in your own eyes; Fear the LORD and depart from evil. Proverbs 3:5-7*

Check out this simple yet profoundly important quote by Andrew Murray:

> *Beware in your prayers, above everything else, of limiting God, not only by unbelief, but by fancying that you know what He can do. (Christian Reader, v. 32, n. 4.)*

We are all too often guilty of praying for what we can see or imagine. The dynamic life of prayer and faith doesn't even really begin until we venture outside of the realm of human senses. It's too easy to get consumed with what seems to be obvious and natural in our pursuits while forgetting that the majority of our answers and adventures sit just beyond the reach of our human understanding.

If this is true (which it is), then we must agree that God's picture of the Church is also painted with colors that exist outside of our earthly realm. This invasion of Heaven on Earth will result in an explosion of brilliance that we could never have imagined.

This is precisely what happened in the Upper Room. God was birthing the Church as only he could with revelation and power that only he had. There was no way for anybody in that room to possibly imagine what was coming no matter how creative they may have been.

In fact, their human futility was obvious just prior to the outpouring in the Upper Room. They were required to fulfill the mandate to find a replacement for the fallen Judas. Their process actually looks a lot like the decision-making processes of Christians today. They prayed and then cast lots.

> *And they cast their lots, and the lot fell on Matthias. And he was numbered with the eleven apostles. Acts 1:26*

They were so limited in revelation because the Holy Spirit had not yet been given to them—that they relied on human methods of decision making. They could do no better than pray and cast lots. Today's church is much like that—there's little revelation and little power so we do what is humanly understandable. The coming Church is both ancient and emerging. It's ancient because it's the Church founded through an empty tomb and a burning Upper Room. It's emerging because it's been largely forsaken. Humanism has replaced supernatural power. Humanistic efforts result in a limited, disappointing life.

However, when the Holy Spirit is in the mix, what is humanly impossible becomes the launching pad of Kingdom life. The transition that is coming will result in a shift of manifestation. Instead of hoping for God to manifest in our natural realm alone we will begin manifesting in God's supernatural realm!

As wonderful as it is, when we focus solely on God touching life as we know it in our earthly realm, we limit God. But when we venture beyond this world into the great expanse of the heavenly world, the possibilities of encounter, adventure, abundant life and Kingdom living are limitless.

I trust the idea of the Church being defined by a Sunday service with some worship songs and some teaching is looking quite ludicrous right about now.

~ *Two* ~

Celestial Elements

The Coming Church will be supernatural.

The day after I received the vision of the coming Church I was still processing through it. As I shared in the previous chapter, I decided to share the vision along with my clear, yet still limited interpretation with the class of interns at theLab.

It's not uncommon for me and others to receive prophetic revelation such as dreams, visions and words, especially during the feverishly hot spiritual environments when theLab is in session, and it can be at least somewhat common to share those impressions with the class. It's a prime environment to learn how to be intimately connected with the lover of our souls, and to hear the beating of his heart. It's quite powerful to communicate just what that beat feels and sounds like!

This particular class was different in every way. I was suddenly carrying a burning coal from the embers of God's heart, and I was undone from the inside out. A tremble was resonating throughout my being, and I knew I at least had to communicate what was happening. The problem was that I honestly didn't have full understanding of what was going on. My spirit was burning with revelation, but how would I put it in human language? What would I say? Would it even make sense to these growing and hungry students? Little did I realize, it was about to make perfect sense to all of us very quickly.

I addressed the students and let them know that something terrifying, yet desirous beyond description was revealed to me the previous evening. I had their attention. I proceeded to share the events just as I did with you in the previous chapter. I was in a state of burning and sobriety. It was quite clear that all attention was to be on what I was saying, and that it certainly wasn't time for interruptions.

I wasn't long into the encounter when one of the students, Kathy, suddenly got quite animated. She was popping her hand up and down, clearly wanting to be heard. I wasn't ready for any type of break because I was in the middle of sharing the revelation, so I asked her to wait until I finished. Throughout the remainder of the story, she was respectful as she waited her turn, but it was clear that something was awakened within. She was about to come out of her skin.

I ended by saying something like, *"I'm not sure what any of this means specifically, but I do know this—the Church as we know it is about to end. There is a fearful burning that is about to replace today's church culture with the supernatural force of God himself."*

Now it was Kathy's turn. Our unsettled student was about to bring revelation with great clarity.

Kathy said something along the lines of, *"I have been about to explode the entire time you were talking! I have to share with you something that I saw on National Geographic just before I left for class tonight!"*

What she shared next launched this revelation into an entirely different realm. She shared what she saw and later sent me the link to watch the documentary myself online. It was a brilliantly produced special on the ramifications of a massive asteroid crashing into the Earth.

The parallels to the encounter I had were remarkable. The question that was being considered in this documentary was this:

I was stunned as I found myself in the middle of one of the most significant revelations of my life.

What would happen to the Earth if a massive asteroid collided with it?

After listening to Kathy explain what she saw, I was provoked! I went home and watched the National Geographic special myself. I was stunned as I found myself in the middle of one of the most significant revelations of my life. As I watched, it was easy to see what God was saying. There is a coming collision and it will change everything. Here's the specific takeaway as I compared my vision with the very timely National Geographic special:

The Collision

The Size

The first point of interest was quite interesting indeed. When the asteroid collided with the Earth, it was so massive in size that the top of it was 30,000 feet in the air—where commercial jets fly! This documentary revealed the shocking ramifications of an alien rock that size colliding with the Earth. Shock and awe would not be sufficient to describe it.

Spiritual Application:

God is coming in such force that it will impact not only the Earth, but the Second Heaven (the atmosphere where the enemy moves freely) as well. The strong demonic influence on the Earth from the Second Heaven will take a mighty blow as Heaven invades Earth–on a path that takes it right through his domain. This doesn't mean the enemy will be disarmed. In fact, the demonic activity will intensify with great power, but the Church will be awakened into its authority and will see many demonic attacks thwarted. Confidence to advance the Kingdom of God will be at an all time high as a burning Church is broken and activated into its true authority. When God's forceful entry is experienced, everything that can be shaken will be shaken.

A Pillar of Fire

The documentary went on to dramatically explain that when the asteroid hit the Earth, a pillar of fire instantly exploded and reached from the surface of the Earth up into the heavens.

Spiritual Application:

The connection between Heaven and Earth, between God and his Church, will be a conduit of fire. The burning of the Holy Spirit will be raging as the Church and God are in constant encounter at a level never before known to man.

Regional Impact

Next, balls of fire shot out from the pillar and scorched regions far away from the point of impact.

Spiritual Application:

An impacted and supernaturally reformed Church will be so volatile, so explosive, that it will ignite fires in regions far away. A single impact in a single region will be so powerful that other cities will not only feel the Earth shake, but will be hit with the otherworldly fire as well.

World-Wide Impact

As I watched the dramatic presentation continue, the global impact became clear. A cloud of smoke then rose and actually surrounded the entire planet. The entire Earth was covered by the residual impact of the asteroid.

Spiritual Application:

The glory of God will cover the Earth! The residue of his activity will be felt all around the planet, capturing the attention of every nation. Nobody will be able to escape the impact, though many will resist it.

Heaven Impacting Earth

Celestial elements, parts of the asteroid that don't exist on this planet, were implanted into the ground.

Spiritual Application:

This is powerful! Heaven was brought to Earth! The Church will be infused with the very DNA of God. God himself will be coursing throughout.

Earthquakes

The narrator went on to explain that such a cataclysmic impact would result in earthquakes rocking the Earth all around.

Spiritual Application:

Everything, including the Earth itself will be shaken under the weight of God's presence. The Earth will groan.

Continual Burning

Molten rock filled the massive crater created by the asteroid.

Spiritual Application:

The coming Church will no longer be a place simply to hold human events while acknowledging God. It will be a place of burning that will destroy flesh and threaten kingdoms of man. The Church will be known by never-ending fire that won't be diminished for the apathetic or cautious.

After watching the documentary, I was shaking. How can we prepare for such an ominous, cataclysmic, life-altering and unavoidable event? The answer: we can prepare our hearts, but we can't stop its arrival.

We will all be crushed under the weight of God's coming Church–some gloriously, some tragically.

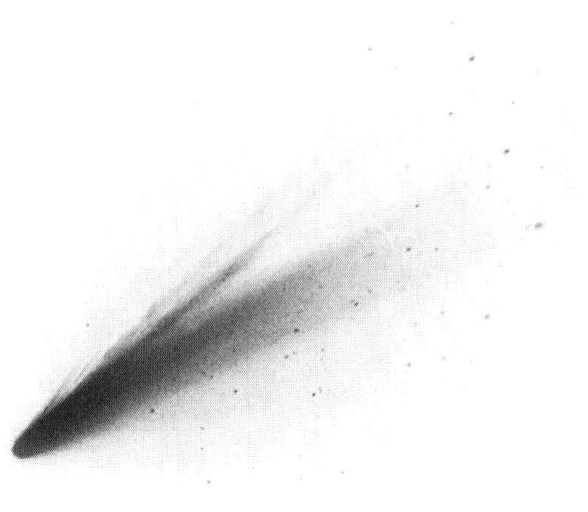

~ *Three* ~

A Troubling Shift

The Coming Church will bring sudden, surprising change.

The revelation that Kathy shared, and that I later saw for myself in the National Geographic video, was stunning to put it mildly. God was revealing his plans to crush most of what we know as the Church (in the Western culture at least) and replace it with a terrifying and wondrous new experience with God himself.

While the revelation is a picture to aid in interpretation, the extreme feeling that I was overwhelmed with reveals to me that it's less symbolic than we may think. There truly is a collision coming, and there's nothing we can do to stop it—though many will try.

We soon won't be able to define *going to church* the way we do now. God is coming to reform, to crush structures of old for what is to be introduced very soon. Our call isn't to stand strong until the

shift comes, it's to prophetically sound the alarm and awaken those at risk! God is coming!

The force from Heaven, the celestial asteroid, is going to impact the Church, and most pastors and people will resist with everything that's within them. Man-made support systems will be removed. People's financial and relational structures will be threatened by this strange new spiritual invasion.

The human wisdom and natural common sense that have been involved in the development of the current church structure will not be usable in the new. Those who walk by sight are in danger.

We will have to rely on a new set of senses as we, in faith unlike any we've ever allowed ourselves to embrace, begin to walk blindly into a fearful new Church reality.

> *No one sews a piece of unshrunk cloth on an old garment. If he does, the patch tears away from it, the new from the old, and a worse tear is made. And no one puts new wine into old wineskins. If he does, the wine will burst the skins—and the wine is destroyed, and so are the skins. But new wine is for fresh wineskins." Mark 2:21-22*

However, if we have false expectations and a wrong understanding of who God is, we will soon be offended.

> *And blessed is the one who is not offended by me. Matthew 11:6*

God & Church Confusion

I believe the coming Church is necessary in large part due to a confused and wrongly defined church model that has led to false expectations and a misunderstanding of the person of God. This confusion has put many Christians at eternal risk.

The current church model, generally speaking, has avoided the mandate to call the body into the fires of intercession and ministry to the lost. Instead of being a troubling shock to the current system of the world and to the spirit of the age, the Church has been marginalized.

We should be grieved! The pure Christian message of surrender, repentance, holiness, intercession and rescuing souls from Hell has been replaced by a self-centered gospel that boldly affirms a focus on benefits without cost, on personal gain without sacrifice, on freedom without consecration. The Church has been unapologetically and boldly focused on how to have faith to receive while forsaking the call to have faith to give. The spirit of the age infiltrated churches long ago—and now, all too often, that demonic spirit is the primary counselor.

> The spirit of the age infiltrated churches long ago...

Great offense will come when God doesn't "come through" for us financially or otherwise. Many will experience rejection when God brings correction instead of a pat on the back. Millions of Christians are at risk of falling away when God disappoints them by not giving them what they presumed was a part of the package they signed up for. The call to martyrdom will be a defining mark of true Christians in a quasi-Christian culture that rejects surrender and trumpets its right to be blessed, fat and selfish.

Even today, people are becoming disenchanted with the Church when they don't feel connected or served or edified. If they can't function in their giftings, focus on their desires or fulfill their supposed ministries, the increasing trend is to become offended and cause trouble. If today's disappointed Christian can't withstand this current low level, marginally supernatural structure, what will they do when the fireball from Heaven crushes them fully? What will their response be when they are called into the humbling ministry

of nameless, faceless night and day prayer? How will they react to an atmosphere of groans and cries of deep repentance and Holy Spirit intercession that cuts to the heart? What will happen when they are called to lay down their lives for the ones they are jealously attempting to use?

> *By this we know love, that he laid down his life for us, and we ought to lay down our lives for the brothers. 1 John 3:16*

The Current Church

There's no way I'm going to attempt to present a comprehensive picture of the Church with all of its varying streams and complexities. The point I'm focusing in this segment is on is the simple, common experience that the current structure and function of the Church presents. This will give some moderate understanding of how God is going to touch every system we have. So much of what is common today will be replaced or reformed soon. The coming Church just won't look like our model of church. It will be a threatening, living organism that will force the fear of the Lord upon us as the love of the Lord confounds us.

Many who read this book will be in a stream of ministry that applauds reformation and is currently alive and hungry for more. I want to challenge you, if you are in that camp, to leave significant room for revolution even in your culture of freedom and expectancy. I don't believe any church, no matter how alive or dead it may be, is exempt from severe and shocking change. Much of the change will be initially disappointing and potentially offensive. In fact, much of what we value in Spirit-filled churches will be done away with to make room for more of what we identify ourselves with–the infilling of the Spirit of Christ.

With that in mind, here are some of the simple, practical attributes in today's Church that are up for change:

- **Teaching driven:** In most churches, the Sunday service revolves around the message, the teaching. It's normal today for people to choose a church based on the style or content of the teaching.

- **Sunday only:** The average attendance for a church attendee in America is less than two services a month. Most of those services occur on Sundays.
- **Predictable & scheduled:** Each service and ministry of the church is mapped out and scheduled, and while there is often some flexibility, you can usually have a pretty good picture in your mind of what to expect during each event. Several songs of worship, a few announcements, receiving the offering and a 30-40 minute message is what most have come to expect.
- **Mostly natural:** While some churches do experience a measure of supernatural activity, the overwhelming experience is logical, natural and humanly comprehendible.
- **Locally focused:** Most churches have a vision that is limited to themselves. Their local church is where most of their energy is focused.
- **Centered around fellowship:** Friendships and a secular social culture are the defining factors in the church for many.
- **Seeker focused:** Even churches that aren't identified as *seeker sensitive* tend to be intent on attracting visitors and they gear their ministry to do so.
- **Personal gain highlighted:** God blesses—and that message when presented in appropriate contexts is a necessary one—But most churches highlight personal benefit while keeping the bar of personal surrender and commitment quite low.

The Coming Church

Does all of that feel quite familiar? That and much more is what will be affected in the coming Church. The new Church will look nothing like what we see now. We must learn how to live in the

Spirit if we hope to embrace this uninvited yet deeply needed invasion from Heaven. Everything is at risk. Will you embrace or resist this reformation? Understand, God is under no obligation to explain himself to us. His plans are about to unfold whether we like them or not, understand them or not.

Some of the shifts that are coming will result in a power center that will be a burning, shining light in the darkness. In contrast to the above marks of the current Church, here is some of what we can expect in the coming Church:

- **Encounter driven:** We will gather together with a primary goal of having an overwhelming encounter with an invisible God. The burning of God will engulf us day after day. A fearful and glorious *2nd Chronicles 7* Church will be the normal reality. While experiences will vary (from sobriety, to struggle, to brokenness, to joy, to trembling), the encounter with God, directly via his Spirt and through the enduring Word of God will drive the culture of the Church.

> God is under no obligation to explain himself to us.

- **The 24/7 Church:** The thought of only gathering in the crater, in the lava of God's shocking presence, on occasion, a few times a month, will be laughable. Our entire lives will be empowered by this tent of meeting and our energies will be spent gathering the desperate masses into the fire to experience an otherworldly spiritual force from Heaven together. Most days of the week we will easily make room to be in the church, on our faces, trembling under the weight of God.

> *As soon as Solomon finished his prayer, fire came down from heaven and consumed the burnt offering and the sacrifices, and the glory of the Lord filled the temple. And the priests could not enter the house of the Lord, be-*

> *cause the glory of the Lord filled the Lord's house. When all the people of Israel saw the fire come down and the glory of the Lord on the temple, they bowed down with their faces to the ground on the pavement and worshiped and gave thanks to the Lord, saying, "For he is good, for his steadfast love endures forever." 2 Chronicles 7:1-3*

- **Unpredictable:** Finally we will begin to know a God who is limitless in expression. Every moment with him in our corporate gatherings will be unlike any other. The fierce burning will never stop; the myriad of emotions we experience as God hovers over us will surprise and overwhelm us continually. A gathering of burning ones will result in fireballs of worship that lead to sharp swords of prophetic teaching that shake the people to their core. Wave after wave of fiery shock and awe will never disappoint. Services will be open ended and will overlap each other as room is made for an uncontrollable Holy Spirit to orchestrate the events in his wisdom.
- **Supernatural:** We will take the leap from mostly translating God into our natural language and understanding to allowing the Holy Spirit to lead us out of the natural realm and into a supernatural culture that can only be understood via our spirits. The lost will finally have hope as we stop trying to give them logical reasons to *get saved* and instead start introducing them to the supernatural God whom they have been craving to meet.
- **Regionally focused:** The level of impact that the rock from Heaven will bring will not be confined to local churches. Pastors and leaders will stop focusing mainly on developing their own local ministry and will instead shelve much of what they did in the old church model and focus on serving the regional mission. The local will give way to the regional as leaders lead the people into encounter, into regional mission and into the greater vision of revival and reformation. The spirit of Pharaoh that focuses on personal goals and keeping people locally focused will give way to the spirit of reformation and King-

dom advance that was manifested through Moses and Joshua. *(Read more about this in my book Pharaoh in the Church.)*

- **God focused:** Instead of attempting to grow the church by focusing on visitors and seekers, the leaders will be fully devoted to a *2nd Chronicles 7* strategy of compelling God to show up in extreme, weighty power. The pillar of fire that connects Heaven to Earth is the new goal. In fact, an empty church is a better goal than a full church if we understand that passage of Scripture correctly! Many disgruntled people will leave the church as a more serious devotion to Holy Spirit activity is given, but the supernatural invasion will result in fire, smoke and earthquakes that will rock cities and nations.
- **Personal surrender highlighted:** Instead of compelling people to join our church through the promise of personal gain, we'll highlight the cross. The cost. The Rich Young Rulers will leave, while the end-time remnant will gain confidence in God's leadership and passion for revival. They will flood in and serve with military-level commitment. You will know leaders have turned the corner toward the new model of church when they actually raise the bar so unapologetically that those with money and influence are allowed to go. How many RICH RULERS are in our churches because leaders have compromised the call, just so they don't lose their money?
- **The Word of God rules:** As a Spirit-filled Christian, I absolutely and energetically affirm bizarre, strange and unexplainable manifestations. I am also OK with some silliness from people who just don't understand how to yield best to God in a revival atmosphere. However, I have no patience for hype and exaggeration. If we exaggerate, we limit what God can do by forcing him into our own imagination. That being said, the coming Church will return to a foundation of the Word. We will be students of the Bible, and much of the flaky silliness we see in so called Charismatic meetings will cease as the truth exposes error. Additionally, there will be an increase of

very influential movements that look and feel like God, but that embrace theologies that put people's eternities at risk. The coming Church will be quick to, in humility and love, bring correction to such error as the Word of God is declared in power.

What I shared above is extremely limited, but I wanted to at least attempt to bring some practicality to the discussion, so you have a better idea of some of the changes that are coming. Even attempting to logically communicate in this book some of the dramatic shifts that are coming to the Church is really ridiculously futile. However, my belief and my prayer is that the Holy Spirit will drop a burning coal into your spirit and at least impart a measure of what I am seeing, and what God is about to do. Remember an immeasurable rock is about to annihilate most everything that we know as Church today. The religious will violently resist the Rock as they did when Jesus walked the Earth. But, it's on this Rock that the Church will be built.

Very literally, everything is threatened including pastors' salaries, people's favorite expressions of church life, current church relationships and many other personally important aspects of the experience. When that threat comes, many wonderful church leaders, elders, Sunday School teachers, small group leaders and deeply committed ministers will be saddened, troubled and offended.

This shift is necessary as God not only brings change to the Church, but also to the nation. We are again going to see bold, burning prophets leading our nation in place of humanistic, self-serving politicians.

Where is Prayer?

To the dismay of those who simply want to hear a little worship and listen to good (and short) teaching, services will become more like prayer meetings. This is one of the most critical and most upsetting shifts that will come–and it must come now. Today, most of the energy church leadership teams expend is usually on attract-

ing and keeping visitors instead of training and engaging intercessors. One of the greatest indictments on the Church today is that prayer is not the driving force. Today, people tend to choose churches based on the appeal of the teaching and the worship instead of the fervency of prayer. If the Church was a house of teaching, or a house of worship, that would make sense—but it's not. Scripture reveals that the Church is a House of Prayer for all nations (Mark 11:17) *Every person* in the Church will function as a burning intercessor, and the services will be marked by this unified groan of fiery prayer. It simply does not make sense that people gather together as Christians without prayer being their primary activity!

Christians who aren't invested in fervent, supernatural prayer will be enticed by the natural familiarity of Ichabod churches (where the glory has departed).

Why is this the way it is?

- First, it's uncommon to find a pastor or church leader who is personally consumed by a lifestyle of prayer. The pressure to draw—and keep—a crowd is high, and their energy is most often given to that endeavor.
- Second, it's equally rare to find Christians who are invigorated by a spirit of prayer. Even in some of our most Spirit-filled bodies, you will notice people quickly checking out after even five or ten minutes of vigorous intercession. Simply, the people don't prefer it, and to keep them around, the program doesn't include it.
- Further, the call to prayer is in itself offensive. There is a massive demonic resistance against the prayer movement today. In fact, people are actually creating doctrine that rejects devotion to intercession and affirms a lackluster, casual approach to prayer. Those who are fervent are often labeled as legalistic or elitist. The accusation is that those who pray with extreme devotion presume themselves to be closer to God than the rest of the Christians. My response? They are! Anybody who invests their time, energy, heart and passions into deeply

connecting with God, and allowing him to cut them to the core, is most definitely closer to God than those who have a theological approach to God. Is that so hard to believe? That reality doesn't have anything to do with God's love for us, but boy does it have everything to do with our love of God!

Christians who aren't invested in fervent, supernatural prayer will be enticed by the natural familiarity of Ichabod churches.

Those who pray cause problems for those who don't, and since most don't pray with a fiery spirit, churches focus on those people and, in effect, shut down the spirit of prayer in the church. These churches, more often than we might realize, have Ichabod inscribed above their doorposts.

In today's Church, connection with other people seems to be more appealing than connection with God. While personal relationships are extremely important, especially as it relates to the Great Commission, the coming Church will again highlight a vertical prayer-driven connection with God as the primary call for every believer. That will result in a revelation of mission that takes us well beyond our desire to have friends or to have others meet our needs. Personal need will give way to personal mission. Today, churches are often more like organic, socially-driven hospitals. People tend to use the church as a way to meet their personal needs instead of serving it as a minister of God. This is going to change.

"If I were to live my life over again, I would spend less time in service and more time in prayer." -Adolph Saphir

Of course, there will still be personal ministry and true needs will be addressed. However, instead of the Church functioning as a hospital, it will once again function as a mission-driven military. The mission will take precedence. The saints will be equipped for service, not for personal survival or personal satisfaction. In this ancient and emerging model, there will be MASH units that will take very good care of the wounded with the primary purpose of getting the soldier back into battle. Apostles will again lead with governmental authority and pastors will be seen as the main leader less and less as they focus more on shepherding the soldiers and less on primary leadership. By some estimates, there are over five billion people on the Earth today who don't know Jesus. In fact, my personal belief is that many in churches today who presume themselves to be converted, are not. This may take the number well over six billion! With that in mind, how can we be focused on our personal needs, fitting in and making new friends as the primary motivators of our church experience? It's nonsense! It's a violation of the very purpose of the Church! The coming Church will be changing that with great finality.

Do You Trust Me?

One of the most important shifts in my life as both a Christian and as a ministry leader came as I was in the midst of developing Revolution Church in Colorado. I was relaxing on the couch late one night when God spoke very simply yet profoundly to me. He said, *"John, do you trust me?"*

The question was threatening! I knew he was about to call me out of comfort and into challenge. I wanted to shout back, *"Nope! I love you but right now I know you are up to something that will trouble me! I'm not sure if I trust you!"*

I'm sure God appreciated my honesty. Of course, after I gathered myself, I told him with clarity, *"Yes, God. I trust you."*

The reality is this: What other choice did I have? I either trusted him and embraced the threat of extreme personal loss, or I refuse to trust and attempt to maintain what would be valued, by default, as more worthy than God. The choice was simple, but not easy.

What God said next was confounding. Understand, for those of you who are familiar with the International House of Prayer in Kansas City, Missouri, what God said will sound very familiar. Later, after we joined the staff at IHOP, I was amazed at how so many others were hearing the same thing! However, I had not yet been exposed to the IHOP culture, and what God said was strange indeed!

God said, *"John, I want you to move from ministering to people to ministering to me."*

What? I had never heard of such a thing. After all, isn't the goal to be connected with people? The Great Commission certainly would demand that we focus on people, right?

This life-altering encounter I had with God revealed just how limited my perspective really was. The black-and-white analysis would reveal that first, people are going to Hell, and second, we need to tell them about Jesus. Additionally, we need to invest into the process of discipleship. This is scriptural, right?

The black-and-white answer is, *"Yes."* The reality is, however, that the answer is insufficient. There is so much more to be understood, more revelation to be had.

As a graphic and web designer, I work with images all the time. It's possible to reduce a beautiful, vivid, colorful image down to only black and white. It's the same image, without the detail and without the depth. Take a look at what I mean on the next three pages:

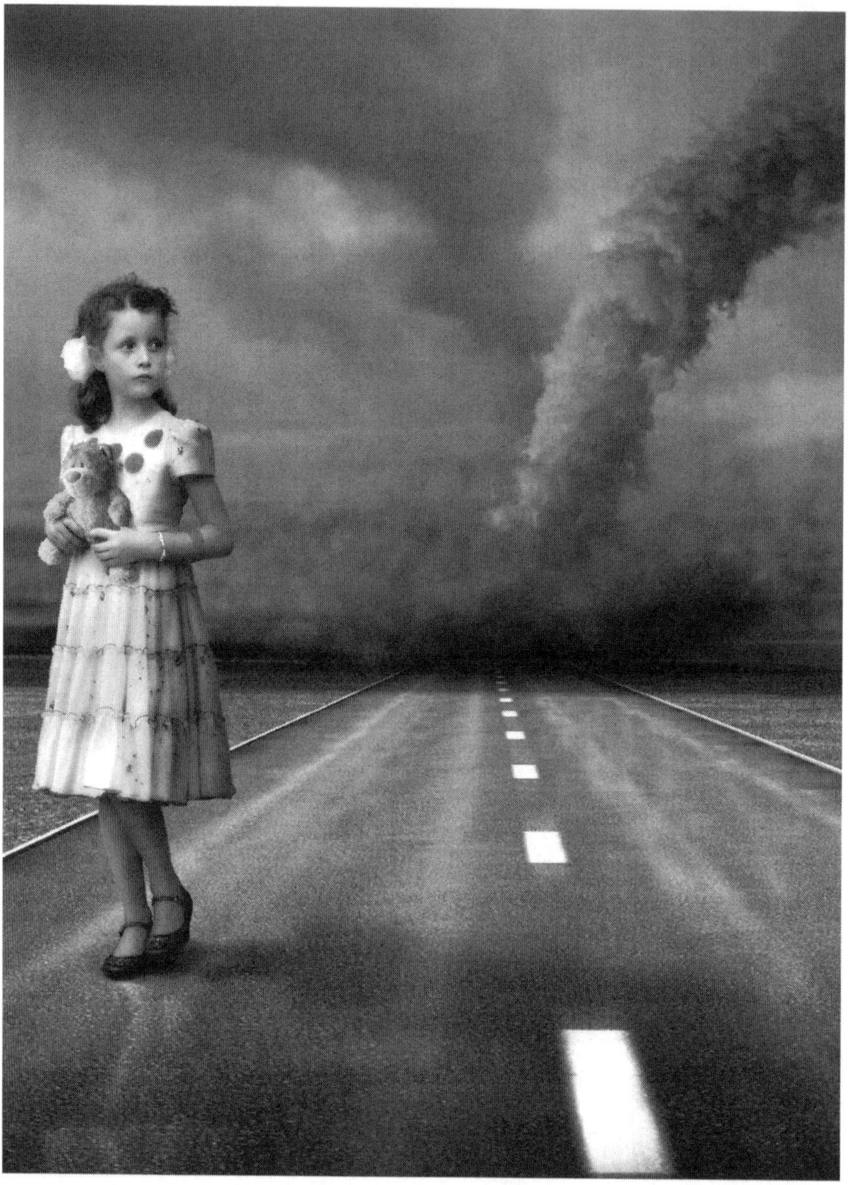

This photo is expressive and full of detail, and, though you can't see it in this book, it's full color. Contrast it with exactly the same photo on the next page.

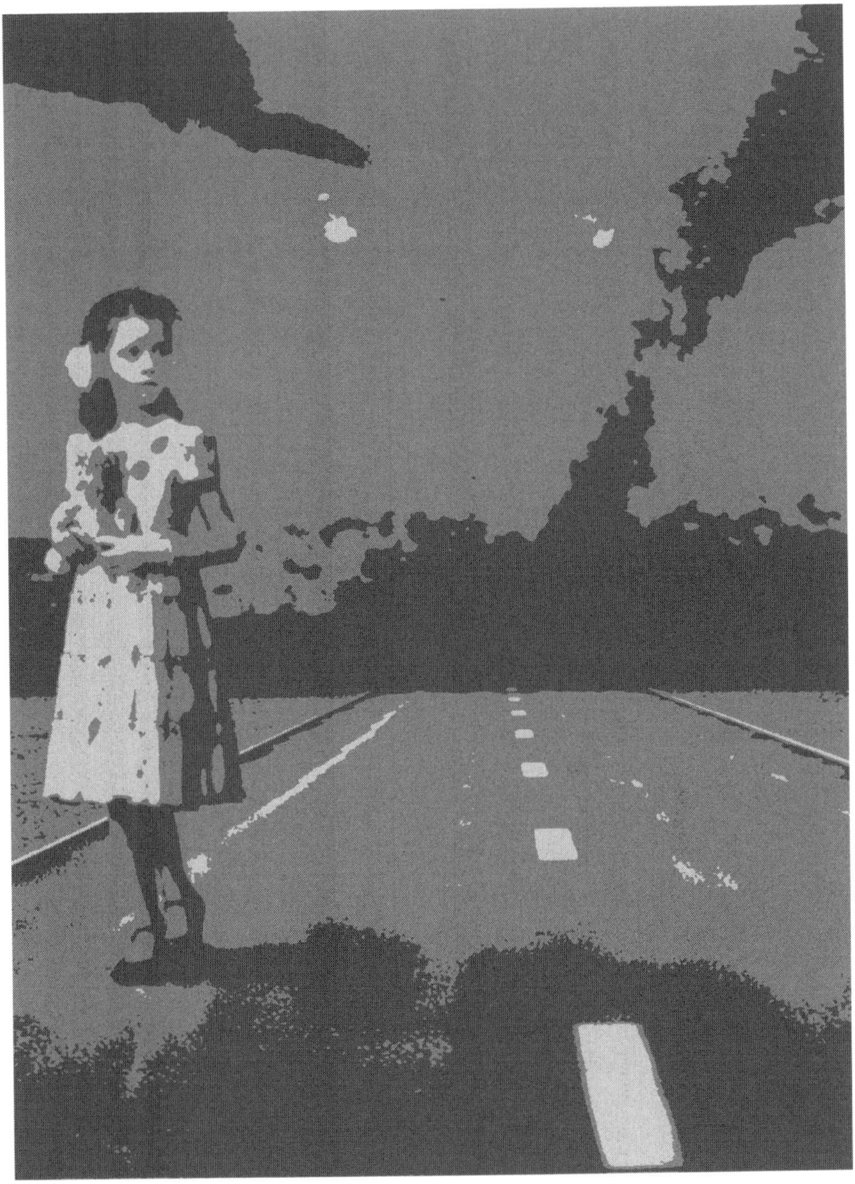

The image has been reduced to three shades. Almost all detail is gone and there is really no sign of the tornado that is quickly approaching. On the next page, you'll see a true black and white photo with only two shades.

Reduced to only two shades, we can see a road and a girl and really nothing more. We don't realize that what possibly appear to be clouds is actually a threatening storm. We can't determine the girl's age or what she is holding.

So the simple answer is this: there is more to the picture. Yes, we must touch people, we must lead them to Jesus, and we must be connected to them. That's the black-and-white reality. But there's more, much more.

In God's wisdom, he knew that a radical shift toward ministering to him—to intercession and the pursuit of a deep, abiding relationship with him—would result in many critical elements added to the mission.

- **Power.** The more we minister to God, the greater the anointing on our lives. You simply gain strength when you are encountering God.
- **Clarity.** When we are intentionally living in the spirit, with God, we see with new eyes. The two shades of our past understanding transform into a beautiful, colorful, more fully revealed image that drastically changes the way we minister.
- **Mystery.** What was previously hidden is revealed to us. Mysteries in the two-dimensional realm morph into brilliant revelation in the multi-dimensional, multi-faceted realm of the spirit.
- **Emotion.** The last photo evokes little emotion. The actual photo demands a reaction to the reality seen only when our eyes are fully opened. As we minister to God we are overwhelmed by God's emotion for the lost and for the people he died for.
- **Strategy.** The image with two or even three shades is too vague to even begin with a strategy. It seems as if all is well and the girl may just want to watch out for traffic as she's standing on the road. In the full color picture, the strategy becomes clear and urgent! *Run! That way! Now! Jump into a ditch and cover your head!* Intimacy with God changes our missions drastically. The low level concern about oncoming traffic gave way to an immediate concern about a deadly twister!

Teaching vs. Instruction

Another shift we will see has to do with teaching. Teaching will be minimized while instruction is emphasized. Teaching is mostly for personal edification while instruction is mostly for corporate assignments.

Today, most churches focus on teaching principles of Scripture, providing truths that will help believers navigate through their lives and on offering nuggets of biblical information. While there will still be important Bible teaching, apostolic instruction will emerge as a necessary new ministry. There is enough Bible teaching online, on CDs, in books and on video to turn every one of us into personal spiritual giants. We need to take it upon ourselves to grow.

Our culture is so lazy. I've actually heard complaints over the years that I don't teach enough on one topic and a I teach too much on another. Come on Church, wake up and grow up! The resources are abounding and there is no excuse to find ourselves lacking when it comes to teaching and personal discipleship. We must grow mostly on our own. How many different potential teaching topics are there? Thousands? Millions? There is no way a single pastor could even begin to teach them all. The responsibility of prophetic leaders is to relay the messages of God and to instruct the people accordingly.

Though teaching materials are in abundance, what is lacking is apostolic leaders, military commanders, who give instruction, assignments, to a ready army. *Teaching is personal growth based while instruction is a call to corporate action for the sake of mission fulfillment.*

An example of apostolic instruction is this: The apostolic leader communicates scriptural truths about prayer and fasting as it relates to city transformation. He then relays a corporate assignment for everybody in the church to fast and pray in a very focused manner for a week and then show up together, full of the fire of God, to prayer walk through the city streets. It's a corporate call to action vs. a simple biblical study. It's mission focused vs. personal growth focused (though I can't imagine a better way to grow personally than by being invested in a corporate mission!). Personal growth will be largely our responsibility between services so we can be ready to respond to the corporate instruction where we will receive our assignments.

Such an intense culture will require an immediate spike in the number of hours we spend together. The missions will require time to complete. In the coming Church, we will gather together on most days of the week. The 24/7 Church will again emerge! The Church will return to driving culture instead of reacting to culture. Cares of life will lose their power as we simplify our lives and put corporate prayer and mission ahead of most everything else. This may be the most challenging change for Christians. Today, Sunday is the day to set aside for corporate worship while we give precedence to our *normal lives* throughout the week. Church and God's corporate mission were never meant to be supplements to our regular lives!

> The Church will return to driving culture instead of reacting to culture.

In the coming Church, the very reason we live will be to pray on fire together every day, receive apostolic assignments and then move out into our lives as equipped, fiery, determined Kingdom ambassadors. It wouldn't be surprising if a tithe of our time is what became the standard. All Believers will give two to three hours a day—whether in the morning, afternoon or evening, or even in the late night hours—to praying on site together, ministering, and giving themselves to intercession-fueled Kingdom ministry. Of course, much of what we have been giving ourselves to in our typical American lifestyles will have to be eliminated so we have the time necessary.

I heard a story of a young Chinese man in current day China who was fully devoted to the advance of the Church in his nation. Every morning at 4AM the entire Church would awaken and gather together in the church building to pray for a few hours before they went to work. Additionally, I talked with an African Christian leader

about the explosive growth in his region. I asked him why it was so effective. He simply said, *"Every Friday night, the entire Church gathers together for an all-night prayer meeting. Many walk for miles every week to be there."*

Are you seeing it? The coming Church will not be a place to pop in and leech teaching nuggets for personal consumption. It will be apostolically driven and there will be calls to action. Can you imagine what would happen in today's American Church if, during next Sunday's sermon, we were instructed to change our schedules on a permanent basis and show up for all-night prayer each week or to 4AM prayer each morning? Few would show. *In the coming Church, everyone will show.*

Groans of Worship

As we become supernaturally changed in a place of extreme intercession, worship will change significantly. It will be supernaturally driven. There is a new sound coming to worship, and it's not simply a new style. There is a supernatural, otherworldly groan of intercessory worship that will explode out of the entire body as a new breed of trembling worship leaders lead the way into the shock and awe of the glory of God.

We will no longer simply sit in a pew or stand with a raised hand while a familiar worship song is sung. The prophetic, groaning sounds of Holy Spirit-facilitated worship will make it normal to shake and fall to our faces as we cry, *"Holy!"* The natural, logical sing-a-longs will be no more. We will have a hard time standing as man's karaoke gives way to God's Shekinah and Kabod glory that takes up residence in his Church. Worship teams will practice less and pray in the Spirit with tears in their eyes more.

Today, along with most other expressions of church life, worship is at least slightly and sometimes extremely marginalized for the sake of the less adventurous attendee. Since most people tend to be adverse to more supernatural forms of worship, and many would leave if the atmosphere became too uncomfortable, the majority has been winning.

I've said it countless times, and have written before that I refuse to tone down the activity of the Holy Spirit out of respect of those less hungry. How is it that the naturally-minded majority has supplanted the supernatural remnant in the Church? How is it that burning, raging, intercessory worship that's driven by the groans of the Spirit himself are not appreciated enough to risk losing people from our churches?

> *For those who live according to the flesh set their minds on the things of the flesh, but those who live according to the Spirit, the things of the Spirit. For to be carnally minded is death, but to be spiritually minded is life and peace. Because the carnal mind is enmity against God; for it is not subject to the law of God, nor indeed can be. So then, those who are in the flesh cannot please God. Romans 8:5-8*

Romans 8 is a very important chapter of Scripture. It's clear that the call to live in the spirit is not a simple suggestion. It's not only for those who want to go unusually deeper in God. If we are to live in sync with God, we must live in the spirit. This is clear for all believers.

> *But the hour is coming, and now is, when the true worshippers will worship the Father in spirit and truth; for the Father is seeking such to worship Him. God is Spirit, and those who worship Him must worship in spirit and truth." John 4:23-24*

True Christians are identified by the way they worship. Is it possible that we have churches and worship ministries that are not fueled by spirit and truth, that are more natural than supernatural? Yes.

The reality is that God is spirit. We have to worship him at his level—what an honor that is!

For we know that the whole creation groans and labors with birth pangs together until now. Not only that, but we also who have the firstfruits of the Spirit, even we ourselves groan within ourselves, eagerly waiting for the adoption, the redemption of our body. For we were saved in this hope, but hope that is seen is not hope; for why does one still hope for what he sees? But if we hope for what we do not see, we eagerly wait for it with perseverance.

Likewise the Spirit also helps in our weaknesses. For we do not know what we should pray for as we ought, but the Spirit Himself makes intercession for us with groanings which cannot be uttered. Now He who searches the hearts knows what the mind of the Spirit is, because He makes intercession for the saints according to the will of God. And we know that all things work together for good to those who love God, to those who are the called according to His purpose. Romans 8:22-28

Creation groans! We ourselves groan! This is the cry of intercession, a literal, thunderous groan that fills a room of intercessory worshipers!

Certainly it must be easy to understand that the supernatural realm is quite different from the natural. Yet, we still can't see ourselves as a Church becoming strangely and wonderfully spiritual in worship. Remember, everything is changing! A small enhancement it is not! Our typical worship experiences will become so humanly bizarre that most will resist it. Why? Because it will raise the bar above where most would be willing to go. The cost to live in the spirit like this is massive, and in today's logical and busy culture, it's not ap-

> We will have a hard time standing as man's karaoke gives way to God's Shekinah and Kabod glory that takes up residence in his Church.

pealing. In fact, it's threatening. However, it's coming, and those who resist will do so tragically of their own volition.

> *When Solomon had finished praying, fire came down from heaven and consumed the burnt offering and the sacrifices; and the glory of the LORD filled the temple. And the priests could not enter the house of the LORD, because the glory of the LORD had filled the LORD'S house. When all the children of Israel saw how the fire came down, and the glory of the LORD on the temple, they bowed their faces to the ground on the pavement, and worshiped and praised the LORD, saying: "For He is good, For His mercy endures forever." 2 Chronicles 7:1-3*

In the coming Church, it will be normal for people to hit their faces and tremble and cry holy as the fire of God's presence rages! Do you see why we can't formulate low level, seeker focused worship services that can be fully understood naturally? Worshipers will be groaning and crying in the spirit, and it's possible we may have to do it on the pavement outside of the sanctuary!

~ *Four* ~

Fierce Religious Resistance

The Coming Church will threaten human systems.

My favorite definition of religion is this:

Man's attempt to use God to get what he wants.

Today's Church is designed, first and foremost, to be appealing to people. It's people-centric. The presumption is that God is always there, and now we have to get the people there. This couldn't be more incorrect.

The simple truth is that people want certain things in life, and by extension, in the Church. Instead of being fully surrendered to Jesus, to the cross of Christ, they place demands and expectations on

God and his Church. A religious spirit will accept God as long as God performs according to expectations.

The moment God fails to meet their spoken, or usually unspoken demands, the religious spirit will embrace a demonic spirit of accusation against God and will look for other means to get what they want.

The coming Church will threaten almost everything we have come to value in the Church of today, because today's Church is largely fashioned by the will of man.

Ichabod

And the word of Samuel came to all Israel. Now Israel went out to battle against the Philistines, and encamped beside Ebenezer; and the Philistines encamped in Aphek. Then the Philistines put themselves in battle array against Israel. And when they joined battle, Israel was defeated by the Philistines, who killed about four thousand men of the army in the field. And when the people had come into the camp, the elders of Israel said, "Why has the LORD defeated us today before the Philistines? Let us bring the ark of the covenant of the LORD from Shiloh to us, that when it comes among us it may save us from the hand of our enemies."

So the people sent to Shiloh, that they might bring from there the ark of the covenant of the LORD of hosts, who dwells between the cherubim. And the two sons of Eli, Hophni and Phinehas, were there with the ark of the covenant of God. And when the ark of the covenant of the LORD came into the camp, all Israel shouted so loudly that the earth shook. Now when the Philistines heard the noise of the shout, they said, "What does the sound of this great shout in the camp of the Hebrews mean?" Then they understood that the ark of the LORD had come into the camp.

So the Philistines were afraid, for they said, "God has come into the camp!" And they said, "Woe to us! For such a thing has never happened before. Woe to us! Who will deliver us from the hand of these mighty gods? These are the gods who struck the Egyptians with all the plagues in the wilderness. Be strong and conduct yourselves like men, you Philistines, that you do not become servants of the Hebrews, as they have been to you. Conduct yourselves like men, and fight!"

So the Philistines fought, and Israel was defeated, and every man fled to his tent. There was a very great slaughter, and there fell of Israel thirty thousand foot soldiers. Also the ark of God was captured; and the two sons of Eli, Hophni and Phinehas, died. Then a man of Benjamin ran from the battle line the same day, and came to Shiloh with his clothes torn and dirt on his head. Now when he came, there was Eli, sitting on a seat by the wayside watching, for his heart trembled for the ark of God. And when the man came into the city and told it, all the city cried out.

> Religion:
>
> Man's attempt to use God to get what he wants

When Eli heard the noise of the outcry, he said, "What does the sound of this tumult mean?" And the man came quickly and told Eli. Eli was ninety-eight years old, and his eyes were so dim that he could not see. Then the man said to Eli, "I am he who came from the battle. And I fled today from the battle line." And he said, "What happened, my son?" So the messenger answered and said, "Israel has fled before the Philistines, and there has been a great slaughter among the people. Also your two sons, Hophni and Phinehas, are dead; and the ark of God has been captured." Then it happened, when he made mention of the ark of God, that Eli fell off the seat backward by the side of the gate; and his neck was broken and he died, for the man was old and heavy. And he had judged Israel forty years.

Now his daughter-in-law, Phinehas' wife, was with child, due to be delivered; and when she heard the news that the ark of God was captured, and that her father-in-law and her husband were dead, she bowed herself and gave birth, for her labor pains came upon her. And about the time of her death the women who stood by her said to her, "Do not fear, for you have borne a son." But she did not answer, nor did she regard it. Then she

named the child Ichabod, saying, "The glory has departed from Israel!" because the ark of God had been captured and because of her father-in-law and her husband. And she said, "The glory has departed from Israel, for the ark of God has been captured."
1 Samuel 4:1-22

In the coming Church, we will be entirely focused on God showing up and visitors being troubled, not the other way around. The only way we can impact the people of the world is if we jealously guard the ark, God's presence.

The coming Church will result in a ferocious invasion of God's presence into the Church, and this will result in a mass exodus of the naturally minded and lukewarm. This reality is what keeps many churches tepid. The "come as you are" sales pitch is another way to say, *"come on in, the water's fine, the temperature is perfect!"*

Not too hot, not too cold. Perfect for everybody to feel comfortable, except God.

If the temperature is too hot, people will flee, and will take their money with them. Many who earn their living from the ministry will be revival's fiercest resisters.

The lukewarm Church will commonly declare that there is no condemnation in Christ Jesus, while not realizing they are condemned and not in Christ Jesus.

> Many who earn their living from the ministry will be revival's fiercest resisters.

Remember, a religious spirit is focused on self, and specifically use God and God's systems for personal comfort, safety and gain. If any of that is threatened, even by God himself, that person will aggressively resist. If the increase of God's uncomfortable burning presence means fewer people will remain, the religious will manipulate the thermostat back down. Fear of man will replace the fear of the Lord.

This is why Ichabod is hanging over the doorposts of many churches today. Leaders have traded God for people. God is currently raising up a new generation of leaders who will not be afraid of people or loss, and who won't give in to the pressure to provide a comfortable, lukewarm environment.

Watch how God rebuked Saul, removed him from position and provoked Saul to react in violence:

> *For rebellion is as the sin of witchcraft, And stubbornness is as iniquity and idolatry. Because you have rejected the word of the LORD, He also has rejected you from being king." Then Saul said to Samuel, "I have sinned, for I have transgressed the commandment of the LORD and your words, because I feared the people and obeyed their voice. Now therefore, please pardon my sin, and return with me, that I may worship the LORD." But Samuel said to Saul, "I will not return with you, for you have rejected the word of the LORD, and the LORD has rejected you from being king over Israel." And as Samuel turned around to go away, Saul seized the edge of his robe, and it tore. So Samuel said to him, "The LORD has torn the kingdom of Israel from you today, and has given it to a neighbor of yours, who is better than you." 1 Samuel 15:23-28*

Remarkable! That doesn't sound like God, does it?

> *"The LORD has torn the kingdom of Israel from you today, and has given it to a neighbor of yours, who is better than you."*

That's not nice at all! Friend, let's be aware of a difficult reality. God is much different than the imaginary image we want him to live up to. God isn't always nice, but God is always right. He is always holy. He is always just. He is not always fair. He is not always pleasant. But he is always a fearful and loving God.

Leonard Ravenhill said:

"A man who is intimate with God will never be intimidated by men."

There are leaders being identified right now who don't fear man. They will be receiving the batons that God has pulled from the hands of some of the previous generation's most celebrated leaders. When their ordination has been lifted by Heaven, people will start to be drawn to other churches led by God's new breed of firebrands. This will not be an easy transition.

I encourage you to read my book *Pharaoh in the Church*. I explain this challenging shift for God's people being violently pulled out of Egyptian, man-made religious systems that are intent on using God's people for their own gain, financial prosperity and legacy. A brilliantly worded lyric to a worship song by Brian Ming sums it up well:

God forgive us for building kingdoms of man on doctrines of demons in your name.

Even Saul's repentance was too late to save his position.

Then Saul said to Samuel, "I have sinned, for I have transgressed the commandment of the LORD and your words, because I feared the people and obeyed their voice."

When Samuel basically told Saul, *"Too late, buddy,"* Saul responded with violence! His livelihood, his reputation, his kingdom was being stripped from him!

Now the LORD said to Samuel, "How long will you mourn for Saul, seeing I have rejected him from reigning over Israel? Fill your horn with oil, and go; I am sending you to Jesse the Bethlehemite. For I have provided Myself a king among his sons." And

Samuel said, "How can I go? If Saul hears it, he will kill me." And the LORD said, "Take a heifer with you, and say, 'I have come to sacrifice to the LORD.' 1 Samuel 16:1-2

The religious intimidation will be extreme when the new breed who are unafraid, humble and surrendered to God are identified. As this story plays out, Saul eventually tries to kill David, though his humble replacement refused to reciprocate. He honored Saul.

Before we get to that point, however, let's watch the story unfold a bit. It's a familiar story, but one worth revisiting.

So it was, when they came, that he looked at Eliab and said, "Surely the LORD'S anointed is before Him." But the LORD said to Samuel, "Do not look at his appearance or at the height of his stature, because I have refused him. For the Lord does not see as man sees; for man looks at the outward appearance, but the LORD looks at the heart." So Jesse called Abinadab, and made him pass before Samuel. And he said, "Neither has the LORD chosen this one." Then Jesse made Shammah pass by. And he said, "Neither has the LORD chosen this one."

Thus Jesse made seven of his sons pass before Samuel. And Samuel said to Jesse, "The LORD has not chosen these." And Samuel said to Jesse, "Are all the young men here?" Then he said, "There remains yet the youngest, and there he is, keeping the sheep." And Samuel said to Jesse, "Send and bring him. For we will not sit down till he comes here." So he sent and brought him in. Now he was ruddy, with bright eyes, and good-looking. And the LORD said, "Arise, anoint him; for this is the one!" Then Samuel took the horn of oil and anointed him in the midst of his brothers; and the Spirit of the LORD came upon David from that day forward. So Samuel arose and went to Ramah. 1 Samuel 16:6-13

The Lord has not chosen thee. We live in a nation where we presume that we can be anything we want. Many parents will tell their children, *"You can be President of the United States if you want."* Mom and Dad, no they can't. There will be but a handful of people out of

all the millions who live in our nation who will be chosen by God to fulfill that role. Humility would demand that we cannot and should not be most things, but we must certainly fulfill the calling that God has for our lives.

Nobody was called to be king except one—David. This type of exclusivity causes problems even today. Many adhere to a false belief system that demands we are all on a level playing field. This just is not so. There are leaders, and there are followers. This is by design. And, as is the case in this story, some leaders will be replaced by others who seemingly have little going for them—except that they are intimate with God and unafraid of man.

Now, the story is about to get interesting! Saul, representing the old, resistant, religious system is about to be visited by a distressing spirit—sent by God! (This isn't the only time God assigns a troubling spirit to someone named Saul. Paul, previously Saul, was given a messenger from Satan to keep him humble. God will use all of his resources to fulfill his plans.)

> *But the Spirit of the LORD departed from Saul, and a distressing spirit from the LORD troubled him. And Saul's servants said to him, "Surely, a distressing spirit from God is troubling you. Let our master now command your servants, who are before you, to seek out a man who is a skillful player on the harp; and it shall be that he will play it with his hand when the distressing spirit from God is upon you, and you shall be well."*
>
> *So Saul said to his servants, "Provide me now a man who can play well, and bring him to me." Then one of the servants answered and said, "Look, I have seen a son of Jesse the Bethlehemite, who is skillful in playing, a mighty man of valor, a man of war, prudent in speech, and a handsome person; and the LORD is with him." Therefore Saul sent messengers to Jesse, and said, "Send me your son David, who is with the sheep." And Jesse took a donkey loaded with bread, a skin of wine, and a young goat, and sent them by his son David to Saul.*
>
> *So David came to Saul and stood before him. And he loved him greatly, and he became his armorbearer. Then Saul sent to Jesse, saying, "Please let David stand before me, for he has found*

> *favor in my sight." And so it was, whenever the spirit from God was upon Saul, that David would take a harp and play it with his hand. Then Saul would become refreshed and well, and the distressing spirit would depart from him. 1 Samuel 16:14-23*

The emerging generation of anointed leaders will bear the burden of loving the previous generation, those they are replacing, and to minister to them from the place of their intimate relationship with God! Only those who are most deeply connected with God will be chosen for this task. This is why the prayer movement is so necessary today. People who know God a lot will be replacing people who know a lot about God.

People who know God a lot will be replacing people who know a lot about God.

Again, this will be a very difficult transition in the Church. Those who are moving into position must, without fail, honor, serve and love those they are replacing.

> *So David went out wherever Saul sent him, and behaved wisely. And Saul set him over the men of war, and he was accepted in the sight of all the people and also in the sight of Saul's servants. 1 Samuel 18:5*

He behaved wisely. As a result, his favor increased, not only with Saul (which would be short lived) but with all of the people. This didn't set well with Saul. Not at all.

> *Now it had happened as they were coming home, when David was returning from the slaughter of the Philistine, that the women had come out of all the cities of Israel, singing and dancing, to meet King Saul, with tambourines, with joy, and with musical instruments. So the women sang as they danced, and*

said: "Saul has slain his thousands, And David his ten thousands." Then Saul was very angry, and the saying displeased him; and he said, "They have ascribed to David ten thousands, and to me they have ascribed only thousands. Now what more can he have but the kingdom?" So Saul eyed David from that day forward. 1 Samuel 18:6-9

> David passed the test with love and a harp while Saul failed the test with fear and a spear.

The resistance has escalated. Young emerging leader, know this: no matter how humble and surrendered and loving you are, the bold advance that is required of you in your developing position in God's Kingdom will result in jealousy, accusation and extreme resistance. Are you ready? Will you still love? Will you use gossip as your weapon of choice, or intercession? David continued to choose intercession. To serve with honor in the coming Church, you must go low and love deeply.

And it happened on the next day that the distressing spirit from God came upon Saul, and he prophesied inside the house. So David played music with his hand, as at other times; but there was a spear in Saul's hand. And Saul cast the spear, for he said, "I will pin David to the wall!" But David escaped his presence twice. Now Saul was afraid of David, because the LORD was with him, but had departed from Saul. Therefore Saul removed him from his presence, and made him his captain over a thousand; and he went out and came in before the people. 1 Samuel 18:10-13

Fear of loss of money, loss of reputation and loss of influence with people will strike many. Again, how will you respond? David continued to intercede for Saul. David held a harp with the intent to deliver while Saul held a spear with the intent to destroy.

Scripture reveals that David continued to exercise wisdom, and that in itself resulted in great fear coming on Saul. Saul's days were numbered.

> *And David behaved wisely in all his ways, and the LORD was with him. Therefore, when Saul saw that he behaved very wisely, he was afraid of him. 1 Samuel 18:14-15*

I know this is quite a long, dramatic story, but I'm compelled to keep with it at least for another moment. I believe it's critical that we see over and over again the heart of David as he was under continual threat of death at the hand of the one he was serving, and ultimately, replacing. This process is about to hit the current day Church, and this lesson cannot be underemphasized.

> *And there was war again; and David went out and fought with the Philistines, and struck them with a mighty blow, and they fled from him. Now the distressing spirit from the LORD came upon Saul as he sat in his house with his spear in his hand. And David was playing music with his hand. Then Saul sought to pin David to the wall with the spear, but he slipped away from Saul's presence; and he drove the spear into the wall. So David fled and escaped that night. Saul also sent messengers to David's house to watch him and to kill him in the morning. And Michal, David's wife, told him, saying, "If you do not save your life tonight, tomorrow you will be killed." 1 Samuel 19:8-11*

So, God continues to provoke the outgoing leader by sending a distressing spirit, and God continued to test David's heart at the same time.

David again passed the test with love and a harp while Saul again failed the test with fear and a spear. Intercession was the stronger weapon.

As Saul's mission intensified, he became relentless as he broadened his attack to include anybody who was faithful to David. The lesson? God will send people your way, young emerging leader, to stand with you, and they will have to be equally prepared to respond rightly, as Jonathan did.

> *For as long as the son of Jesse lives on the earth, you shall not be established, nor your kingdom. Now therefore, send and bring him to me, for he shall surely die." And Jonathan answered Saul his father, and said to him, "Why should he be killed? What has he done?" Then Saul cast a spear at him to kill him, by which Jonathan knew that it was determined by his father to kill David. So Jonathan arose from the table in fierce anger, and ate no food the second day of the month, for he was grieved for David, because his father had treated him shamefully. 1 Samuel 20:31-34*

The coming Church will divide families and will result in extreme anger. We see the true motive of Saul's heart in the above passage.

> *For as long as the son of Jesse lives on the earth, you shall not be established, nor your kingdom.*

Saul's plan was to be established and to lead the kingdom. That same spirit is driving many leaders today. It's a *Saul spirit* and it's a *Pharaoh spirit.* It's a religious spirit. Personal gain was their motivation.

Now, read this last, somewhat lengthy, portion of the story closely. Take note of the attitude of David and his willingness to go through great, inconvenient process and to continually honor the one he would replace. His heart qualified him and equally important, Saul, who had God given authority, declared David to be king.

Just as God had to put extreme pressure on Pharaoh, the established leader of Egypt, to be the one to make the decree that the Israelites may go, he caused King Saul to do the same. The current authority validated the incoming authority. This is significant.

> *Then Saul took three thousand chosen men from all Israel, and went to seek David and his men on the Rocks of the Wild Goats. So he came to the sheepfolds by the road, where there was a cave; and Saul went in to attend to his needs. (David and his men were staying in the recesses of the cave.) Then the men of David said to him, "This is the day of which the LORD said to you, 'Behold, I will deliver your enemy into your hand, that you may do to him as it seems good to you.' " And David arose and secretly cut off a corner of Saul's robe.*
>
> *Now it happened afterward that David's heart troubled him because he had cut Saul's robe. And he said to his men, "The LORD forbid that I should do this thing to my master, the LORD'S anointed, to stretch out my hand against him, seeing he is the anointed of the LORD." So David restrained his servants with these words, and did not allow them to rise against Saul. And Saul got up from the cave and went on his way. David also arose afterward, went out of the cave, and called out to Saul, saying, "My lord the king!"*
>
> *And when Saul looked behind him, David stooped with his face to the earth, and bowed down. And David said to Saul: "Why do you listen to the words of men who say, 'Indeed David seeks your harm'? Look, this day your eyes have seen that the LORD delivered you today into my hand in the cave, and someone urged me to kill you. But my eye spared you, and I said, 'I will not stretch out my hand against my lord, for he is the LORD'S anointed.'*
>
> *Moreover, my father, see! Yes, see the corner of your robe in my hand! For in that I cut off the corner of your robe, and did not kill you, know and see that there is neither evil nor rebellion in my hand, and I have not sinned against you. Yet you hunt my life to take it. Let the LORD judge between you and me, and let the LORD avenge me on you. But my hand shall not be against you. As the proverb of the ancients says, 'Wickedness proceeds from the wicked.' But my hand shall not be against you. After*

whom has the king of Israel come out? Whom do you pursue? A dead dog? A flea? Therefore let the LORD be judge, and judge between you and me, and see and plead my case, and deliver me out of your hand."

So it was, when David had finished speaking these words to Saul, that Saul said, "Is this your voice, my son David?" And Saul lifted up his voice and wept. Then he said to David: "You are more righteous than I; for you have rewarded me with good, whereas I have rewarded you with evil. And you have shown this day how you have dealt well with me; for when the LORD delivered me into your hand, you did not kill me. For if a man finds his enemy, will he let him get away safely? Therefore may the LORD reward you with good for what you have done to me this day. And now I know indeed that you shall surely be king, and that the kingdom of Israel shall be established in your hand. 1 Samuel 24:2-20

There's the declaration. David would be king. Saul, after great and grievous pressure, relents. The religious resistance, as with Pharaoh, surrendered and God's Kingdom would advance.

~ *Five* ~

Their Freedom is Your Mission

The Coming Church will prepare us for the end.

I was rocked. I was on the platform during a powerful night of encounter at a Bay of the Holy Spirit event with John Kilpatrick and Nathan Morris in Detroit. As I stood there and looked at the jam-packed church with at least 1200 people on the main level and in the balcony, I had a vision.

It was simple, but overwhelming. I saw the walls of the church disappear, and the tightly packed crowd of 1200 expanded to the left, right and straight ahead as far as I could see, all the way to the horizon. There were millions upon millions of people.

As I was awestruck by the sheer magnitude of the vision, and by the innumerable sea of people, God spoke.

"John, your mission is their freedom."

The feeling of extreme responsibility was nearly unbearable, but the most weighty emotion was of brokenness. I felt sadness consume me. I knew it would require a reformation in our churches and in our methodologies if we were to even have a glimmer of a hope of rescuing these people from an eternity in Hell. But the mandate was clear. I had been commissioned to ensure the millions (or whatever the number might be) are rescued. Their freedom was now my mission. I started to have an understanding of just how great the Great Commission truly is.

The fear of the Lord has vanished and the groans and cries of a desperate people have gone silent.

There are billions of people on the Earth today who will most likely enter Hell. One hundred years from now, they will be burning in torment. One billion years from now they will be in the same place, in the same horror. Seconds will feel like decades and the decades will never stop coming.

It's clear that the current church structure, which is not anywhere near the biblical model that Jesus initiated with his death and resurrection, simply cannot serve this Great Commission. Attempts at relevance, surrender to the fear of man, submission to the spirit of the age and a focus on gathering people instead of on the Spirit of God, have resulted in a mostly impotent Church, where it is embarrassingly rare to experience God's pure power.

The positive, sugary messages in our pulpits today rarely have the unction of the Holy One behind them. The fear of the Lord has vanished and the groans and cries of a desperate people have gone silent.

The false/hyper/distorted-grace movement is putting millions at eternal risk as they buy into satisfying deceptions that are carefully crafted and marked with the name of God—yet are in reality treacherous doctrines of demons. The message is that we no longer should focus on sin, we don't need to confess because as Christians it's impossible to have sin in our hearts. Thus, no repentance is offered and we now have an emerging army of people following Jesus under the leadership of demons in an unsaved condition. The millions that God has put on my heart are mostly those who have been deceived into a false relationship with Jesus through a false grace and false love message.

I will talk more about that dangerous doctrine in a later chapter, but I needed to mention it now so you understand the extreme need for awakeners and prophetic messengers who will sound alarms and rescue the confused.

Lying Prophets

> *Thus says the LORD of hosts: "Do not listen to the words of the prophets who prophesy to you, filling you with vain hopes. They speak visions of their own minds, not from the mouth of the LORD. They say continually to those who despise the word of the LORD, 'It shall be well with you'; and to everyone who stubbornly follows his own heart, they say, 'No disaster shall come upon you.'" Jeremiah 23:16-17*

I have been absolutely grieved by movements that are lulling hungry Christians into a false-love theology that reduces God to Cupid.

In mythology, Cupid is the god of desire, love, attraction and affection. Cupid in Latin means "desire."

The problem? It's a myth. God is not limited to manifesting warm, fuzzy feelings. He is also fierce. He's the Judge. Without experiencing the fear of the Lord, we simply cannot experience the love of God in fullness.

Interestingly, Wikipedia reveals this:

> *Cupid continued to be a popular figure in the Middle Ages, when under Christian influence he often had a dual nature as Heavenly and Earthly love.*

We can't be Jeremiah 23 lying prophets that function in the spirit of Cupid and proclaim false-love to an immature love-stricken people.

That influence has been reawakened in our modern culture and has resulted in theologies and philosophies that refuse any expression of God that doesn't feel good. It's an immature picture of God, much like a junior high school student might write with her pencil the name "God" replacing the letter o with a scribbled heart. People are so longing for affection, that they are hoping for a happy, all-powerful boyfriend that always tells them what they want to hear.

That is not God. He is both a Lion and a Lamb. He is both ferocious and tender. He will manifest diverse emotions that, yes, are all driven by pure, supernatural love—yet supernatural love is very different than natural love.

Have you ever heard someone discount a possible attribute of God because they argue, *"Would you as a father ever think of doing that to your child?"* What they are saying is that because we as humans might never discipline someone in a certain way, then, of course, God would never do that either.

Let me ask you this: would you ever, as you look into the depths of Hell, cast a human into that place for eternity? Wouldn't it seem to be deep love to grant that person, no matter how defiled they are, access to Heaven? If we define love with our human understanding, we would agree with that. However, God's supernatural love transcends our human understanding.

True love will warn, with tears in our eyes, the sleepers and the deceived! We can't be Jeremiah 23 lying prophets that function in the spirit of Cupid and proclaim false-love to an immature love-stricken people while ignoring the often troubling, offensive truth. It's true love and pure truth that will lead people into life. That is true love.

The coming Church will explode with the full range of the emotions of God, including a love that simply shocks us to the core. The burning, trembling atmosphere that existed in *Acts 2* and in *2nd Chronicles 7* and other places in Scripture will hit the Church when the fireball of his glory impacts it.

The impact will bring revelation of the cross of Christ and the power of the resurrection in such clarity; it will strike us with the supernatural mix of fear and love that will introduce a new understanding of just who God really is.

Compliance

The coming Church will be announced by prophetic messengers who are deeply surrendered and broken before the Lord. While much of today's prophetic ministry is quite embarrassing to say the least, we cannot silence true prophecy. We need the baby, but not the bath water.

> *Do not quench the Spirit. Do not despise prophecies, but test everything; hold fast what is good. 1 Thessalonians 5:19-21*

We are to actively listen to prophecy, test it and receive what passes the test. We cannot turn a deaf ear to prophetic voices due to skepticism, unbelief or frustration with the prophetic movement. God has a lot to say, and much of it will be delivered through other

people. The coming Church is going to be a powerfully prophetic Church—more than at any other time in history.

Today, prophetic voices are neutered by a culture that is extremely suspicious, indifferent and independent, and, as a result, they are declaring the critical words of the Lord less and less. Many of those with prophetic ministries have abandoned the call for compliance to a correction or redirection of God for words that tickle ears and communicate positive destinies even for those who are in direct rebellion to truth.

I was at the Detroit Prayer Furnace recently, and God dropped a very clear, weighty word into my spirit: *compliance.*

I immediately knew that we as a nation were moving into a very troubling and dangerous time where prophetic voices must unapologetically call the Church into compliance with God's very costly, inconvenient calibration. No longer can we act as salesmen, forming our words in such a way that people will buy what we are saying! Prophetic messengers will be shunned, assaulted, resisted, cursed and accused due to their demands that the Church vacates theologies of comfort and independence.

It is absolutely critical that these prophetic messengers that to whom God is entrusting some of the most critical, invasive and troubling words in history, are living holy and are sensitive to the leading of God.

Their calls to compliance must be pure. They won't be suggestions but rather messages of life and death for an at-risk culture.

Minor is Major: Two of My Sins

Minor is major with God. Two recent minor sins had a major impact on my life. I'm about to confess those sins to you.

With the emergence of the false grace message, there is an increase in those who believe that their sin is little more than temporarily troubling. They believe sin issues for Christians are eternally benign.

Additionally, there's a decrease of the fear of the Lord and any concern at all over eternal destinies.

An increasing number of Christians believe that, while it's best if we do not sin, we in fact can sin without any fear of judgment. This belief is sending so many to Hell.

As I said above, minor is major with God. So often we hear in the argument regarding the *big sins* of homosexuality, murder, etc., that *all sin is the same*. The argument is that God can forgive a murderer just as quickly and completely as he can forgive one who gossips, lies or lusts. I do agree with that. (For the record, I don't believe all sin is the same, but, for the sake of this point, let's certainly agree that the blood of Jesus is sufficient to cover sin.)

What if we turned the argument around? If all sin is the same, then the sin of gossip is as detestable and eternally destructive as the sin of murder. Lying can send one to Hell just as quickly as premarital sex. Minor is major. And, no, we aren't exempt from eternal threat simply because we consider ourselves to be Christians. That is one of the greatest, most devastating fallacies in the Church today. *Christians who sin absolutely are at risk of eternal separation from God.*

> *"You have heard that it was said to those of old, 'You shall not murder; and whoever murders will be liable to judgment.' But I say to you that everyone who is angry with his brother will be liable to judgment; whoever insults his brother will be liable to the council; and whoever says, 'You fool!' will be liable to the hell of fire.*
>
> *So if you are offering your gift at the altar and there remember that your brother has something against you, leave your gift there before the altar and go. First be reconciled to your brother, and then come and offer your gift. Come to terms quickly with your accuser while you are going with him to court, lest your accuser hand you over to the judge, and the judge to the guard, and you be put in prison.*

> *Truly, I say to you, you will never get out until you have paid the last penny. "You have heard that it was said, 'You shall not commit adultery.' But I say to you that everyone who looks at a woman with lustful intent has already committed adultery with her in his heart. If your right eye causes you to sin, tear it out and throw it away. For it is better that you lose one of your members than that your whole body be thrown into hell. And if your right hand causes you to sin, cut it off and throw it away. For it is better that you lose one of your members than that your whole body go into hell. Matthew 5:21-30*

Anger is murder. Lust is adultery. Unforgiveness results in Hell fire. Minor is Major.

> *For if we go on sinning deliberately after receiving the knowledge of the truth, there no longer remains a sacrifice for sins, but a fearful expectation of judgment, and a fury of fire that will consume the adversaries. Hebrews 10:26-27*

Sin Number One

I know a key assignment for me is to call the Church back into radical holiness and consecration, and my authority to do so comes via the blood of Jesus. When I sinned recently in what I would consider a minor way, my assignment was compromised. I temporarily lost my authority to prophetically call the Church to corporate holiness when I myself didn't respond to God's call to personal holiness. I no longer could impact the major because of my failure in the minor.

> "We need prophetic people who don't wash their mouths out with soap, but with the blood of Jesus!"

A couple of weeks ago I was writing a post for my website and email subscribers. Many people presume that I haphazardly write and say anything that comes to mind in a cavalier way due to the provoking topics I tackle. This couldn't be further from the truth. Every word that comes out of my mouth is measured and ordered in the fear of the Lord. It's a daily, weighty matter for me to ensure I'm not withholding anything due to the fear of man and that I'm not saying what I should not due to the fear of God. To be a prophetic messenger requires this wrestling match.

As I was writing the message, I boldly said what I felt the Lord would want me to, and I was making some sharp points.

As I was writing, I was at the same time casually listening to a teaching about how certain sins can manifest in our bodies as sickness. For example, if we gossip and don't repent, it's not uncommon to have tooth pain or even to need expensive dental work such as a root canal. Gossip out of our mouth affects our mouth. As I continued writing, I was thinking to myself, *"We need prophetic people who don't wash their mouths out with soap, but with the blood of Jesus!"* I kept seeing pure mouths of bold messengers filled with the blood of Jesus as they declared truth.

I came to a point in the article where I relayed an extremely minor, common issue that can come up in a messenger's life. I wrote in an extremely generic, careful manner about a personal situation that happened in my life recently. The content wasn't the problem, but the attitude of my heart was. Again, it was so minor. You'd laugh if you knew just how minor it was! But, as I wrote it, God gave me a gentle check in my spirit. I considered the check, wondering if it was just my own emotions—then I ignored the check. After all, there was nothing that I wrote that would raise alarms whatsoever.

So, I finished the article and prepared to send it out. I always post articles to my website first, and then immediately after I will send it to my email list.

When I was finished, I got up from my office chair and I felt something strange in my mouth. I went to the bathroom and looked in the mirror. Directly under my tongue, right in the center, I saw a blood blister! It was not there five seconds prior! God immediately reminded me that his prophetic voices must have their mouths filled with the blood of Jesus, and I was instantly convicted. I ignored Jesus.

I instantly repented of my minor sin that had a major effect on my relationship with God from a deep place of my heart. I was wrecked!

I went back to my office, troubled that the tainted message was now all over the world, sitting in email in-boxes ready for people to see. But, then, I noticed something. I had actually forgotten to send the message to my email list, which would have been a point of no return! I never forget to do that! Reprieve! I quickly removed the questionable sentence, re-posted it to the website and then sent it to my email list. The pure prophetic message was delivered.

Less than three hours later, the blood blister in my mouth completely disappeared! God is so kind as he is training us in righteousness! I learned, as a seasoned minister of 22+ years, that promotion to new assignments requires trust of God that we will respond immediately and exactly to him, no matter how minor we believe the issue may be. I learned that lesson…or so I thought.

Sin Number Two

About a week later I had a great meeting with two state prayer leaders in Dearborn, Michigan. I can't explain it, but God was really getting my attention that day. It was as if there were an open heaven over me and God was calling me to engage with him. It really was quite amazing. After I left the meeting, I felt compelled to stop by the Detroit Prayer Furnace on my way home and get alone with the Lord. I craved him, and I could tell he craved time with me.

> I was in rebellion. My minor sin was major. My rejection of God was real.

I had also wanted to go to Best Buy at some point that day to buy something I really wanted, so that was definitely in the back of my mind.

I spent about 45 minutes getting into the zone in the prayer room trying to hear what the Lord had for me that day. I was still extremely stirred.

A friend unexpectedly showed up and we talked for just a little bit. He then decided to leave, and, with the desire to head to Best Buy increasing, I did too.

I felt a minor check in my spirit that I needed to stay put and keep seeking after God. Instead, I responded casually and thought that I could pray in the car and possibly reconnect with God later that night or tomorrow.

Well, I couldn't connect in the car, and my spirit was increasingly grieved, but I excused it away. I got to Best Buy, and almost left without buying what I wanted, and I felt that's what God wanted. Keep in mind, this is all low level stuff. It was minor. I didn't see an angel with instructions from Heaven. I was discerning something that felt more like the story of the Princess and the Pea. That small irritating pea wouldn't go away.

Before I left Best Buy, I checked one more aisle, and there it was—exactly what I wanted! And, they price matched Amazon.com, so I saved $20! I bought it, and my grief increased.

For one week my life was a swirl of God, Satan and flesh—all assaulting me. A very minor decision to casually respond to God and ignore his gentle prompts resulted in sleepless nights and non-stop feelings of demonization. Trust me, I am not exaggerating.

I was in rebellion. My minor sin was major. My rejection of God was real. He had called me up to the mountain to meet with me and I chose to remain at the bottom with a spirit of Egypt compelling me to worship a golden calf. I actually had a picture of my rebellion resulting in an eternity in Hell—just me, demons and that stupid item I bought at Best Buy! I was tormented!

You might try to encourage me by saying that there's no condemnation in Christ Jesus. That's true. But, I'm sober enough to admit that, in that moment of minor/major rebellion I really wasn't in Christ Jesus, I was in the flesh and unrepentant—and that's why the shouts of condemnation by the enemy were piercing me so effectively. Now, I believe God knew this trial would hit me, and he knows my heart is so deeply in love with his, so I wouldn't be dying in that state of rebellion. It was a Peter-denying-Christ type of moment. However, I'm also convinced that continued rebellion by me, someone who leads ministries, has written books, teaches on holiness, goes to church, pays my tithe, prays continually—would absolutely put me at risk of Hell.

> *Take care, brothers, lest there be in any of you an evil, unbelieving heart, leading you to fall away from the living God. But exhort one another every day, as long as it is called "today," that none of you may be hardened by the deceitfulness of sin. Hebrews 3:12-13*

After several days of wrestling with this issue, I was exhausted as I kept trying to connect with Jesus whom I love so much, and who loves me so much. I prayed, I worshiped, I listened to anointed music. Nothing worked. I had my intercessors praying for me. I was in darkness and I was wiped out. I cried out to God, *"Please talk to me! Give me something that will reveal what I am to do! I can't go on feeling alone and separated from you!"*

Within moments, my good friend Julia Palermo posted this on Facebook:

> *Any place in our lives and heart where we are exerting our will and ways over God's will and ways will inevitably drain us of energy and resources. Exertion=Exhaustion. On the other hand, death to self requires only that we lay down at the foot of the cross and give up the right to run our lives. We say with Christ, "Not my will but Yours be done Father." The Crucified life is the entrance into true rest. #ComeAndDie*

Jesus immediately answered me—and he did it on Facebook! I instantly packaged up what I bought at Best Buy to take it back. I crucified my flesh and returned my idol. Peace flooded my soul. The life and love of Jesus immediately returned in overwhelming fashion. I felt him instantly! The anointing spiked.

It's absolutely stunning how simple, minor sins can have such a profound impact on those called to serve the Lord!

Minor is major! The sins of apathy, gossip, independence, selfishness, materialism, idol worship, homosexuality, murder, rape and all of the others, major or minor, required the same death of Jesus.

Sins that are repented of, that have the blood of Jesus applied

We must refuse to be entertained by sin in media that required the mutilation and savage killing of the one we so passionately love.

to them, are eradicated! But, if we refuse to repent and confess and allow Jesus to have Lordship again, we cannot presume to be in a safe place.

God is going to hold ministers to a much higher standard. This is why we must pursue holiness and refuse to participate in the sins of culture through media, rebellion, materialism and independence.

We must refuse to be entertained by sin in media that required the mutilation and savage killing of the one we so passionately love. I rebuke the emerging spirit of the age that calls holiness and consecration legalism!

It's time to embrace a spirit of repentance. God is extremely kind. He was in my two back-to-back sins. But, he's equally serious. He will discipline those he loves. I am so thankful that he loves me.

Remember the miraculous appearance and disappearance of the blood blister under my tongue? It was God's loving kindness that instructed me in righteousness.

In Numbers 12 you can read about the story of Miriam and Aaron. They handled their words wrongly, as I did in my message, and they were struck, by God, with leprosy. After they repented, it cleared up.

Something also happened after I repented of my second sin by returning the item, which cost $50, to Best Buy. I was blown away! Immediately after I returned it, I received an email from Amazon. I received a totally surprising, unexpected $50 voucher!

Previously, I had rejected God and blessed myself. Now, I was obedient to God and he blessed me! When I rejected God's call to be with him, not only did I lose out on that encounter, I was out $50 of my own money. When I turned toward God and enjoyed him, I kept the money in my pocket as God blessed me with the exact same gift!

I ordered it and now have a story of how God can bless instead of a story of how I chose an idol over him!

The coming Church will gloriously be held accountable unlike ever before.

Compliance to God's Mandates

This brings us back to compliance.

God is raising up voices that will walk in true consecration and holiness. Not perfect people, but responsive people. People who will quickly repent and who will walk in true authority—authority to call the Church into compliance to the Word of God. Remember, their freedom is our mission! They are awaiting bold and obedient end-time deliverers!

When this generation's true prophetic messengers sound an alarm, it won't be open for discussion. We won't have the option to consider whether we want to obey or not. We will have to comply or suffer very real consequences. Are you one who will awaken the Church and call it to holiness, to prayer and to consecration? Are you walking in holiness? Are you listening to God, or are you casual, as I was in the two above stories? Pray for your discernment to increase, and get ready to gather the ready, responsive remnant that will offer no excuse as they respond to the alarms of the Lord as they are shouted through your blood-filled mouth!

> *Blow the trumpet in Zion; consecrate a fast; call a solemn assembly; gather the people. Consecrate the congregation; assemble the elders; gather the children, even nursing infants. Let the bridegroom leave his room, and the bride her chamber. Between the vestibule and the altar let the priests, the ministers of the LORD, weep and say, "Spare your people, O LORD, and make not your heritage a reproach, a byword among the nations. Why should they say among the peoples, 'Where is their God?'" Joel 2:15-17*

A Troubling End-Time Dream

Here is a clear example of a sharp, prophetic message. Will we respond to the call or casually watch from the sidelines?

It would be nice if all of our dreams, visions and communication from God had the feel of running and dancing through a field of daisies, but it's more important that we receive accurate data than imaginary, feel good stories.

This dream was anything but candy canes and ice cream. To date, other than my encounter with Hell in the early 1990s, I've never received such an urgent and troubling dream of God.

The first scene in my dream represented a typical American day. I was in my basement in a really comfortable leather recliner, sitting in front of a large television. I was excitedly watching my favorite NFL team, the Chicago Bears, play in a nationally televised evening game. I was thoroughly entertained and was settling in for a great night of football.

The scene then suddenly changed. I found myself in the captain's seat of the largest commercial airplane I'd even seen. In fact,

this jet was capable of holding over 1000 people. Everybody in the airplane was excited and ready for the journey—and they were all blood-bought Christians. They represented an end-time remnant being prepared by God for the days ahead.

In the cockpit, I was overwhelmed by the magnitude and majesty of the airplane. I put my hand on the throttle as we were sitting on the runway, ready to depart. Simply touching it revealed a power that was sobering indeed.

I understood that, as the captain of the airplane, my responsibility was immense. I felt completely incapable of fulfilling my duties, but at the same time, I felt such an overwhelming confidence. I had the grace to do what I was called to do, even though I didn't understand even how to take the first step.

In that grace, I gave the throttle a push. Every inch that I carefully moved the throttle forward it seemed that the power increased one hundredfold or more. The slight vibration that was caused by multiple jet engines kept increasing as I moved 1000 people down the runway.

Suddenly, we were airborne, and we were catapulted into our unknown mission.

Almost immediately, as I followed the flight plan, we were flying over an ocean. As I looked down, something unusual had caught my attention, and I yearned to move in for a closer look. I brought the jet down and flew just above the surface of the water. What I saw was remarkable. All around, sea life was leaping out of the water. Everybody in the airplane was glued to the windows as they were captivated by the same view. Dolphins and whales were jumping high into the air as were innumerable other creatures, many of which I had never seen before.

As I watched, my desire for greater revelation and encounter with this seeming other-worldly exhibition was rapidly increasing. I wanted more!

I then did what makes no sense in the natural—I nose-dived and took the giant airship under the water. The moment I did, the power of the engines rapidly increased. The deeper I went, the greater the power. Under the water, I saw things I had never seen before. It was dark, but all of the sea life was easily visible as they glowed in various brilliant colors. Needless to say I, along with my passengers, would never be the same again.

I then reemerged at the surface of the water and took the aircraft back up to cruising altitude. It was time to move on to our destination.

Just as we reached the appropriate altitude, I received an urgent radio transmission:

> *The airport you will soon arrive at has been overtaken by terrorists. When you land, you and your passengers will deplane and will be confronted by them. You have no option to divert to another airport. If you do, the missiles that are currently locked on to your aircraft will be launched and you will all perish. You have no option but to continue according to your original flight path and land.*

I then passed that information along to the 1000 passengers. In a moment, our joyful awe of what we experienced just moments ago shockingly changed to sobriety. We were about to land.

When we did, my two older boys (who at the time were approximately 10 and 12 years old) and I left the plane and entered the terminal.

I expected to see mass chaos, but I did not. Though there were many thousands of people in the terminal's various public areas, it was so quiet that you could hear someone cough from one hundred yards away. Fear had gripped everybody. They were scared silent.

Each public area looked the same. People were ordered to line up along the walls by a terrorist who was standing in the middle of the room. The terrorist was dressed fully in black and had a machine gun in his hands.

We were ushered into a room, and as we entered, my oldest son thought he saw someone he knew on the other side of the

room. Before I could do anything, he broke away from me, oblivious to what was happening, and ran across the room to see his friend. I knew it was the last time I'd ever hold my son.

I then held my younger son closer than ever as we took our place on the wall.

The terrorist then started addressing people as he walked along the wall. He slowly, methodically moved closer to where we were standing. He then stopped and ordered the man who was standing next to us to move to the center of the room. The terrorist asked this terrified man a question, *"Have you ever stolen anything?"*

The deeper we go, the more power and wonder we will experience.

He didn't know how to answer. Should he tell the truth and reveal that, yes, he had stolen something at some point in his life? Would that earn him favor with the terrorist? Or, should he lie and attempt to convince him he was pure and should not be executed?

I knew that it didn't matter how he responded. He was about to take his last breath.

What I saw next was grisly. I shielded my younger son's eyes as the terrorist pulled out a machete and started hacking the victim's fingers, a half an inch at a time. He dismembered this man and was ready to move on to the next—us.

Then I woke up.

What did it mean?

Football. In America, football is one of the enduring symbols of passionate, cultural entertainment. Of course, there is nothing inherently wrong with watching a football game, but the game's place in my dream was significant. It represented life as usual. I was happily distracted and nothing else existed on my grid that night.

The sudden shift to the cockpit is key. Vehicles often represent ministry when they occur in dreams. We must, as the remnant Church, be ready for a sudden move into critical end-time ministry. We have to be instant in and out of season. Our ears must be attentive to the prophetic voices that are sounding alarms in our nation.

Supernatural power and grace is coming to the true, remnant Church. The 1000 passengers represented the true Church—Christians who were ready to be carried by God and who were not doing so for their own enjoyment. The massive airplane and the immeasurable power that it produced was there for a purpose—to carry people into a mission. The coming Church will be marked by people, as in the first century Church, who are mission minded and willing to lay down their lives. They aren't there for the benefits alone.

When the remnant Church is in position, the adventure will begin! As in the dream, the first phase will include such glorious, supernatural revelation that we will be forever transformed. Those who are distracted by the offerings of the world will miss out on this remnant call into the shock and the awe of the glory of God! There is a consecration that's required for those who are interested in going into the deep places with God.

The deeper we go, the more power and wonder we will experience.

> *Then Joshua rose early in the morning and they set out from Shittim. And they came to the Jordan, he and all the people of Israel, and lodged there before they passed over. At the end of three days the officers went through the camp and commanded the people, "As soon as you see the ark of the covenant of the LORD your God being carried by the Levitical priests, then you shall set out from your place and follow it. Yet there shall be a distance between you and it, about 2,000 cubits in length. Do not come near it, in order that you may know the way you shall go, for you have not passed this way before."*

Then Joshua said to the people, "Consecrate yourselves, for tomorrow the LORD will do wonders among you." And Joshua said to the priests, "Take up the ark of the covenant and pass on before the people." So they took up the ark of the covenant and went before the people. Joshua 3:1-6

God is raising up captains, leaders who will, like Joshua, call everybody into position. They will lead the remnant Church out of typical, deadly desert life across the water and into promise.

The end-time company represented by the 1000 on the airplane will be those who, as priests of the Lord, will carry the ark of his presence into the mission.

We have never been this way before. It is a mystery, but a mystery well worth the trouble to discover. We must consecrate ourselves on this side of the unknown as we, in faith, get ready to experience the wonders of the Lord!

As we emerge out of revelation of the glory of God, we will be functioning from a place of power and radical transformation. We will then be ready for the troubling warnings of God.

I believe the terrorists in my dream are less symbolic than we might hope. Fear is about to grip our land as the enemy puts his boots on the ground. We must stand firm in the grace of God, even when horrific trouble comes, as it did for me as a father, when in my dream, my older son broke away from my care.

Very troubling times are ahead of us. The enemy's primary weapon will be the spirit of fear. God's primary weapon? The shock and the awe of the glory of God. The coming Church will be a Church that has gone deep in God together and my friend, this is the only Church that will be able to stand against the wickedness.

Interestingly, I discovered after I had this dream, that it is known that Islamic terrorists will actually chop off the fingers of thieves just as I witnessed in my dream. I had never heard of this before and it was further confirmation that the dream was communication from the Lord and that we must be ready for an assault against his Bride.

> *"As to the thief, Male or female, cut off his or her hands: a punishment by way of example, from Allah, for their crime: and Allah is Exalted in power." Quran 5:38*

Perfect love casts out fear, which is why we know the kingdom of darkness cannot win. This is all the more reason for the Church to go deep into God! We need a revelation of Jesus! The coming Church will have that revelation of deep, glorious love, and the enemy knows this. This is why he is unleashing a false-love movement that is actually founded on fear...

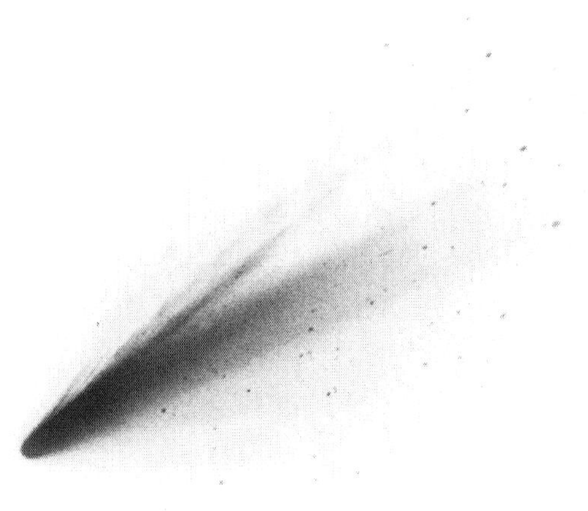

~ Six ~

The Great Love Deception

The Coming Church will demonstrate true love.

A deeper, weightier revelation of God's love is coming—and it will look much different than we realize. The coming Church will be marked by burning love, but before we can experience that, we must allow God to deconstruct any false image, any false idea of what love really is.

Are you ready for a deep, heavy, absolutely overwhelming revelation of God's love? So many are, and God is listening to their cries.

As I write this chapter, I'm sitting in a powerful session with Barbara Yoder, Cindy Williams and a ministry team from Catch the Fire (Toronto) at Shekinah Church in Ann Arbor. It's all about encountering the love of God, soaking in his presence and preparing to serve in love in a revival atmosphere. I'm yearning for more of this presence!

There is a massive increase in revelation of the love of God, the experience of his presence coming and much of it will fulfill the yearnings of our heart. I'm convinced that much of it will also be quite surprising to us regarding how it manifests. Just as the raging fire of God's power and love in the crater in my vision was both threatening and compelling, God's love will alert us, provoke us and woo us closer.

In order for there to be a false representation of anything, there must be a true, pure reality. Those of you who are longing for a pure, love-driven move of God, get ready! We are about to have the opportunity to go deeper than we ever have. True love will change the world. The burning, churning crater is filled with molten, liquid love!

We could spend trillions of years learning about and discovering and encountering the love of God. In fact, we will do so throughout all eternity. The Bible itself exhorts us to learn about love:

> *So this is my prayer: that your love will flourish and that you will not only love much but well. Learn to love appropriately. You need to use your head and test your feelings so that your love is sincere and intelligent, not sentimental gush. Live a lover's life, circumspect and exemplary, a life Jesus will be proud of... Philippians 1:9-10 (MSG)*

We are to learn to love appropriately. This Scripture is a critical exhortation! Why? It means there are inappropriate ways to love. There are deceptions that feel right but are poor representations or even counterfeits of truth.

As God's love begins to manifest in such amazing, deeper ways at the end of the age, we have to be aware that the enemy will work hard to redefine, misrepresent and twist true love. He has a castrated version to offer us.

The enemy is so terrified of pure love being revealed that he is willing to promote and endorse a compromised, lesser version of it. Love defined by human emotion instead of the Word is his plan.

Free Love

In the 1960s and 1970s we saw the emergence of free love.

From Wikipedia:

> *Free love is a social movement that rejects marriage, which is seen as a form of social and financial bondage. The Free Love movement's initial goal was to separate the state from sexual matters such as marriage, birth control, and adultery. It claimed that such issues were the concern of the people involved, and no one else.*
>
> *Much of the free-love tradition is an offshoot of anarchism, and reflects a libertarian philosophy that seeks freedom from state regulation and church interference in personal relationships.*

The free love movement was not a love movement at all. It was focused on self-satisfaction, personal experience and relational connections. The intimacy they sought after was never found. Sexual promiscuity served as a destructive, unfulfilling counterfeit.

I believe we are experiencing a similar free love movement in the Church today:

- **Rejecting marriage**: This speaks to a resistance to covenant. The desire is to control the love connection, the experience. When the emotional rush is gone and relational intimacy is disappointing, so many of today's Christians sever that connection and move on to more satisfying relationships. They move from partner to partner, driven by selfish ambition, seeking to be served instead of to serve.
- **Social and financial bondage**: Free love seeks after social and relational euphoria, and if this is not experienced, people tend to flee from the threat of bondage. True investment into others is resisted unless there is an exchange, unless what they are seeking after is given to them. The problem? This is relational prostitution. Many Christians will invest into others only if friendship is given in return.

- **Separation from the state**: Just as those in the free love movement several decades ago sought after liberation from governmental control, many Christians today reject biblical government. Government requires submission, and submission doesn't feel like love—though it is. Kingdom order requires submission, respect of boundaries and a surrender of personal rights. This is love! We hear so much about human rights today, as if it's the purest manifestation of love. It is not! The homosexual movement demands the government stays out of their intimate pursuits. The pro-choice movement demands the government stays out of their wombs. 1 Corinthians 13 reveals that love is not self-seeking! It's not about human rights. It's about serving God's government, his purposes and his people.

False-Love Myths & Deceptions

Keep in mind that false or tainted love doesn't flow mostly from an evil, debased heart. It also doesn't mean that there is nothing about the argument or viewpoint that is true. A person who craves pure love can, in their zeal or in their weakness, allow impurities into their expression of love that twists and compromises it. The reason I needed to say this is to encourage you if you've been hit by the false-love spirit. Your desire for manifested love is probably true, yet the enemy can come in and confuse the process.

The coming Church will be introducing pure, true love and it's important that we are ready for this shift.

With that in mind, here are some false-love (or tainted love) myths and deceptions that have hit the Church:

Expecting or demanding love from others

Remember, love is not self-seeking. Have you ever been wounded by someone who didn't act in love toward you? It

is normal to desire to be loved, but true love doesn't expect or demand others to be the one to fulfill that desire. Pointing our fingers at others who aren't acting in love is evidence that we ourselves do not love.

If someone isn't acting in love toward you, isn't relationally close to you, won't befriend you, how will you react? Will you refuse to invest into them unless you get something in return? You have actually fallen into relational prostitution. Jesus laid down his life for those who hated him and we must do the same.

Focusing on God's love is all we need

This is a disturbing trend in the Church, but it's actually not mostly incorrect. It's mostly right! The argument is that when we focus on experiencing the pure, true love of Jesus, everything else in life just falls into place. If we focus on love, sin won't be an issue. Maturity will just happen. Not so. What is mostly right? Well, the greater the revelation of God's love for us, the more we want to be holy, respond in obedience and mature. Love is a great motivator! However, experiencing love is not all we need! The Bible is filled with instructions and mandates and focuses that we are responsible to respond to even if the love connection isn't there one day.

Additionally, the Bible is filled with stories of people who loved God, and who sinned. Being with Jesus, loving Jesus, being intimate with Jesus is worthy of most of our energy and focus. However, even in a deep, intimate place with Jesus, obedience can be hard. Flesh can rise up. Satan can tempt. We can be deceived. Our theologies can be off. This is why we must continually let God search our hearts for any wicked way in us. We must be in the Word! We must be submitted to authorities who watch out for our souls. We can't just enjoy God and presume our job is done.

Love initiated pride

There seems to be a rapid emergence of those who are going after the love of Jesus and who are resisting discipline and discipleship. The reason? Pride. The presumption is that their encounter with the love of God has elevated them to a point where they no longer need to be a student of the Word, to focus on the sin potential in their lives or submit to others. They wouldn't say that they are above others, but their arguments reveal their hearts more than not. When the call for holiness, brokenness, study, obedience, etc. is presented to them, they become puffed up and in turn, while rejecting your "inferior focuses", call you to come up higher and just focus on love. Their response very often is, *"If you really understood the Father's love, you would see what I mean."* It's arrogance masquerading as spirituality. The very fact that this is happening is a revelation that they have not truly experienced love the way they claim.

Love must always manifest a certain way

In Scripture, we do have a great definition of love in 1 Corinthians 13. So, it is true that, for example, love is always patient. If you aren't patient, then that is a specific issue that you can analyze in yourself. However, there is a spirit of accusation in the camp that moves outside of this scriptural definition and declares that if you don't function a certain way, then you don't love the way God loves. For example, someone might say to an intercessor, *"If you truly loved people, you would move out of your prayer closet and hit the streets and feed the homeless!"* It's an accusation against a child of God that they don't love, because they don't fit into an imperfect definition of what love really is. Can you really imagine someone looking at a sweet, passionate grandma who prays with tears every day that she that doesn't love people because she isn't street witnessing? On the flip side, an intercessor might say, *"If you truly loved people, you would spend hours a day praying for them!"*

Additionally, love will manifest through the different offices. Love looks different when delivered through a pastor than it does when delivered through a prophet. As a church leader, I have had to expend a lot of energy explaining to people what type of love and connection they might expect from someone like me. Most people think I'm a pastor when they first meet me (because church leaders in America are almost always called "Pastor"). If people presume that I will express love like a pastor, they can actually get very offended when that doesn't happen.

Accusations can fly. But, if we simply understood that, in addition to the 1 Corinthians 13 definition, different people, different offices and different cultures will express love very, very differently, it will be easy to honor and love them instead of making demands of them.

> Today, sharp, provoking preaching is rejected, because it doesn't feel good. They might say in their disturbed state, "That's not the Jesus I know."

Love always feels good

Oh boy, this one is big. When we encounter love, we will be presented with a view of God that is quite different than what we previously understood to be true. God's love can be expressed in a very direct, uncomfortable way that breaks you, and you may even make you wonder how a loving God could act that way. God's expression of love will often put you at risk, threaten you and trouble you. Jesus' expression of love on the cross put Peter at risk of the same grisly death! How could

Jesus do this? Peter was confused as he was presented with a side of Jesus he never saw—and he denied that expression of Jesus and his love for the world! I guarantee that Peter did not feel good as Jesus loved him by rescuing him from Hell by dying on the cross.

Today, sharp, provoking preaching is rejected, because it doesn't feel good. They might say in their disturbed state, *"That's not the Jesus I know."* The risk is, like with Peter, rejection of God when the feelings aren't warm and intimate. This is one reason why being people of the Word is non-negotiable. We can't afford to call good evil and evil good. We must learn about Jesus and how he functions so that our emotions don't lead us astray. Remember, God is love. All of him, not just the parts that feel nice.

God is always in a good mood

Not true. Period. I've said it this way: If God is always in a good mood, he would be a monster, laughing and doing a happy dance as he casts people he loves into Hell.

If we believe God is always in a good mood, we will reject messages and revelations that don't result in us being in a good mood. We will associate the love of God with the hate of Satan. We know that God is still wrathful. He still gets angry. He is saddened. He is joyful. He is happy. He has moods, and the deepest place of love exists when we partner with God in his emotions. What is on God's heart? How can we serve him and minister to him?

For the sake of qualifying this point, there are some who might say that God isn't moody—meaning, God isn't tossed around emotionally, having mood swings like those so common to humans. However, he does have moods, he does have emotions, and they often change based on what is going on in the world and in his heart.

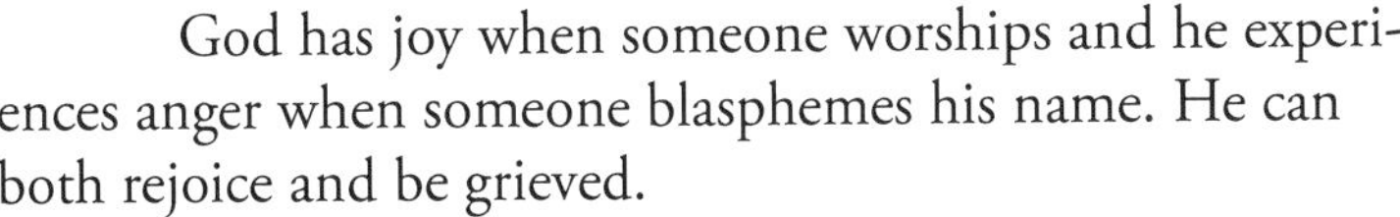

God has joy when someone worships and he experiences anger when someone blasphemes his name. He can both rejoice and be grieved.

Love requires that you are emotionally connected

Again, not true. Humans have the ability to love many but can only befriend a few. Different people have different capacities, but the principle remains the same. Don't presume someone doesn't love you if they don't get close to you at a heart level. In fact, may I be so bold as to say, they might not like you! To love someone does not require that we like them. So we can love the masses and only connect at a close, friendship level with a few. Think about it. Do you want to be friends with everybody? Nope. Why would you expect the same from another? A rejection complex has really done a lot of damage to people—and they look for their healing to come from others loving them the way they want instead of dying to self and refusing to place that burden on them.

> If God is always in a good mood, he would be a monster, laughing and doing a happy dance as he casts people he loves into Hell.

I remember a mega-church pastor who was extremely popular. He felt like your best friend though you really didn't have a real personal relationship with him. People often wanted to get close to him, and they actually had a bit of a system in place to handle that! An associate would approach those who were a bit overzealous in their attempts to befriend the pastor. He'd say, *"The Pastor will serve you well and express love by leading you, teaching you and helping you connect with Jesus. However, don't expect him to be a personal friend of yours."* The same scenario is true for small churches. The pastor may be an introvert, may have

limited emotional energy or simply may be called to focus on different things! Don't presume that someone doesn't love you just because they aren't serving you the way you want. How potentially offensive and seemingly arrogant is this passage?

Now in these days when the disciples were increasing in number, a complaint by the Hellenists arose against the Hebrews because their widows were being neglected in the daily distribution. And the twelve summoned the full number of the disciples and said, "It is not right that we should give up preaching the word of God to serve tables. Therefore, brothers, pick out from among you seven men of good repute, full of the Spirit and of wisdom, whom we will appoint to this duty. But we will devote ourselves to prayer and to the ministry of the word." Acts 6:1-4

They were saying that they would not be connecting to people who needed help! They would focus on connecting to God and their very specific tasks! And, my good friends, that is love! They weren't to feed the widows. They weren't to make hospital visits. They weren't to answer their phones every time someone needed them. They were to pray and preach, and that was deep, fiery love!

You have to convince people that you love them

We are to be kind, without question. However, we aren't to modify our messages, to soften our speech or to attempt to convince people that we love them. We should simply love them! How's this statement of love:

Men of Israel, hear these words: Jesus of Nazareth, a man attested to you by God with mighty works and wonders and signs that God did through him in your midst, as you yourselves know— This Jesus, delivered up according to the definite plan and foreknowledge of God, you crucified and killed by the hands of lawless men. God raised him up, loosing the pangs of death, because it was not possible for him to be held by it. Acts 2:22-24

"You killed him!" He was in their grill! He was bringing correction with a bold, fiery spirit! He wasn't worried about hurting their feelings—he was proclaiming the power of Jesus! His goal wasn't to sit down and ask how their heart was, how they were feeling, or if they feel OK. He was in another mode, functioning in love, rocking their world and exposing their thinking that would lead them to Hell! I'm sure they didn't feel loved, but if they responded to Peter's message, they would have been flooded with the experiential, burning love of Jesus!

Hard messages aren't driven by love

This is attached to the above point, but it's worthy of some extra attention. Jonathan Edwards' message "Sinners in the hands of an angry God" is largely dismissed by today's ultra-sensitive, thin-skinned culture as unloving. I've heard it said that he didn't have a revelation of the Father's love. This is not only wrong, it's a violation of scriptural truth! We cannot avoid the hard messages of sin, Hell and repentance out of fear that we'll be rejected by those who are offended. We can't modify our messages to sound loving—we must trust that the Word of God is a message of love! Truth delivered in love doesn't always feel great, and it will offend many, but those who receive it are changed forever!

We could go on and on for quite a while discussing myths and deceptions regarding love. The enemy is terrified of the manifestation of true love, and he's offering a castrated version of it to those who are seeking after good, happy feelings. Castrated love feels good, but it has no ability to bring forth life!

It's time for us to trust God as he is, not as we want him to be. It's time to dive into the Word, and embrace Jesus as he manifests a variety of emotions which are all rooted in love. The coming

Church will be literally burning in liquid love—and we cannot fall for any lesser or counterfeit expression of it!

Almost Homosexual: A Crisis in the Church

The false-love movement is in full force, and we see arguments for it coming from several camps, including the homosexual camp. However, allow me to offer a deeper viewpoint regarding this. There is a crisis in the Church, and it might surprise us how it's manifesting.

After I woke up from a significant dream about Ellen DeGeneres, I read my verse of the day… here it is:

> *Be wise when you engage with those outside the faith community; make the most of every moment and every encounter. Colossians 4:5*

I felt God had a message of love for Ellen that I should try to get to her.

I decided to email Ellen. I have no idea if she will ever get it, but I pray she does.

Here's what I sent to Ellen DeGeneres:

> *Here's a strange story for ya! I'm a pastor & author, and I had a dream about you last night. It was crazy long and detailed and the first two part dream I've had (I got up to go to the bathroom in the middle and the dream continued after I went back to sleep).*
>
> *You aren't someone I think about often at all (sorry!), so I have a feeling God may have dropped that dream on me. It started with you at the Academy Awards (or something similar) and you called me on stage from the audience. I was overwhelmed with grief and whispered to you, "Please forgive me for judging you."*

Later, you went on to share with me from your heart about some pain and you talked about your mom. Later on I met your mom and your brother at their home. (I didn't realize you had a brother until I googled it just a moment ago.)

There were other pieces to the dream, but I thought I'd leave it at that for now.

A little about me; I may appear to fit the stereotype as I do believe any lifestyle that embraces activities that God, in his wisdom, deems unhealthy must be avoided. Homosexuality included. However, what's also included is pride, which the Christian Church is often steeped in. So is selfish ambition and having cold love. All deadly, all have hit the Church at large. Again, please forgive me.

After the dream I decided to preach tonight on a crazy controversial message calling the Church to repentance titled, "Almost Homosexual: The Church in Crisis."

God likes you, he loves you. Me too.

As I share this particular urgent and troubling prophetic message, I must do my best to make several points extremely clear.

> God is passionately jealous and zealous for his beautiful bride, the Church.

God is passionately jealous and zealous for his beautiful bride, the Church. His emotions are extreme and deep as he yearns for love-fueled intimacy with those he laid down his life for. His affection cannot be described by even the most romantic or poetic language.

When I mention the Church in this message, I am referring to the global body of Christ. The global bride of Christ. I'm fully aware and thankful that there are many local expressions of the Church that are radically surrendered and given to the lover of their souls—Jesus Christ.

The primary points I will expound on have little to do with sexuality, or sexual sin. You will have to intentionally keep this in mind so as to ensure you understand the issues when I deal with the spirits behind homosexuality and how these spirits are being embraced in the Church (again, the global Church or the Church in general). It's also important to understand that demonic strategies can manifest differently depending on the setting. The thought of a homosexual spirit infiltrating the church is a potentially offensive suggestion. However, if we understand that demonic attacks can manifest in very different ways depending on who is being attacked, this session will be easier to understand.

A spirit of anger can cause one to murder and another to simply be angry. It's the same spirit with different manifestations. Jesus was communicating this truth when he compared murder to anger:

> *"You have heard that it was said to those of old, 'You shall not murder; and whoever murders will be liable to judgment.' But I say to you that everyone who is angry with his brother will be liable to judgment; whoever insults his brother will be liable to the council; and whoever says, 'You fool!' will be liable to the hell of fire. Matthew 5:21-22*

Massive Repentance

> *The heart is deceitful above all things, and desperately sick; who can understand it? "I the LORD search the heart and test the mind, to give every man according to his ways, according to the fruit of his deeds." Jeremiah 17:9-10*

This is a powerful verse, and the more time we spend on our face in the presence of God, the more we realize how true it is.

Before we can go any further, we have to all agree on the above point that is found in Jeremiah 17: *Our hearts are both deceitful and wicked.* What does this mean? Very simply, it's possible and common for impure motives to be rooted deeply in us even though we may be devoted followers of Christ.

The more time I spend in prayer the easier it is for the Lord to dig deep and bring to the surface issues that wouldn't normally be evident. My heart has harbored pride at times though at the surface I felt meek. Other times I've verbally forgiven people, but then the Holy Spirit revealed to me a deeper reality—that I hadn't truly done so.

This is why we must not only be OK with messages like this one, but we have to eagerly invite God to shine his burning light into every part of our lives.

> *And I said: "Woe is me! For I am lost; for I am a man of unclean lips, and I dwell in the midst of a people of unclean lips; for my eyes have seen the King, the LORD of hosts!" Isaiah 6:5*

When God is in our midst, a revelation of our own sin and issues are made known. A key problem today is that God's manifest presence isn't with us as He should be! Jesus is the Spirit of Prophecy. He is the Revelation. He is the Word. Where God is, revelation is. You can't separate the two.

As God, in his burning love for us, reveals our hearts to us, we will find ourselves falling to our knees.

God is calling the Church to massive repentance.

Almost Homosexual?

God has suddenly revisited me with a prophetic word that shocked me and those I shared it with a few years ago—and he's added to the revelation.

Trust me, I've waited several days before deciding to write this (I usually write prophetic words the moment I receive them). I have considered the trouble it may bring. I've also considered God's thoughts about the matter and I've chosen to trust his wisdom that this revelation will free many more people than it will disturb. God's word and his wisdom must return to the pulpits again.

> *"If Jesus had preached the same message that ministers preach today, He would never have been crucified." — Leonard Ravenhill*

> *Take care, lest you forget the covenant of the LORD your God, which he made with you, and make a carved image, the form of anything that the LORD your God has forbidden you. For the LORD your God is a consuming fire, a jealous God. Deuteronomy 4:23-24*

God is jealous of his Church—and the spirits that have not only invaded the Church but have been embraced by the Church have made him jealous indeed.

As I was on the airplane flying into Colorado a few years ago, the Lord surprised me with a strong and striking word for the Church. I was shaking.

The Church is almost homosexual.

This is a word that I'm confident is tearing at the heart of God…he's watching his bride become bewitched.

The massive collision of a spiritual asteroid will bring correction to the current Church, and the resulting fire-filled crater will bring purity. The coming Church will be a pure Church that's eager for God's loving judgment.

With that in mind, here's a question—*is it possible that we in the Church are close to embracing the same spirits that fuel the homosexual agenda? Is it possible we, at least in part, already are?*

As I was watching the mountains of Colorado draw closer during the final approach to the airport that day, the Lord revealed three drivers of the homosexual agenda:

Pride
Identity
Lust

We can't cast out the same demonic spirits we embrace.

Understand—*the primary driver of the homosexual agenda is not same-sex attraction*, but rather strong deceiving spirits of pride, self-promotion and identity, and lust.

I was on a train where I saw two homosexual girls very visibly hanging on each other, making it very clear that they were together. Their actions were not a result of raging hormones, but rather, they were making a bold declaration, a prideful pronouncement of their chosen identity as lesbians.

They wanted to force affirmation, be noticed and demand acceptance and equality.

The Church has been bewitched by the same spirits that give fuel to the homosexual agenda—and this is a primary reason we have not had success in winning homosexuals to Jesus. *We can't cast out the same demonic spirits we embrace.*

Pride

We've all heard of gay pride. Pride is a hallmark of the homosexual movement and all too often, it's a driver of the Church as well.

I hear continually that it's rare to find a church where the tangible, manifest presence of God can be experienced. I believe, sadly, there are more Ichabod churches than we realize. An Ichabod church is simply a church that is devoid of God's glory. The ark of God's presence has been captured. It doesn't mean God hates that church. Quite the opposite—He is grieved that he must be removed from his lover, his bride.

> *And she named the child Ichabod, saying, "The glory has departed from Israel!" because the ark of God had been captured and because of her father-in-law and her husband. And she said, "The glory has departed from Israel, for the ark of God has been captured." 1 Samuel 4:21-22*

> *...Clothe yourselves, all of you, with humility toward one another, for "God opposes the proud but gives grace to the humble." 1 Peter 5:5*

You may not have thought about it this way, but God, though he loves so deeply, actually opposes or resists those who are proud. God's glory departs.

We live in a culture where we fight for success, we jockey for position, and we can't imagine being hidden or failing. Compromise has consumed the Church as it seeks success, a larger building, more people, more influence, more money and other demands. Pride has resulted in worship of images made of gold. Humility demands the gold is given as worship to God. Pride has resulted in worshiping a packed house. Humility calls for laying down our lives for even one.

We wonder why the Church isn't having more success in the culture.

I believe a key reason is that we are attempting to attack worldly pride with religious pride. We are actually retaining the services of the very same demons that we are attempting to battle! A spirit of pride! God resists the proud! Is it possible that we are attempting to change culture from a position of religious pride all while God is not standing with us?

When humility reigns, the Church will have the grace that God promises in 1 Peter 5.

Identity

This point is the most burning issue in my spirit right now.

I am fully given to seeing people step into their destinies, discover their true identity in Christ and discover freedom from lies and emotional scars that the enemy has given them. It's a significant focus of my own ministry.

However, we have a growing problem.

Focus is on self more often than it is on God.

Focus is on living more than it is on dying daily.

We are fools for Christ's sake, but you are wise in Christ. We are weak, but you are strong. You are held in honor, but we in disrepute. To the present hour we hunger and thirst, we are poorly dressed and buffeted and homeless, and we labor, working with our own hands. When reviled, we bless; when persecuted, we endure; when slandered, we entreat. We have become, and are still, like the scum of the world, the refuse of all things. 1 Corinthians 4:10-13

Please understand, I believe we are seated in heavenly places with Christ Jesus. We are kings and priests. We have great authority. We have overcome. We are the head and not the tail, above and not beneath.

But, our identities, when rightfully understood, don't lead us to focusing mostly on personal benefit. When we embrace the cross of Christ, which is where our identities originate, we are now focused on going low, humbling ourselves, serving with passion, and identifying with the scum of the world—so that they might have life and have it more abundantly.

A focus on our own benefits, our own healings, our own identities as it relates to personal gain, has actually resulted in us aligning with a key spirit that drives the homosexual movement.

Just as with homosexuals, God loves them and us too deeply to affirm a false identity—no matter how desirable and convincing that identity may be! God's wisdom is much higher than ours, and it takes humility to admit that.

This is a huge, huge point!

When we fight for a false identity that feels so overwhelmingly a part of us, and when our focus is on acceptance, affirmation and human rights, we give up the call to die to our own desires. Suddenly securing our own identity is more important than serving the masses.

The goal is not to be affirmed, accepted, liked, or honored. We aren't to look for equality. We don't compare ourselves with others. We can't make demands when life is unfair. The Church is to die so that others may live. Our identity is to be fully and entirely in Christ.

An improper attention given to the pursuit of identity (acceptance, affirmation, etc.) causes us to forsake the call to focus on our mission, for the sake of devotion to narcissism. This is where the temptation to disobey God and submit to the demands of man can happen.

> *For where jealousy and selfish ambition exist, there will be disorder and every vile practice. James 3:16*

Lust

Lust is oozing through the Church today. Yes, it's true that sexual lust is rampant. Some reports reveal pornography has been viewed by as many as 50% of Christian men recently while others state as many as 95% of Christian men are involved.

However, lust is not limited to the sexual variety.

Simply ask the question, *"What causes you to get excited, to come alive?"*

Many honest Christians would admit that everything from money, to fame, to popularity, to sex, could be the answers.

> *But each person is tempted when he is lured and enticed by his own desire. Then desire when it has conceived gives birth to sin, and sin when it is fully grown brings forth death. James 1:14-15*

Lust results in death. It really is that simple. The life is sucked right out of people. Suicide is on the rise. Eternal death is another threat as well.

The bride is becoming intimate with the bride.

This is a tragic reality in the Church today—we've lost our first love! False intimacy in the form of lust has taken the place of a deep, satisfying, truly intimate and never ending encounter with Jesus! He yearns for us while his beautiful bride is yearning for other lovers!

The Church has lost its desire for intimacy with Jesus. Many Christians don't even know what it is to be overwhelmed by his deep, burning love. Jesus is more of a principle or a foreign character in a book than he is a real, tangible, literal person you can feel.

This lack of revelation and encounter in a very intimate, life-giving way with Jesus has resulted in one more comparison with the homosexual movement:

The bride is becoming intimate with the bride.

What does that mean? Does it mean we can't have close relationships with other people? No, not at all. In fact, closer, deeper friendships with people are coming—but they can never be a substitute for our jealous Bridegroom.

The problem? We have become more interested in reproducing after our own kind than in receiving a fresh impartation directly from God himself. How does this play out? Several ways:

We become enthralled with a certain stream in the body (Word of Faith, House of Prayer, etc.) and want to have a relationship with that stream hoping that it produces life.

We turn to other people in the Church instead of to God through prayer and study of the Word, in the hopes that the union can result in the outcome we are looking for.

We are more connected socially to people than we are spiritually to God.

We believe our church growth comes through people, so we compromise the mission, cancel prayer, water down the message and get intimate with the body!

An intimate union with God will result in a fresh stream birthing through your ministry!

A deep encounter with Jesus will bring the results that a million human counselors never could!

"You can have all of your doctrines right—yet still not have the presence of God." — Leonard Ravenhill

The Solution

Intimacy. Repentance. Falling in love with Jesus. Humility.

"A sinning man stops praying, a praying man stops sinning" — Leonard Ravenhill

Yes, fervent, zealous prayer must return to our churches again!

if my people who are called by my name humble themselves, and pray and seek my face and turn from their wicked ways, then I will hear from heaven and will forgive their sin and heal their land. Now my eyes will be open and my ears attentive to the prayer that is made in this place. For now I have chosen and consecrated this house that my name may be there forever. My eyes and my heart will be there for all time. 2 Chronicles 7:14-16

We cannot anymore develop systems that enhance our own identities, stroke our pride or fuel our lust for power, recognition or anything else. The coming Church will be a humble Church.

It's time again to declare the cross, holiness, humility and passion from our pulpits and on our faces!

The core call is for a movement of humility and holiness.

It's a call to become broken and undone, desperate and deeply intimate with Jesus.

It's a call to a fasted lifestyle, to full surrender and complete saturation in the advance of the Kingdom.

It's a call to the deeply humble, yet powerfully bold life of John the Baptist.

Are we ready to let the lover of our souls invade the deepest parts of our inner man? He is wooing his glorious bride back to him…will we respond?

Draw me after you; let us run. The king has brought me into his chambers. Song of Songs 1:4

Shock Christianity

You might be of the opinion that the previous section was quite provocative, that it went too far. The times are far too urgent to remain passive, silent and to deliver moderated messages that feel good but do little.

A prophetic alarm is sounding as a code blue Church is under the shock paddles of the great Physician.

I'm going to take the opportunity to lay some very important things out on the table—in the hopes that God will bring clarity to what is expected in this end-of-the-age season that we are in.

I will also share very important information about why I personally focus on such a narrow, offensive, troubling message. It's important that you hear my heart on this.

> A leader's responsibility is not to connect to everybody. It's to connect everybody to God.

I had planned on writing an article dealing with the issue of love as it's revealed through prophetic voices for the last week, and since then I've had at least a few key unexpected discussions regarding what one called "Shock Christianity."

I believe this is evidence that it's time to both humbly ask God to inspect our hearts (as I always do when I find myself in such active and controversial seasons) and clearly communicate what is truly to be expected.

It's extremely easy to point out self-defined lack in another's life with the accusation that they are not acting in love. This is an accusation that I and many other aggressive and prophetic leaders, who shock, rock, tear down idols and altars, have received more than once.

The problem? There's confusion about what love is, and also about how to react when someone isn't manifesting love in the way we think they should. Remember, the coming Church will be burning in supernatural love that is so pure that it will transform us for eternity. It's all about love! Or better said, it's all about true love.

Friendship & Emotional Intimacy

For many, especially those with a high mercy gift, the seemingly obvious, non-negotiable manifestation of love is close friendship and deep, emotional intimacy.

This isn't an inappropriate desire—it's the way many are wired. But, it is inappropriate to presume that a lack of emotional intimacy is evidence of a lack of love.

It's too easy to point a finger at someone who has established healthy boundaries and accuse them of not loving you. The accurate analysis would actually be that they most probably do love you, but they don't desire emotional intimacy with you.

In fact, it may hurt, but we have to understand that not everybody wants to be our friend! That doesn't mean they don't love us, it just means that they don't feel impressed to develop that type of relationship with us. They are limited in their ability or desire to befriend certain people, and that's OK. It's normal.

I personally know that not everybody will like me, and not everybody will want to be my friend. It would actually be really bizarre if that weren't true!

Additionally, for many leaders, their primary goal isn't to connect with everybody, but rather it's to connect everybody to God. That is a valid and important ministry.

I think of Mike Bickle who isn't going to just befriend anybody who walks into IHOP, but he absolutely will invest every ounce of his energy to help you connect to Jesus. What love that is!

What is Love?

That's a loaded question. I feel all of us would agree that the answer is wildly expansive and multifaceted.

And that it is. If the definition of biblical love is so deep and wide, why is it that we get offended when someone doesn't fit our shallow and narrow definition of love?

If you search for "God's Love" on Amazon, it returns 311,863 available books. It's an inexhaustible topic!

When you read Scripture, it is again, inexhaustible. Of course, we do have quite a wonderful definition here:

> *If I speak in the tongues of men and of angels, but have not love, I am a noisy gong or a clanging cymbal. And if I have prophetic powers, and understand all mysteries and all knowledge, and if I have all faith, so as to remove mountains, but have not love, I am nothing. If I give away all I have, and if I deliver up my body to be burned, but have not love, I gain nothing.*
>
> *Love is patient and kind; love does not envy or boast; it is not arrogant or rude. It does not insist on its own way; it is not irritable or resentful; it does not rejoice at wrongdoing, but rejoices with the truth. Love bears all things, believes all things, hopes all things, endures all things. 1 Corinthians 13:1-7*

I personally consider this passage often. Really, I do so continually. For me, loving with God's love is non-negotiable, though it is so easy to fail. The fear of the Lord is on me regarding the issue as this passage reveals a sharp warning to those who minister without loving. For someone with a "shock Christianity" mandate, this is all the more sobering. I must love without fail while shaking the sleepers. If love doesn't drive the shaking, if it's selfish ambition or greed that does it, I am in big trouble.

Now, this passage isn't to be used as ammunition against others who don't measure up, but instead it's to be a sword to our own hearts. We need to let God break us. Don't look to others who seem to be failing in love and accuse them of failure. You love them without reserve! Cover them as Noah was covered by two of his three sons. Don't be the son that exposed his father's nakedness! That results in a curse!

> *Noah began to be a man of the soil, and he planted a vineyard. He drank of the wine and became drunk and lay uncovered in his tent. And Ham, the father of Canaan, saw the nakedness*

of his father and told his two brothers outside. Then Shem and Japheth took a garment, laid it on both their shoulders, and walked backward and covered the nakedness of their father. Their faces were turned backward, and they did not see their father's nakedness.

When Noah awoke from his wine and knew what his youngest son had done to him, he said, "Cursed be Canaan; a servant of servants shall he be to his brothers." He also said, "Blessed be the LORD, the God of Shem; and let Canaan be his servant. May God enlarge Japheth, and let him dwell in the tents of Shem, and let Canaan be his servant." Genesis 9:20-27

Love According To The Bible

There are questions we have to ask ourselves to ensure we are personally living in the love of God:

- **Am I patient?** This doesn't mean we aren't bold or that we don't challenge people to pick up the pace. This is a heart issue. Can we advance with determination while also honoring people who are slower than us?
- **Am I kind?** This is also an attitude of the heart. It doesn't mean we are passive or soft spoken. It just means we are looking out for the needs of others.
- **Do I envy others?** Jealousy divides. Enough said.
- **Do I boast?** Do I have pride that results in attempting to outshine others?
- **Am I arrogant?** Boldness and arrogance are closely related. One is Holy Spirit driven, the other is not. I'm sure people might accuse me of arrogance due to my aggressive, urgent focus on life, and my unwillingness to entertain lukewarm theologies, but I am consistently asking God to search my heart on this. I desire to be bold without reservation, even if it looks like arrogance. I'm not out to prove I love people. I'm to

love them, and sometimes it can get testy as I promote God's messages that irritate the resisters.

- **Am I rude?** I post a lot on Facebook and Twitter. My goal is to be extremely provocative (to shock!), and I'll talk about that more in a bit. But it is always extremely important for me to not be rude. It's critical that, while I provoke, I also honor and refuse to react in a rude or condescending manner.
- **Do I insist on my own way?** This is about selfishness. Am I self-centered and demanding? Or, do I prefer others above myself?
- **Am I irritable?** I will admit that I wrestle with this one at times! It's usually because of small but nonetheless meaningful issues. I have to be sensitive to my family by not getting irritated when they aren't in the car ready to go on time or when the kids' chores aren't done. I have improved greatly, but I must remain sensitive to this.
- **Am I resentful?** When life doesn't go as planned, do I resent God or other people who didn't live up to my expectations?
- **Do I rejoice at wrongdoing?** Or do I do the opposite as revealed in Ephesians 5 by exposing the fruitless deeds of darkness? Even when accusations of lacking love fly, we can humbly go to prayer, let God search our hearts and review the above scriptural revelation of what love looks like.

So, if someone is aggressive, bold, focused, not easily approachable, confrontational, controversial, troubling or intent on tearing down false ideologies that people hold dear, does that reveal a lack of love? Not according to the Bible. In fact, they may love with such a passion that they are more focused on loving than on convincing people they love.

False Expectations

In our culture, love is defined in a way that is often different than what we see in Scripture. For example, there is a false-love movement on the rise that presumes that relational friendship is a required manifestation of true love. I disagree. That false expectation will leave many wounded when someone who does truly love doesn't show it the way they would prefer. Offense will follow, and division, hard hearts and cold love are next.

This is an eternal issue! We cannot allow false expectations to result in cold love! If others don't love us the way we want, do we ourselves lose our love for them?

> *And then many will fall away and betray one another and hate one another. And many false prophets will arise and lead many astray. And because lawlessness will be increased, the love of many will grow cold. But the one who endures to the end will be saved. Matthew 24:10-13*

I'll say it again—true love doesn't demand that others respond lovingly. True love is seen on the cross where Jesus didn't demand any affirmation, friendship, encouragement or any outward manifestation of affection. We know from the encounter in the garden just prior to his arrest that he desired relational closeness, but he didn't get offended when his friends slept while he sweat and bled.

True maturity comes from our garden experiences. If we can't escape the lonely bleeding in the garden without offense toward the unconcerned selfish sleepers rising up in our hearts, how can we expect to take up our cross for them? Do we demand that they manifest love toward us, or do we simply love them unto death?

People who struggle with fear and rejection are often hit by the enemy regarding this. They so crave affirmation (which feels like love), that when they don't get it, it's easy to accuse the person of not loving them. The problem? Affirmation and love are not the same.

You can love someone without affirming them, befriending them or even talking to them!

John Doesn't Love People

I told you I was going to lay it on the table!

This one hurts so deeply!

There was a situation in Colorado many years ago that resulted in an underground "spirit of Absalom" situation (when someone close to us stole the hearts of those under our care; 2 Samuel 15) that was fueled by offense. I started to hear the rumors: John doesn't love people. Amy and I felt like we were hit by a train.

Someone on my staff had a false expectation about something I considered to be incredibly minor. I was unable to meet that specific request due to needing to be somewhere later that night. It wasn't until months later that I put two and two together and realized that an underground movement of gossip was setting some on my staff and team against me. The accusation? I don't love people because I wasn't there for them that day. Further, since that situation, according to their analysis, revealed my true, unloving heart, and my motives in ministry were now compromised, there must be an effort to resist the ministry—and, for them, it was in the name of *love!*

My initial split-second reaction when I received knowledge of the situation was this: *That doesn't make sense! I love that person and the others so much. Of all things how could that be the accusation?*

I was really saddened that those who I expressed love to by welcoming them onto our team, supporting them in their ministries, encouraging them to be free to lead with passion, etc. were rejecting my expression of love! Wow! Isn't it interesting how it all works together—how the enemy can twist and turn things in such a dastardly way!

This was the same individual that had come to me previously with a dilemma. She had to deal with a situation in the church, but she didn't want to make waves. She asked, *"John, how in the world can I handle this explosive situation and convince the person that I love them?"* I simply responded, *"Why are you trying to attempt to convince them you love them? Simply love them."*

If we try to convince people we love them, we won't actually love them when administering true tough love, biblical discipline and other challenges are called for. True biblical love at times does not feel like the love our culture has defined.

This is the power of love languages at work. We can't expect someone to respond in love according to our love language. They will naturally respond according to their love language.

Of course, we can try to reach out to people according to their love language, but, here's the point I'm trying to make—a failure to manifest love according to another's language doesn't mean they don't love—it means they aren't expressing or manifesting love the way that seems obvious to us. That accusation must come to an end.

Can an introverted recluse so deeply love people he has never even met by writing checks for millions of dollars to charities? Yes! That is love though he would never hug you, seek friendship or even smile when you enter the room!

My heart breaks over situations like this. Can I love better? Oh man, YES! But, I also need to help bring this issue to the surface. Too many leaders are not living according to their calling, because they are so busy modifying their personality and mandate to match what others expect!

We must love according to how God designed us. The cross wasn't welcomed, but it was the method Jesus was mandated to use. It didn't feel like love then, but boy was it.

The Test

I will never get over how God works. He is beyond amazing. Both my wife and I will admit that we were deeply wounded

when this individual rose up against us. We instantly had to humble ourselves and allow God to work on our hearts. Though we feel we handled it well, God will always test us. That test is not for God, but for us—it will clearly show where we really are with a situation.

The coming Church is going to be jealously guarded by God, a loving Bridegroom. There won't be room for bitter, unforgiving leaders, and we have to be willing to be continually tested by God. We must crave his involvement!

Our staff member finally decided to move from Colorado to another far away state. We thanked Jesus! What a wonderful moment that was! Though we had forgiven her, it felt good that the drama was over.

A year or so later, Amy and I were called to leave Colorado and move to Kansas City to join the staff of the International House of Prayer. Though we loved Colorado and the ministry there, we couldn't deny that God was opening doors to Missouri, and we also couldn't deny that a fresh new season was quite welcome.

We thought we'd only be there for the three month internship, but ended up staying for two years as we gave leadership to that very same internship as Directors. It was a very exciting time for our family—until...

...the crisis. I won't go into the entire dramatic story, but please understand we were suddenly blindsided and the pain was real.

We lost an unborn baby (we've lost a total of seven) and were replaced as Directors of the internship in the same week. Suddenly, a lot of life and joy was replaced by very real, unexpected and confusing pain. Now, understand, though we were in another trial, we were processing very well. Being replaced in the internship did make sense, even though we enjoyed serving in that ministry so much! That role called for a very different personality type and gift mix, and I didn't realize this when Mike Bickle offered me the position. They were so gracious in the entire process, and we love that ministry deeply!

However, again, the pain was legitimate. You might wonder how this story connects with the story of pain in Colorado. Get ready for this.

Remember, God will go to great lengths to ensure we are operating in love, and that we are humble and teachable.

At this time, God began opening doors for ministry in Detroit, Michigan. In those meetings he began to move in a very dramatic and powerful way, confirming his Word with signs following. So after much prayer, we felt led that we should move to Detroit. Now in the natural, this was not the best time to sell our house in Kansas City. The economy was bad and Forbes Magazine had recently called our city the eighth fastest dying city in America! So my wife put out a fleece: if God wants us to move to Detroit, he will have our house sell for our full asking price within seven days of placing it on the market.

Miraculously, God sold our home after being on the market for only six days!

Glory to God! We were in another exciting, miraculous season!

About thirty days before we were to move from Kansas City to Detroit I sat in my last all-staff meeting at IHOP. There was over a thousand people in that meeting, and I sat in the very back, on the floor, kind of bored and ready to get on with my day. Then it happened. The impossible happened.

From the platform I heard the leader of the meeting say something like, *"We would like to introduce a new staff member who will be giving leadership to a new ministry on our base. Everybody welcome..."*

No way! No way! No way!

It was impossible! When I heard her very distinct, unusual name, and saw her welcomed onto the team, I was speechless. I think my jaw hung down for quite a long time. My head was spinning as I was witnessing an invasion into our fragile world.

There was simply no way that this person, who had done so much damage to our ministry in Colorado, who had moved to a far away state, could suddenly converge with our life in Kansas City!

I stepped outside and called my wife. I'll never forget her response to my news. After I told her who was now on staff, all I heard her say, with defeat in her tone, was, *"No."*

Do you realize what happened? God set up this encounter, this trial, to test our hearts.

When I got home that afternoon, we talked and resolved that it was indeed a test, and we endeavored to pray for this person and to ask God to bless her deeply!

I never did see her over the next month. Amy, however, had a very important chance encounter with her. The very last day we lived in Kansas City, as the moving truck was being loaded in the driveway, Amy went to the bank to close our account. You guessed it. Standing in line right in front of her was our former staff member.

My wife smiled big and gave her a huge hug! Amy felt so good that it was so easy to love this person!

That was the last time we ever saw her, and to this day we pray for her to be wildly blessed!

Love will certainly manifest in many different ways, but for those who are called of God, that love will be tested. The coming Church will be a love-bathed Church, and we must welcome the testing, no matter how painful it is. My wife would say the freedom and abundant life she feels regarding the Colorado/Kansas City crisis is well worth the trial she and I went through.

True Expectations: Same Love, Different Manifestations

I once considered that it would be powerful to have a resource that explained how we can relate to various personality types, giftings and offices. What type of manifestation of love is typical in a pastor?

What about a prophet? How will an apostle and a teacher relate to others, taking into account their different emotional expressions? I was hoping someone would write this book on interactive Christian love, but maybe I'll have to tackle that at some point!

For example, I often hear people slander the prayer movement by shouting that those who lock themselves in the prayer room for hours a day don't love people. If they did, they would be out on the streets feeding the homeless or doing something else that's relational and meets an immediate need. This couldn't be further from the truth. While certainly some people who pray all day might struggle with issues of love, the same is true across the board. It has nothing to do with the manifestation (intercession, serving the homeless), but rather it has to do with the condition of the heart.

So, what should we really expect from others? Here's a short, extremely simplified explanation that should set you free. If you don't expect someone to express love in a certain way, you won't be offended when they don't! The coming Church will be a church of governmental order, and we will learn how to relate to various expressions of love:

Pastor

In America, church leaders are almost always called "Pastor." We need to fix this. Why? There are expectations associated with the offices, and if someone is not truly a pastor, when you call them pastor you are putting a burden on them they can't bear.

In a true pastor, you might expect someone who loves to listen to your story and is ready to encourage you in it. They may be very relational, conversational and invested in people one-on-one.

Teacher

A teacher might spend most of his time behind closed doors in study, and might not have a relational bone in his body—

but he loves people by rightly dividing the Word. His love is manifested not through smiles and handshakes but through hours of investment in you through study and prayer.

Evangelist

An evangelist will show love by leading people to Jesus. This can get confusing for some who get saved, and then don't understand why the evangelist isn't his best friend. After all, they shared a life-changing moment together! The reason? The evangelist is off loving the next person!

Prophet

A prophet will show love through irritating you! I'm a prophetic Apostle, so this is my area of expertise. Prophets may have tears in their eyes and fire in their veins in the place of prayer that results in an uninvited confrontation. In fact, you can consider a prophet an uninvited teacher. He delivers what is not desired to a people who are asleep. Whenever you awaken someone from their sleep, you can expect them to be irritated—yet this irritation is a result of a man or woman of God who loves you so much that they can't leave you in your condition.

So, you can expect sharp words of warning that are love-fueled alarms designed just for you. You probably wouldn't expect a prophet to be ultra-relational (they make too many enemies for this to work!). They make horrible counselors most of the time. They love you much as the teacher does—through prayer-driven messages from God.

Apostle

Apostles are always on the move. They show love by inviting you on the journey. However, they usually don't wait too long for you to catch up. For some, that feels unloving, but the opposite is true. Their love compels them to move and build and advance into new territory so that many can be saved! While an apostle may not wait long for you, he will always be there to pick you up on his next loop through!

Don't expect apostles to be locally minded. If you need someone to help with your current life situation, an apostle will show you his love by inviting you on a journey regardless of your current situation! You may need to find a pastor if you aren't looking for that quite yet!

A One-String Banjo

As someone who's not a pastor, I find myself, by design, extremely limited in my message. I'm a one-string banjo. Maybe two-string.

> "Many Christians will be shocked to find themselves in Hell one day."

If I asked you what a particular pastor's life message is, you probably wouldn't be able to answer. He will usually teach on many different topics.

But, if I were to ask you what John the Baptist's message was, you'd have an answer—REPENT! PREPARE THE WAY OF THE LORD! Like John the Baptist, prophetic leaders are one string banjo players.

For me, everything I do in ministry stems from one experience and one message. After an encounter in the early 1990's of being dragged toward Hell, God spoke this to me: *John, many Christians will be shocked to find themselves in Hell one day.*

My love for mostly nameless, faceless people burns so hot that I simply cannot deviate from my message of warning. I am loving

through provoking people into safety. I am, as has been suggested, a shock Christian. I'm a prophetic messenger that sees time running out.

The horrific confusion regarding the issue of salvation in the Western Church is the key reason why I am so intense. I am intentionally extremely off balance as a heavy counterweight due to current off-balance theologies. People are going to Hell. They think they are saved.

Just so you know how I see things, due to this encounter that I had 22 years ago: when I'm in a vibrant, Spirit-filled church of, lets say, one thousand people—people who are lifting their hands, worshiping Jesus and paying their tithes—I see maybe 100 of them, on average, ending up in Heaven. That's not a judgmental statement, as I have no way of truly judging that on a person-by-person basis. It's simply a statistical, analytical reality for me based on my encounter with Hell. How can I stay silent even for a day if billions of unsaved people are going to Hell—not to mention many others in churches who are following Jesus in an unsaved condition?

In fact, I've often said that I give myself only an 80% chance of making Heaven. If I were to die today, I'm about 99.9% sure I'd be there. However, the Bible is clear that there will be a great falling away. Even the elect will be deceived. If I presume myself to be exempt from that, I am presuming myself to be among the elect—and I am surely deceived. I absolutely can fall away from Jesus, and I don't take that lightly.

My mandate is simple—love people by communicating truth, sounding alarms and tearing down doctrines of demons and humanistic religious idols.

Additionally, as a prophetic Apostle, those warnings come with an invitation—to get equipped to do the same, and to run with me as I charge ahead. I'm looking for modern day reformers who will love people through shocking and shaking deadly systems!

Running with me will be a joy if you want to be rocked and challenged as your destiny is called out of you.

The label of *shock Christian* fits the movement I'm a part of. I'd rather you be shocked with truth now than shocked to find yourself in Hell one day.

I am extremely thoughtful, prayerful and boldly intentional with what I communicate. Do I always do it perfectly? No way. But I try. But you can know that I love you deeply and will be in prayer continually as I get the *now message* of the Lord. The message will probably trouble you at times. It is supposed to. The paddles must be placed on all of us at times to shock to life a dying part of our hearts.

You may wonder why I don't deviate from this approach. I hope you now know why. The coming Church will consist of a remnant that has tears in their eyes and fire in their mouths as they prepare the way of the Lord in these end days.

And, I'll add one last thought. It's an indictment on our passive, timid culture when what I consider to be mildly jarring truths seem to be so extreme and impacting. It's an indictment on the church when truth is shunned as hatred when it troubles or causes discomfort. What I write—honestly—is simple, old school Christianity. I'm saddened that people find it drastic—but so be it. I will continue preaching it until drastic becomes normal again.

~ SEVEN ~

HELL, HOLINESS AND THE FEAR OF MAN

The Coming Church will be a prophetic Church.

I have no patience for the current trend in the church that ensures hearers of its messages suffer no troubled emotions or theological crisis.

If we read the Bible, and believe it is our blueprint for ministry, we cannot buy into this strategy. The Gospel troubles.

Ignoring Hell does not keep people from Hell—it increases the number who will perish. Ignoring sin in media, music and entertainment must stop—the Church is devouring the vomit of Satan in media and is unconcerned about the effects because of an unbiblical view of an indifferent God.

We as Christians have NO OPTION but to shine the light on works of darkness, of unholiness—especially within the camp of the church!

> *Take no part in the unfruitful works of darkness, but instead expose them. Ephesians 5:11*

There is a growing resistance by shepherds to the idea that the judgment of God is in force today. They argue that the better approach to the issue of unholiness is to attempt to minimize its potency, to affirm that it's not really a big deal.

> *For the wrath of God is revealed from heaven against all ungodliness and unrighteousness of men, who by their unrighteousness suppress the truth. Romans 1:18*

Strong delusion has hit the church—and many in Spirit-filled environments are on a path to Hell, and they have no idea.

Christians are watching R and PG-13-rated movies, inappropriate TV shows and are listening to unholy music.

Yes, being entertained by sin by watching and listening to such media ABSOLUTELY PUTS PEOPLE AT RISK OF HELL—Christian or not.

This is why the prayer movement is so critical! You cannot be fervent in prayer, devoted to obedience to the Word and be fervent in sin at the same time. One of those devotions will lose its appeal.

A lifestyle of fervent, burning prayer and legitimate salvation are more closely related than today's religious teachings reveal.

Fear of Man

God is raising up a people who have the boldness of the Holy Spirit, and who will, in humility, stare the enemy in the face and renounce him and his strategies! It's time to tear down our father's altars! The coming Church will be an altar-destroying Church!

You will lose friends! Family will shun you! Are you OK with that?

> *Then the men of the town said to Joash, "Bring out your son, that he may die, for he has broken down the altar of Baal and cut down the Asherah beside it." Judges 6:30*

It's time we stop using Facebook to post pictures of kittens and start using it as a platform to expose darkness and to declare the word of the Lord! End-time warriors awakened in the fire of the coming Church will use every vehicle they can to awaken others!

The evidence of a life devoted to declaring truth is not a growing sphere of friends, but a growing revolt by those who want you shut down. I'm talking about other Christians. Truth presents a clear and present threat to the lukewarm, casual lifestyles of the majority in the church today.

It's time we stop using Facebook to post pictures of kittens and start using it as a platform to expose darkness and to declare the word of the Lord!

Fear of man will keep you silent with a sleeping prophetic spirit as you embrace false humility and false love in the hopes of maintaining friendships.

Have I then become your enemy by telling you the truth? Galatians 4:16

I refuse to honor immorality. I will not respect darkness. I won't befriend the lukewarm and rebellious. Instead, I will love those bewitched by the enemy with a spirit of disturbing awakening!

Will You Sound the Alarm?

Use Facebook, Twitter and other outlets daily to shake and provoke the sleeping church! Here's the message:

Enjoying media and participating in activities that promote sin will result in a delusion that puts even seasoned ministers and other Christians at clear risk of going to Hell. This is not a rare situation in the American church, but, rather is the norm! Many will be shocked to find themselves in Hell one day!

"There is reason to think, that there are many in this congregation now hearing this discourse, that will actually be the subjects of this very misery to all eternity." -Jonathan Edwards speaking on Hell

Jonathan Edwards had no fear of man, none that we could see anyway. Read on:

"It is everlasting wrath. It would be dreadful to suffer this fierceness and wrath of Almighty God one moment; but you must suffer it to all eternity. There will be no end to this exquisite horrible misery. When you look forward, you shall see a long for ever, a boundless duration before you, which will swallow up your thoughts, and amaze your soul; and you will absolutely despair of ever having any deliverance, any end, any mitigation, any rest at all. You will know certainly that you must wear out long ages, millions of millions of ages, in wrestling

and conflicting with this almighty merciless vengeance; and then when you have so done, when so many ages have actually been spent by you in this manner, you will know that all is but a point to what remains. So that your punishment will indeed be infinite. Oh, who can express what the state of a soul in such circumstances is! All that we can possibly say about it, gives but a very feeble, faint representation of it; it is inexpressible and inconceivable: For "who knows the power of God's anger?"

"How dreadful is the state of those that are daily and hourly in the danger of this great wrath and infinite misery! But this is the dismal case of every soul in this congregation that has not been born again, however moral and strict, sober and religious, they may otherwise be. Oh that you would consider it, whether you be young or old! There is reason to think, that there are many in this congregation now hearing this discourse, that will actually be the subjects of this very misery to all eternity. We know not who they are, or in what seats they sit, or what thoughts they now have. It may be they are now at ease, and hear all these things without much disturbance, and are now flattering themselves that they are not the persons, promising themselves that they shall escape. If we knew that there was one person, and but one, in the whole congregation, that was to be the subject of this misery, what an awful thing would it be to think of! If we knew who it was, what an awful sight would it be to see such a person! How might all the rest of the congregation lift up a lamentable and bitter cry over him! But, alas! instead of one, how many is it likely will remember this discourse in hell?"

"Therefore, let every one that is out of Christ, now awake and fly from the wrath to come. The wrath of Almighty God is now undoubtedly hanging over a great part of this congregation. Let every one fly out of Sodom: "Haste and escape for your lives, look not behind you, escape to the mountain, lest you be consumed."""

And the reaction of the people that day? It is what we must see in today's Church! It is what we'll see in the coming Church!

"Before the sermon was done there was a great moaning and crying out throughout the whole house, "What shall I do to be saved?! Oh, I am going to Hell! Oh, what shall I do for Christ?!" etc. etc. So that the minister was obliged to desist. Shrieks and cries were piercing and amazing. After some time of waiting, the congregation were still so that a prayer was made, and after that we descended from the pulpit and discoursed with the people, some in one place and some in another, and–amazing and astonishing!–the power of God was seen, and several souls were hopefully wrought upon that night, and oh, the pleasantness of their countenances that received comfort."

Lest one believe that Jonathan Edwards was dour and sad, here is the text of his sermon, Heaven, A World Of Love:

"...But heaven is his dwelling-place above all other places in the universe; and all those places in which he was said to dwell of old, were but types of this. Heaven is a part of creation that God has built for this end, to be the place of his glorious presence, and it is his abode forever; and here will he dwell, and gloriously manifest himself to all eternity. And this renders heaven a world of love; for God is the fountain of love, as the sun is the fountain of light. And therefore the glorious presence of God in heaven, fills heaven with love, as the sun, placed in the midst of the visible heavens in a clear day, fills the world with light. The apostle tells us that "God is love;" and therefore, seeing he is an infinite being, it follows that he is an infinite fountain of love. Seeing he is an all-sufficient being, it follows that he is a full and over-flowing, and inexhaustible fountain of love." (from http://the-end-time.blogspot.com/2013/07/sinners-in-hands-of-angry-god-not-so.html)

The Church's Diminished Authority

Hosea 4:1-3 Hear the word of the LORD, O children of Israel, for the LORD has a controversy with the inhabitants of the land. There is no faithfulness or steadfast love, and no knowledge of God in the land; there is swearing, lying, murder, stealing, and committing adultery; they break all bounds, and bloodshed follows bloodshed. Therefore the land mourns, and all who dwell in it languish...

We have a controversy in the land!

Swearing, lying, murder, adultery, bloodshed! It results in the Earth crying out! The Earth is waiting for a holy army of sons of God to emerge!

For the creation waits with eager longing for the revealing of the sons of God. For the creation was subjected to futility, not willingly, but because of him who subjected it, in hope that the creation itself will be set free from its bondage to corruption and obtain the freedom of the glory of the children of God. For we know that the whole creation has been groaning together in the pains of childbirth until now. Romans 8:19-22

I know that I will have no authority to preach in the anointing of the Holy Spirit on holiness if I enjoy anything that is unholy. The Spirit is holy, and for him to minister through us requires that we too are holy.

Let the evildoer still do evil, and the filthy still be filthy, and the righteous still do right, and the holy still be holy." "Behold, I am coming soon, bringing my recompense with me, to repay each one for what he has done. I am the Alpha and the Omega, the first and the last, the beginning and the end." Blessed are those who wash their robes, so that they may have the right to the tree of life and that they may enter the city by the gates. Outside are the dogs and sorcerers and the sexually immoral and murderers and idolaters, and everyone who loves and practices falsehood. Revelation 22:11-15

Be holy!

As obedient children, do not be conformed to the passions of your former ignorance, but as he who called you is holy, you also be holy in all your conduct, 1 Peter 1:14-15

Again, my authority to speak on holiness relies on my agreement with holiness! If I watch a sitcom that has homosexuality as a theme, whether overt or subtle, I simply need to know that I will not be able to speak to that with anointing in my ministry. Why do you think it was so important for the homosexual agenda to overwhelm media with homosexual characters and situations? So the Church would become entertained by that spirit, and, in turn, become sympathetic to it—and made impotent by it.

Did you know that a popular Disney show is introducing a lesbian couple? *Good Luck Charlie* has been extremely popular, and now, when hooked, Disney knows they won't lose viewers when they introduce immorality into the story line.

Do you wonder why the Church has near zero impact on the increase of violence in the world? Pastors and their flocks are playing first person shooter video games, watching violence in movies and ignoring calls to holiness.

The current Church is deceived! People are being given up by God to a debased mind! A falling away has begun in the Church!

And since they did not see fit to acknowledge God, God gave them up to a debased mind to do what ought not to be done. They were filled with all manner of unrighteousness, evil, covetousness, malice. They are full of envy, murder, strife, deceit, maliciousness. They are gossips, slanderers, haters of God, insolent, haughty, boastful, inventors of evil, disobedient to parents, foolish, faithless, heartless, ruthless. Though they know God's righteous decree that those who practice such things deserve to die, they not only do them but give approval to those who practice them. Romans 1:28-32

Every time we are entertained by a sin that required the death of Jesus, we are approving of those sins, and our future is terrifying.

> *...and try to discern what is pleasing to the Lord. Take no part in the unfruitful works of darkness, but instead expose them. For it is shameful even to speak of the things that they do in secret. Ephesians 5:10-12*

If even talking about sin is shameful, how can we presume God is indifferent to us being entertained by it in media?

To approve of being entertained by sin in media, and to communicate that there is no fear of punishment, no repercussions, is to function as an end-time false prophet.

> **The moment we start preaching against something that we are participating in, we are devoid of power.**

The moment we start preaching against something that we are participating in, we are devoid of power. But, we can preach the same message from a place of holiness, brokenness and Holy Spirit anointing and it will explode in power out of us! Though some would accuse such a focus on sin as being legalistic, it's not. It's not legalistic to call people to holiness. It is legalistic to call people to coerce God to love us as a result of our human works. (He already loves us!)

Sin hardens hearts, and deception and darkness will overwhelm us if we entertain it (or it entertains us!).

> *The coming of the lawless one is by the activity of Satan with all power and false signs and wonders, and with all wicked deception for those who are perishing, because they refused to love the truth and so be saved. Therefore God sends them a strong delu-*

sion, so that they may believe what is false, in order that all may be condemned who did not believe the truth but had pleasure in unrighteousness. 2 Thessalonians 2:9-12

Pleasure in unrighteousness will result in great apostasy and falling away—in the church!

Telling people only about the love of God without also discussing the fierce judgment of God not only won't work, it's not biblical. We see warnings from cover to cover, Old Testament and New Testament.

We actually need to crave and appreciate God's judgment. If God was evil, his judgment would also be evil. But, God isn't evil. God is love, which means judgment is an expression of his love! We can trust him!

~ *Eight* ~

A Civil War in the Church

The Coming Church will be resisted by the current Church.

A civil war in the Church is drawing near—and it will be centered around the fear of the Lord.

As I shared previously, I am absolutely intentional regarding my "unbalanced" approach on the end-times, the Church and the call to reformation. The reason is simple—the situation in the Church is so dire that an urgent, radical response is necessary.

We cannot casually sit back and initiate Christian small talk as we seek to find common ground anymore. Billions are headed to Hell, and in their ranks are an alarming percentage of those who call themselves Christians.

Many believe the Church is mostly doing well with a few minor, non-essential issues to address, and an upgrade in positive, encouraging messages will help nudge us back on course. The thought is that a focus on God's goodness and love alone will be enough to convince people to veer back on course. If that were the case, I would absolutely be more subtle in my approach. However, it is not. The Church is way off balance, and an extremely weighty counterbalance is necessary.

I let my son Skylar get behind the wheel of the car for the first time in a parking lot the other day to begin to teach him how to drive. He was getting used to the steering, gas pedal and brake responsiveness, and, under my watchful eye in the passenger seat, he would jerk the car left and right, brake too hard, step on the gas too quickly and give us quite a ride. My response? Subtle, encouraging words to straighten it out, to ease up on the gas and to brake more softly. He was on the right track but was simply learning how to stay on it.

That is not where the Church is today. Things are not mostly good. We are not on the right track.

How would you react if the person driving your car decided to go the wrong way down a highway, at 100 miles per hour, at night with the headlights off, with his eyes closed and not a care in the world?

You would scream! You would grab the wheel! You would not passively, subtly encourage him to straighten it out. You would not talk about how lovely an evening it is. It wouldn't be the right time to teach him how to parallel park or how to change the oil. You both are near death and immediate, continuous cries and alarms must be sounded! Not only are you near death, but others will be crushed by your wayward vehicle as they come over the next hill!

The current Church is also near death—and is putting many others at risk. Many in the Church are on their way to Hell—and they have no idea. This is why I sound alarm after alarm after alarm. If you choose to turn a deaf ear, so be it.

However, I challenge you to be receptive and responsive, and not shut out the warnings of the Lord, no matter how irritating and repetitive they are. In fact, join me in my cry. Cry out, *"Repent! Turn around!"* The coming Church will be marked by alarms from Heaven as the end-time crisis grows more dire.

> *In those days John the Baptist came preaching in the wilderness of Judea, "Repent, for the kingdom of heaven is at hand." For this is he who was spoken of by the prophet Isaiah when he said, "The voice of one crying in the wilderness: 'Prepare the way of the Lord; make his paths straight.'" Matthew 3:1-3*

A Coming Civil War

I needed to explain what I did in the opening section to help you understand what I'm going to share next.

Entire popular movements today are in the wrong lane, going the wrong way and putting the Church at risk of eternal death.

We are going way too far with our ecumenically driven strategies of unity within the Church. The false-love movement that focuses on friendships and affirmation has led to a false-unity movement where we presume anybody who goes to church and professes Christ to be a legitimate Christian worthy of our alliance.

I do not presume people to be saved simply because they say they are.

I've said before and I'll say again—I will love everybody with the fiery love of Jesus, but I absolutely, unapologetically refuse with bold resolve to unite with anybody who isn't carrying their cross, dying daily and burning hot for Jesus Christ.

I do not presume people to be saved simply because they say they are.

We are all in process, and as long as we, in our weakness, in our struggles and in our brokenness are truly running after Jesus, I will be right there with you. However, if that is not the case, you heard me right—I will not run with you.

I will love you. I will pray for you. I will honor you. I will encourage you. But I won't run with you. I won't unite with you.

You might be wondering how, with that type of resolve, we can avoid a civil war in the Church. We can't. We don't want to.

The sickle is about to be taken to both the wheat and the tares, so we will all be hit with the judgment of God. This will be a very difficult season for everybody, but it is a necessary one.

> *Let both grow together until the harvest, and at harvest time I will tell the reapers, Gather the weeds first and bind them in bundles to be burned, but gather the wheat into my barn.'" Matthew 13:30*

> *"Do not think that I have come to bring peace to the earth. I have not come to bring peace, but a sword. For I have come to set a man against his father, and a daughter against her mother, and a daughter-in-law against her mother-in-law. And a person's enemies will be those of his own household. Whoever loves father or mother more than me is not worthy of me, and whoever loves son or daughter more than me is not worthy of me. And whoever does not take his cross and follow me is not worthy of me. Whoever finds his life will lose it, and whoever loses his life for my sake will find it. Matthew 10:34-39*

Jesus boldly revealed what a true believer looks like. His sword of truth is about to strike the Church and those who are not fully his will be revealed.

The true remnant will rise up with spiritual violence to liberate masses from the slavery that has been granted them through inappropriate theologies and religious systems.

From the days of John the Baptist until now the kingdom of heaven has suffered violence, and the violent take it by force. Matthew 11:12

No longer will we gather around a fire to warm our flesh, but rather we'll lay across it as burning ones who allow the Consuming Fire to do just that—consume us.

There will be great confusion in the nation as the world watches this happen in the Church, yet it will only be for a season. The true Church will eventually emerge, finally, with the power and love they have been craving to see.

Great leaders will rise up in the spirit of Elijah and John the Baptist to initiate conflict (instead of avoid it) and to wrestle with spiritual forces of darkness.

For we do not wrestle against flesh and blood, but against the rulers, against the authorities, against the cosmic powers over this present darkness, against the spiritual forces of evil in the heavenly places. Ephesians 6:12

"The will of God prevails. In great contests each party claims to act in accordance with the will of God. Both may be, and one must be, wrong." — September 1862 — Abraham Lincoln — Meditation on the Divine Will

Assisted Suicide

> **The prayer movement is at risk of agreeing with its own death!**

I recently had a dream that really shines the light on the coming battle in the Church. As I've said, the Church is to be a House of Prayer. Any other dominant defining attributes than intercession dilute and compromise the Church's mission.

The Church isn't to be a house of teaching, a house of friendships or a house of evangelism. It's a House of Prayer, a place that facilitates a lifestyle of night and day intercession. We are all called to pray at that level, not just some mystical, elite group of prayer warriors. The coming Church will be a Church on fire. No longer will we gather around a fire to warm our flesh, but rather we'll lay across it as burning ones who allow the Consuming Fire to do just that—consume us.

As we pray and live on fire, much trouble will come. We will threaten those who don't choose to pray, those who don't see the need. There are already strategies and theologies that are opposing and assaulting the prayer movement, and my dream brings clarity to that reality.

In the dream, I was walking up a dirt hill where my dad was. In the dream, my dad represented the prayer movement. In the Branson, Missouri area he founded and gave leadership to a significant regional prayer effort called the Uninterrupted Prayer Team (the UP Team).

My dad was on the top of that dry, dirty hill for a very specific reason. He was going to be executed. It was a public execution. I was shocked at how passive my dad was. He was on a bed, like a hospital bed, and he was submitted to the demand that he die.

I sensed that the forces were too strong for me to fight against them. He was to be executed, and there seemed to be nothing I could do about it.

I asked my dad what in the world was going on. He was pleasant in his demeanor, and in fact, most of the people around him who were helping facilitate the public execution were casually going about their day, and they were good friends of my dad. They were "good Christians" who were focused on having a great day and did what they could to eradicate anything that would threaten that.

My dad said, *"John, this is going to be an assisted suicide."*

I couldn't believe it! The pressure of the Church as it opposes the prayer movement will be so great, that many will be overwhelmed and will lose hope that their mandate to pray will have impact. *The prayer movement is at risk of agreeing with its own death!*

The Church today is threatened by the prayer movement, and it will do much to embrace the spirit of the age and execute the spirit of intercession.

As the dream continued, I then left his side and walked down the dirt road in deep, troubling thought. I looked down and saw a lighter, that looked like it was broken. I picked it up and I understood that if I could only get it to light, the execution would be called off.

If we pray, the fire of God will burn, and the opposing spirits will lose their strength.

Believe me, this is a very real situation. Someone actually contacted me online recently and arrogantly told me that they and others in a local church were actually praying for a local house of prayer to close down—and it did close down.

It's absolutely stunning that supposed Christians can oppose prayer with such zeal that they actually pray against the prayer movement!

The coming Church will be marked by constant prayer, and there will be a divide along this line. If we don't pray, I do believe it's a serious issue with eternity hanging in the balance. If we truly know

God, we will understand the desire and need to connect with him in prayer.

The Fear of the Lord

Please consider what I'm about to communicate very carefully. We must be humble, teachable and repentant. As prophetic messengers, we cannot move in the flesh and come against what may be a true move of God. Take your viewpoints to God, and ensure he confirms them to you. Allow your theologies to be challenged by the Holy Spirit. Let the Spirit of Truth reign in your life.

That being said, we cannot stay silent when there is a clear and present danger in the Church. To do so would be treason! When God sounds an alarm in your spirit, you must respond to that alarm!

The coming civil war in the Church will hinge on the issue of the fear of the Lord (among a handful of other issues).

There are entire movements that are vocally opposing the validity of the fear of the Lord today. The civil war in the Church will form as the camp divides on this primary issue.

Of course, the false grace movement and the false-love movement (that refuses anything that doesn't feel like love) are devoid of the fear of the Lord. There are other significant movements out there that may not be as extreme as this but are at least silent, if not resistant, to any discussion of the fear of the Lord.

Many who are driven mostly by what they feel, those who seek out experiences, will be deceived by anointings that feel good but are not God.

Spiritual pride is a direct result of the absence of the fear of the Lord. So is apathy, a focus on personal experience, the rejection of the call to live a repentant life and having a benefit and blessing mindset.

The fear of the LORD is hatred of evil. Pride and arrogance and the way of evil and perverted speech I hate. Proverbs 8:13

And his mercy is for those who fear him from generation to generation. Luke 1:50

While I understand and even affirm the desire of many to call God *"Daddy,"* I am at least a little troubled at how casual we have become with such a fearful, mighty God.

God is not our personal, emotional, *warm fuzzy*. He cannot be limited to that. He is mighty indeed!

Does he comfort? Oh my, YES! Does he encourage? Yes! Is he your Daddy? Absolutely! But, my friend, he is so MUCH more.

We can and must experience both comfort and fear simultaneously! The civil war in the Church will result in a departure on this issue. Many will reject this mandate to fear God.

So the church throughout all Judea and Galilee and Samaria had peace and was being built up. And walking in the fear of the Lord and in the comfort of the Holy Spirit, it multiplied. Acts 9:31

Without the fear of the Lord, his true nature cannot be discerned. Without the fear of the Lord, there is no friendship of the Lord.

The friendship of the LORD is for those who fear him, and he makes known to them his covenant. Psalm 25:14

And if you call on him as Father who judges impartially according to each one's deeds, conduct yourselves with fear throughout the time of your exile, 1 Peter 1:17

This fear of the lord is indeed the beginning of wisdom. This consciousness of sin is the straight pathway to heaven. -Joseph Barber Lightfoot

Having sin consciousness is glorious if we truly believe in the power of the blood of Jesus to set us free! It is critical that we allow the fear of the Lord to expose issues of our heart that put our relationship with him at risk! This is very good! This is desirable! And, the fear of the Lord is not simply "respect" of the Lord. The Bible calls it dread. Terror. It's quite the mystery indeed that we can experience both terror and love at the same time! How mighty is our God!

Having sin consciousness is glorious if we truly believe in the power of the blood of Jesus to set us free!

> *Since we have these promises, beloved, let us cleanse ourselves from every defilement of body and spirit, bringing holiness to completion in the fear of God. 2 Corinthians 7:1*

> *The fear of the LORD is a fountain of life, that one may turn away from the snares of death. Proverbs 14:27*

Vision of a Chess Board

I once had a vision of a chess board, and on the appropriate squares stood actual humans, Christians. They each were fervent and focused as devoted warriors. They all seemed to be spiritually mature and responding to their call of duty.

Suddenly, the chess board began to shake violently. It was clearly a tremor from Heaven as God was causing everything to be hit by his loving judgment. He will shake everything that can be shaken.

What happened next was remarkable. Most of the Christian soldiers remained standing, while a few hit their faces in humility and brokenness. Those who stood, in pride, were suddenly shaken so violently that they turned to dust.

This shaking is coming to the Church. Those who pridefully reject the fear of the Lord are in great danger, though they are fervent in their religion.

A Concentration of Government

I shared at a recent regional church leader's prophetic prayer meeting that we must be careful.

There is a lot of pride in this region—especially within the Church of Detroit.

> *...but in every nation anyone who fears him and does what is right is acceptable to him. Acts 10:35*

It's right to respond to God's mandate to focus on our region and on the state of Michigan. I am friends with some phenomenal leaders who are spearheading a movement of prayer in this state, and they are doing so with great humility.

We must follow their lead, and we cannot allow the pride of Detroit to manifest in our zeal to see a great end-time revival land here.

While geographic boundaries do have extreme significance, we have to understand the greater reality.

Washington DC is not important to this nation because of its geographic boundaries. In fact, it's a very small area. The reason Washington DC is significant is because of the concentration of government. It is our governmental center, and the governmental activity is greater there than anywhere else in the nation.

Yet, the Pentagon is also important and strategic to our nation. So are our military bases. Why? Because of their affiliation and alliance and responsiveness to the governmental leadership in Washington.

We need more troublers to arise!

Michigan is no different. Pride would cause us to presume that there is something special about our geography. Humility and an accurate analysis of the situation would reveal something very different—Michigan will be special because of the concentration of humble, cross-bearing, anointed, Kingdom government officials and offices that will be established here. Heaven's authority is coming, I believe, to Michigan. Our impact will be determined by our willingness to humbly respond to God's governmental leadership.

Just as with Washington DC, it's not about making Detroit famous. We have been given a sober mandate—to serve our nation in the midst of a coming national, civil war.

This is true for every region. The coming Church will be a regional Church, expressed on a city level. The local expressions will be important, but only as they are connected regionally. The regional Church will be important, but only as it is connected with God's Kingdom government.

The competition with and resistance to the coming Church will be extreme, and the only way to advance is via God's governmental authority. Babylonian systems in the Church will give way to the true Church, though it will come through Elijah style fire from Heaven in the midst of great crisis.

> *When Ahab saw Elijah, Ahab said to him, "Is it you, you troubler of Israel?" And he answered, "I have not troubled Israel, but you have, and your father's house, because you have abandoned the commandments of the LORD and followed the Baals. 1 Kings 18:17-18*

We need more troublers to arise! Why? Based on what we see in Elijah's story, the prevailing culture is actually what is troubling the Church, and it's the prophets of God that MUST stand boldly in the face of their accusations. Truth will prevail. God will answer by fire.

Prophetic Fire

The coming Church will be marked by those who will preach truth without moderation.

I want to directly address fellow pastors and leaders with both brokenness and boldness—open your mouths!

When people tell me that I have guts to say what I do in teachings, on Facebook, Twitter or YouTube, I am shocked! Really? They can't be serious! I barely reveal even a small percentage of what is burning within me. The messages are minor and obvious, yet somehow in our passive, ultra-sensitive culture they come across as sharp and risky. We have to open our mouths and deliver the troubling truth! No more messages designed to grow churches. No more sermons that result in us looking good, smart and polished.

If we are out to save face, we may do just that—as we ultimately lose our soul in Hell.

The raw, irritating, offensive messages of the Word of God must explode out of us with the full understanding that many of those under our care will revolt! That is true love-based preaching!

We can't even call people to prayer today due to the fear that they will leave our churches! My God! How can we presume revival is near?

I met with a House of Prayer network leader the other day who said that people leave churches when leaders shift time, energy and attention from them to God. I've watched that happen myself,

and it rips me up! In our church in Colorado we shifted from pot lucks to prayer meetings, and there was a mass exodus. We lost people and money. I had to get a part-time job. It was disruptive. It was heartbreaking that people ran from the call to pray.

Where are the ones who aren't looking first for human friends, personal affirmation or a sense of belonging but who are seeking after every available minute to minister to God in prayer? The prayer rooms must be full—and the main prayer room in the American Church is the Sunday morning sanctuary!

And don't you even think of using the excuse that you need to create a non-threatening environment for the new believer! Every person, young or old, immature or seasoned must be in the prayer room—and it must be their primary focus! What if the Upper Room were toned down in the hopes of drawing a bigger crowd and interested seekers?

We must absolutely refuse to tone down the activity of the Holy Spirit out of respect of those less hungry! God is a consuming fire, and he is about to consume what is unholy and compromised. Who are we to presume we know better how to facilitate a service? Is inviting the Holy Spirit to step aside as we give preference to human wisdom the way to go? I've heard it said that the main Sunday service should be a toned-down meeting so as not to freak out visitors and seekers. Apparently the meeting where the Holy Spirit has liberty to move in freedom should be reserved for a night when there's little risk of the unconverted showing up.

This is humanistic religion at its best! Did those in the Upper Room tone down the Holy Spirit so as not to confuse and trouble the seekers in the city? Absolutely not! In fact, the power was so extreme and so unusual that the people were provoked to wonder and proclaim, *"they must be drunk!"* What was happening was off of their grid.

When man moves, it's naturally familiar. When God moves, it's supernaturally shocking. Keep in mind, there's always a spirit giving leadership in a service—the spirit of man, a demonic spirit or the Holy Spirit.

I told God one day many years ago that if I responded to his extreme call to facilitate a white hot environment of prayer in our church I would lose my reputation. People would sever relationship with me and hurl accusations my way.

"My Son was of no reputation, why should you be?"

God said, *"Good. My Son was of no reputation, why should you be?"* I was rocked. It was that day, many years ago, that I stopped trying to look good and build a ministry and make people happy about running with me. Selfish ambition died that day. The moment we make decisions based mostly on attracting people, keeping people or raising money is the moment we have failed as leaders.

> *...but emptied himself, by taking the form of a servant, being born in the likeness of men. And being found in human form, he humbled himself by becoming obedient to the point of death, even death on a cross. Philippians 2:7-8*

I'm not trying to build a ministry—I'm devoted to obeying God and delivering the messages he has given me. I know these messages will directly hit theologies and ideals that so many hold dear. That's the point. I crave people's freedom from those harmful ideals! I desire the truth of Jesus to invade everybody's life!

> *"Do not think that I have come to bring peace to the earth. I have not come to bring peace, but a sword. Matthew 10:34*

One reason I'm OK with this divisive strategy (that Jesus affirmed above) is that it clearly reveals who's for and who's opposed. I'd

rather make the message clear and know who I'm running with than to tone it down and have those who are opposed to it in our camp. So, we love and serve everybody in the camp, but we can't get sidetracked from our mission for the sake of their comfort.

Trust me, the resulting remnant of burning ones will rejoice at such an atmosphere of clarity and fire! Those who are lukewarm today just may awaken and burn tomorrow—if we have the courage to preach the very difficult, costly truth!

I'm sure there are some who translate boldness and refusal to soft step issues as arrogance—but I do not apologize. Yeah, I know that sounds arrogant! The reason I don't apologize is because I wrestle with the call to humility continually, and I check my heart non-stop. The possibility of pride and arrogance is there, without question, and I take that very seriously. I check my heart to ensure I'm humble and full of love. It's wisdom to receive insight from your critics, at least to a point!

People that are close to me do know my heart—and they know I'm broken before the Lord. My call is to aggressively sound alarms, gather people around the mission of revival and provoke people to pray night and day. It can't be a soft spoken suggestion if we hope to awaken a great end-time army!

Several years ago in Colorado, the Lord directed me very urgently to learn how to walk in extreme humility and extreme boldness at the same time. It was a full year of intense prayer and discovery—a personal school of the Holy Spirit. In that school, I learned much, including this—I was not to attempt to appear humble, I was to be humble. Why was this important? Because the Elijah-level boldness that is required to impact a region would often look like anything but humility. It would appear as arrogance and selfish ambition.

We are not in a season where we need to gather around a table and water down the message in the hopes of finding common ground that results in handshakes and smiles. The message of the hour will overturn that table with violence.

I endeavor to love every person deeply, but I refuse to affirm systems, methodologies, theologies and lifestyles that are an offense to the Word of God. I will, in humility and boldness, be relentless in provoking the sleepers to awaken and those given to a lukewarm life to be shaken. Prophetic threats against human systems and unholy altars results in accusation, gossip and resistance.

> *When the men of the town rose early in the morning, behold, the altar of Baal was broken down, and the Asherah beside it was cut down, and the second bull was offered on the altar that had been built. And they said to one another, "Who has done this thing?" And after they had searched and inquired, they said, "Gideon the son of Joash has done this thing."*
>
> *Then the men of the town said to Joash, "Bring out your son, that he may die, for he has broken down the altar of Baal and cut down the Asherah beside it." But Joash said to all who stood against him, "Will you contend for Baal? Or will you save him? Whoever contends for him shall be put to death by morning. If he is a god, let him contend for himself, because his altar has been broken down." Judges 6:28-31*

I know the accusations will continue, but you need to know that, if you are bold, you will provoke. You must be OK with that! Love people deeply, hate the enemy powerfully and know there will be a crisis in the middle as God, people and demons step into the ring. Don't wrestle against flesh and blood! Be innocent! But don't presume a passive spirit is the same thing as a humble spirit.

False Unity

Today I hear a lot about leaders, churches and movements in a region unifying for the sake of revival. I have been disturbed by that strategy for years.

First, it's imperative that we honor people. That's a heart condition issue that will either qualify or disqualify you from ministry. But, honor and unity are not at all the same.

I commit to serve all, but I refuse to strategically align with someone who doesn't embrace fervent prayer as a lifestyle, holiness as a principle and dying daily as a goal.

Today we have worship leaders who listen to secular music and go to secular concerts. There are pastors who are entertained in media by the very sins that required the death of the Jesus they preach about. It makes you wonder just what they are ministering to us!

I'll say it plainly—we cannot align with those who are operating in the spirit of Baal. We must confront them in the spirit of Elijah!

There is so much fear today that messages of holiness will result in accusations of legalism. I say, bring on the accusations!

Take no part in the unfruitful works of darkness, but instead expose them. For it is shameful even to speak of the things that they do in secret. But when anything is exposed by the light, it becomes visible, for anything that becomes visible is light. Therefore it says, "Awake, O sleeper, and arise from the dead, and Christ will shine on you." Ephesians 5:11-14

There is so much fear today that messages of holiness will result in accusations of legalism. I say, bring on the accusations! You have to be kidding me if you think it makes sense to lessen the call to purity for the sake of unity! The coming Church will be a Church that is consecrated and focused on holiness and purity.

When preaching holiness results in accusation of legalism you can know darkness is increasing in strength in our culture—and in the Church.

No, it's NOT OK to watch movies that have cussing, nudity, violence or crude humor in it. It's NOT OK to soak in secular music in one moment and with worship music in the next.

It's so hard for so many to encounter God today—and this is the main reason! Media! Holiness! Prayer!

I have a high value for true unity and am looking for those in the Detroit region that will truly gather in a spirit of humility, brokenness, intercession and passionate, unhindered focus on the goal of God's heart—revival that transforms a culture.

The call today is first for consecration, not liberation! First comes holiness and a resolve to be single-minded in our pursuit of a holy God—and then the power to set the captives free will come.

> *Then Joshua said to the people, "Consecrate yourselves, for tomorrow the LORD will do wonders among you." Joshua 3:5*

No, it's NOT OK to watch movies that have cussing, nudity, violence or crude humor in it. It's NOT OK to soak in secular music in one moment and with worship music in the next.

Listen closely: the lukewarm, casual Church must be shaken! Yes, the true Church is one that is burning hot, in love with her Bridegroom. I risk offending a lot of people when I deal with this issue of fervency and costly discipleship as it's an assault against their theologies and lifestyles. It is NOT OK to be casually committed, loosely connected and given to the apathy that is destroying the Church. I'm calling awakeners to rise up! We must

pray and burn non-stop! You can do this! There is no better way to live—and there is no other option!

I know this is why some don't connect well in houses of prayer, or even in my own church—the call to burn hot is beyond what most are comfortable with. The call over the edge is unsettling for those who don't even want to come near the edge. Listen—your eternity is at risk! Be fervent and radical in your love of God and commitment to his mission! The coming Church will be a burning hot crater of searing fire. It will be pure and it will be rejected by most in today's culture.

A Dividing Line

As God's government increases, no matter where it is, the division will increase. Gray will become black and white. People will have to choose where they stand. It sounds terrible, but in a wheat-and-tare season it is absolutely necessary. God is bringing judgment to the Church, and people will absolutely choose sides.

> *For it is time for judgment to begin at the household of God; and if it begins with us, what will be the outcome for those who do not obey the gospel of God? And "If the righteous is scarcely saved, what will become of the ungodly and the sinner?"*
> *1 Peter 4:17-18*

This is why the fear of the Lord is so critical! We are scarcely saved, and judgment is coming!

Those with a casual disposition, a resistance to the fear of the Lord, and a focus on "Daddy God" without also acknowledging him as "Fearful Judge and Father" will be disturbed beyond description.

Their understanding of who God is will be threatened, and they will end up choosing to resist the one they say they know! My God!

Thus, the civil war will commence.

The false-unity, "can't we all just get along" hopes will be crushed as the fearful reality of the Judge brings his sword of division. His love will provoke him to call the true bride of Christ out, and give those compromised by faulty foundations a clear and compelling chance to run to him.

The false grace, false love, false unity movements are radically resistant to the fear of the Lord, yet they won't be able to escape it when it all comes crashing down.

Nephilim Doctrine

I recently had a troubling and urgent dream.

Before I share the dream, I'd like to share a short portion from a book titled *Baptized by Blazing Fire* by Pastor Yong-Doo Kim. It's an account of his multiple journeys into Heaven and Hell. This part rocked me:

> *Even later that night, as I continued to pray in tongues, I was taken down to hell. I was in a place where there was some devil jabbing a long, sharp spear into rectangular shaped boxes. With foul language, it shouted, "You think you are a pastor? What kind of life did you live? I am ecstatic that you are here with me." The evil spirit continued to jab the boxes as it cursed. Loud, painful screams came from the boxes, as blood flowed out. I noticed the tops of the boxes were covered with canvass, with a large cross portrayed on it. The boxes were lined up in an orderly fashion, and they stretched endlessly. I could not see where they ended. I realized that they were coffins. Evil spirits were jabbing their long, sharp spears into the holes unmercifully. I asked the Lord, "Jesus, why are the caskets of former pastors here?" Jesus replied, "These pastors did not preach My gospel. They preached another gospel, and those who followed became depraved. This is their end result, a place in hell." Jesus said, "Depraved pastors will be judged greater."*

This is why we must ensure we are preaching the cross, the gospel. We are in very serious times in the Church.

Note that this isn't titled "The Doctrine of Nephilim," as that would take us into an entirely different direction. This isn't about the controversy surrounding Nephilim that existed in Scripture. As I share my dream and the interpretation you will understand clearly why this is titled "Nephilim Doctrine." Keep in mind, this is a symbolic parallel. I'm using the story of historic unholy mixture to shine the light on how deadly that can be to us. This principle will become vivid as you read on.

As most of my prophetic dreams tend to be, the atmosphere was urgent, dark and apocalyptic. It was night time with dark clouds covering the area I was in.

I was terribly disturbed and confused regarding two children that were in my house. I didn't recognize them, but I knew somehow that they belonged to me.

One was ten months old, but looked full grown with a neatly trimmed beard. I would have guessed him to be 50 years old, but I knew that he was only 10 months old. I believe the other child was younger.

The older child was extremely intelligent and thoughtful. He spoke as a 50-year-old man with "wisdom." He looked quite disturbing and dead inside however—almost like a child that's the product of incest. Something just wasn't right.

I didn't have much contact with the younger child, but he was also malformed and looked older than he actually was. This child didn't appear to have wisdom or anything remarkable about him. He was just out of place.

I was so troubled and I couldn't figure out what had happened. Who were these "children" and what was I to do?

I was driving around frantically looking for help (I don't even know what type of help I was hoping for). I kept trying to call my wife Amy on her cell phone, but no matter what I did the phone kept ringing through to Imago Dei, which is where Amy works.

Then I woke up.

The Interpretation

I immediately knew that the children in the dream were Nephilim. In Scripture we know that the Nephilim were the offspring of fallen angels and humans. Many believe demons are the spirits of dead Nephilim (as opposed to fallen angels). Regardless of that, we clearly know that they were unholy offspring. Demonized children. A different breed altogether.

> *The Nephilim were on the earth in those days-and also afterward-when the sons of God went to the daughters of men and had children by them. They were the heroes of old, men of renown. Genesis 6:4*

The Nephilim were great in size, so its no wonder the 10-month-old child appeared as a grown man, though that has more of a spiritual than literal application here.

As the interpretation of the dream continued, God warned me about demonically inspired doctrines. Doctrines of demons.

> *Now the Spirit expressly says that in later times some will depart from the faith by devoting themselves to deceitful spirits and teachings of demons... 1 Timothy 4:1*

The warning was even more specific as he revealed that children of God, people made in God's image, must not, under any circumstances, become intimate with doctrines of demons. That mixture is deadly. When what is holy unites with what is unholy the union produces what I'm calling *Nephilim doctrine.*

I as a leader must ensure people under my care are not seduced by teachings that feel great, and seem right, but are as evil as Satan himself. I must ensure the demonic seed, demonic theology, is

not deposited into the people I'm serving. The fear of the Lord struck me.

> *There is a way that seems right to a man, but in the end it leads to death. Proverbs 16:25*

When mankind becomes intimate with doctrines of demons (instead of becoming intimate with Jesus, the Word), unholy doctrine is reproduced. Nephilim Doctrine. Part truth, part deception. Demonic doctrines that are received by people who were made in the very image of God result in mixture and a defiled offspring—children that are part *image of God* and part *image of Satan*. This is extremely sobering! It's possible to embrace some truth and some error and have that result in compromised doctrines. Those doctrines can be extremely alluring, and many will eat of that fruit.

> *Genesis 3:1-7 Now the serpent was more crafty than any other beast of the field that the LORD God had made. He said to the woman, "Did God actually say, 'You shall not eat of any tree in the garden'?" And the woman said to the serpent, "We may eat of the fruit of the trees in the garden, but God said, 'You shall not eat of the fruit of the tree that is in the midst of the garden, neither shall you touch it, lest you die.'" But the serpent said to the woman, "You will not surely die. For God knows that when you eat of it your eyes will be opened, and you will be like God, knowing good and evil." So when the woman saw that the tree was good for food, and that it was a delight to the eyes, and that the tree was to be desired to make one wise, she took of its fruit and ate, and she also gave some to her husband who was with her, and he ate. Then the eyes of both were opened, and they knew that they were naked. And they sewed fig leaves together and made themselves loincloths.*

Adam and Eve allowed a doctrine of a demon to mix with the truth they were walking in. The result? Destruction.

I felt that as the head of my house in the dream (leader of the ministry) that it's my responsibility to ensure that no intimacy with demonic doctrines and schemes is allowed. You have no idea how weighty the fear of the Lord is on this for me! I'm searching my own heart too!

Though I valued Amy's wisdom (in the dream), and wanted desperately to talk with her, God kept redirecting my call. I kept connecting to Imago Dei. My answer would come from another source.

Get this. When I was trying to figure out what Imago Dei had to do with it, I decided to see exactly what those words meant, so I searched online for the meaning. Are you ready? Imago Dei means "Image of God."

That blew me up! The Nephilim were a defilement of people who were made in God's image. There was unholy mixture. God is calling us to intimacy with the Truth of the Word of God which is what will result in us living undefiled in the image of God. The cross of Christ must be preached!

Then, I wondered what the number 10 had to do with it. This is also very interesting.

Ten is the number of perfection or completion of God's "divine order." It is the only one of the perfect biblical numbers in which humans have a part– it is the number of completion based on God's order AND human responsibility.

Wow! It's God and man coming together! The enemy wants to take the place of God and wants us to unite with him! We must ensure divine doctrinal order is in our churches. The coming church will be fervently devoted to the Word of God.

It's possible for us as people created in the image of God to become intimate with doctrines of demons. The result of our ministry then would be people embracing *Nephilim doctrines* who now have a demonic nature in their theological blueprint! There can be people in our church who worship and tithe and serve and read their bible— but who have doctrines of demons in their DNA! These are people who may have been under my care!!! My God.

Just to clarify, again, I'm not talking about the debatable role of the Nephilim in the end-times, or in history. This is all about a symbolic parallel. We want to seek after truth and avoid any mixture with the spirit of the age whatsoever. This is why the coming Church must—and will—initiate a return to preaching the blood and the cross. Satan is doing much today to see impurities injected into the Church. He fears what is coming—as he fears what happened to him 2000 years ago.

The Cross

The cock is about to crow—where will you be when the crisis of the cross is reintroduced to the Church?

> *Matthew 26:73-75 After a little while the bystanders came up and said to Peter, "Certainly you too are one of them, for your accent betrays you." Then he began to invoke a curse on himself and to swear, "I do not know the man." And immediately the rooster crowed. And Peter remembered the saying of Jesus, "Before the rooster crows, you will deny me three times." And he went out and wept bitterly.*

He invoked a curse on himself.

From the Life Application Commentary:

While Peter may have hoped to seem a natural part of the group by joining in the conversation, instead he revealed, by his speech, that he did not belong there. This was too much for Peter, so he decided to make the strongest denial he could think of by denying with an oath, "I don't know the man." Peter was swearing that he did not know Jesus and was invoking a curse on himself if his words were untrue. He was saying, in effect, "May God strike me dead if I am lying."

Peter was running for his life. In the church today the prevailing focus is on our experience and the affirmation and protection of our lives and lifestyles. People so often go to church with the primary motive of enhancing their lives. When their lives, or even their lifestyles, are threatened, people will begin to run for their lives. They will run to safety.

This clear and extreme denial of Christ will invoke a curse!

Jesus was so indignant about this type of reaction that he dealt with Peter in fierce fashion before this event even unfolded:

> *From that time Jesus began to show his disciples that he must go to Jerusalem and suffer many things from the elders and chief priests and scribes, and be killed, and on the third day be raised. And Peter took him aside and began to rebuke him, saying, "Far be it from you, Lord! This shall never happen to you." But he turned and said to Peter, "Get behind me, Satan! You are a hindrance to me. For you are not setting your mind on the things of God, but on the things of man." Matthew 16:21-23*

Peter denied the cross, and Jesus rebuked Satan who was working through Peter (who Jesus had just identified as the rock, the CHURCH!). He made the point clear: Peter was mindful of the things of man and not the things of God. Jesus then said:

> *Then Jesus told his disciples, "If anyone would come after me, let him deny himself and take up his cross and follow me. For whoever would save his life will lose it, but whoever loses his life for my sake will find it. Matthew 16:24-25*

Apostles and prophets must step into their positions of authority and release a great crisis to the church!

This is a necessary crisis as it will result in the true, abundant life of multiplied millions. The offensive, bloody cross must return to the church—and now!

When Jesus was hailed as King at the Triumphal Entry, the masses converged. The focus was self. They wanted Jesus to save them, to make their lives better. They were crying out, *"Hosanna!"* which means, *"save us now!"*

So Jesus complied. The only way to save the ones he loved was to face death on the cross. Yet, the rooster crowed and the crowds scattered and turned on Jesus. His closest friends ran for their lives. One cursed himself in his denial. Another betrayed Jesus and hung himself.

Yes, it's time not to snack on some bread and grape juice, but to eat his flesh and drink his blood!

When the cross is introduced in its full, bloody force again in the Church, we will watch this drama unfold another time. People will flee from the Church when focus changes from personal freedom to personal cost. Betrayal will skyrocket. Fear will grip those who haven't surrendered all.

Where will you be when the cock crows?

The generations must come to the cross

Everybody ran for their lives but mom and son, Mary and John (along with Mary Magdalene), remained. The generations converged.

> *When Jesus saw his mother and the disciple whom he loved standing nearby, he said to his mother, "Woman, behold, your son!" Then he said to the disciple, "Behold, your mother!" And from that hour the disciple took her to his own home. John 19:26-27*

> *...and he will go before him in the spirit and power of Elijah, to turn the hearts of the fathers to the children, and the disobedient to the wisdom of the just, to make ready for the Lord a people prepared." Luke 1:17*

The elder generation must refuse to run. The younger generation must refuse to run. We must converge around the threatening, offensive cross of love. When we do, the harvest will come. The world is watching. The thief was watching and surrendered to the love that could only be revealed at the cross as the two generations deeply loved Jesus together:

> *And he said to him, "Truly, I say to you, today you will be with me in Paradise." Luke 23:43*

Any movement that doesn't take place at the cross is a false movement.

This is one reason I'm so troubled by some events, certain unity movements in a city, pastors' meetings, etc. If a pastor isn't fully ready to resign his mission, to lose his salary, to surrender his sheep, to shut his church down, I have little interest in meeting. The cross demands everything. When pastors of a city gather around the cross and don't focus on personal gain, revival will be at hand. Yes, many will be offended, but the Harvest will come in!

The World is Getting Better and Better?

The glorious fear of the Lord results in radical and continual repentance as we joyfully encounter the lover and judge of our souls at the same time.

The grief and mourning is multifaceted, yet much of it comes from an understanding that great destruction is upon us, and Hell is expanding as millions are sucked into its horrors.

Those who reject this idea are focused on blessing and benefits. The belief is that the world is getting better and better, and we can rest easy—eat, drink and play.

> *And he received the gold from their hand and fashioned it with a graving tool and made a golden calf. And they said, "These are your gods, O Israel, who brought you up out of the land of Egypt!" When Aaron saw this, he built an altar before it. And Aaron made a proclamation and said, "Tomorrow shall be a feast to the LORD." And they rose up early the next day and offered burnt offerings and brought peace offerings. And the people sat down to eat and drink and rose up to play. Exodus 32:4-6*

So many have fashioned a god of their own design—and have given it glory for rescuing them from Egypt! Their plan is to play instead of forging ahead to save the world. They want to stay at the bottom of the mountain with their hands in their ears saying, *"La la la la la!"*

I've heard it said that God is always in a good mood. This is not only ridiculous theology, but it's dangerous. Why? When those who subscribe to this idea experience the fearful shaking of God, they will reject him as a foreigner or as a demon.

> *The Jews answered him, "Are we not right in saying that you are a Samaritan and have a demon?" Jesus answered, "I do not have a demon, but I honor my Father, and you dishonor me. Yet I do not seek my own glory; there is One who seeks it, and he is the judge. John 8:48-50*

I honestly have no patience for the argument that God is always in a good mood, and that he no longer judges. We need his judgment!

How can 4,000 babies a day murdered in our nation, an increase in radical terrorism, absolutely disgusting moral decline, pornography being viewed by most people—in the Church—and increasing suicides, murders and other atrocities cause anyone to presume the world is getting better?

The goal is not to live a great life now—it's to rescue a dying planet and prepare the way of the Lord!

The fear of the Lord will result in a sobriety that will shake us terribly. We will see the heartbreak of God and join him in his distress.

No, God is very often sad, disturbed and heartbroken.

Now what?

Pray. Pray like your life depends on it. It does.

Mourn. Cry out. Sound alarms. Prepare ye the way of the Lord!

Be broken. Be humble. Be repentant.

A civil war is coming. Will you choose the way of comfort and pleasure and personal benefits as you fashion a god of your own design? Many significant movements and churches will do so. The pressure to join them will be extreme. The deception will be convincing. Will you seek after peace and safety with them?

Or will you drop your toys, leave the remote on the couch, let the dead bury their own dead and head up the mountain where the lightning, thundering, shakings—and God himself are?

> *On the morning of the third day there were thunders and lightnings and a thick cloud on the mountain and a very loud trumpet blast, so that all the people in the camp trembled. Then Moses brought the people out of the camp to meet God, and they took their stand at the foot of the mountain. Now Mount Sinai was wrapped in smoke because the LORD had descended on it in fire. The smoke of it went up like the smoke of a kiln, and the whole mountain trembled greatly. And as the sound of the trumpet grew louder and louder, Moses spoke, and God answered him in thunder. Exodus 19:16-19*

~ *Nine* ~

A Call for Reformation

The Coming Church will demand reformation.

God has given the Church every resource necessary to initiate a fire of revival that will burn cities and nations.

We can all agree this fire is not raging—and the current structure of the Church can neither initiate nor sustain a move of God of this magnitude.

It's time for a radical and momentous change in the Church. It's time for a reformation. It's time for a revolution.

The coming Church will cause every one of us to evaluate our lives, and to repent and change course.

I was awakened suddenly one night with a call for reformation, and this call is what follows:

20 Points of Reformation

1. We must repent of prayerlessness.

A call is being made for every believer to pray with hunger and passion to an extreme degree. Spiritual leaders must model such a lifestyle of prayer on a daily basis. It must be our primary activity. Pastors and leaders—let's agree to fill our daily schedules with prayer watches.

Leonard Ravenhill said, *"Pastors who don't pray two hours a day aren't worth a dime a dozen."*

But we will devote ourselves to prayer and to the ministry of the word." Acts 6:4

2. We must repent of competition.

It's time to promote the City Church ahead of our local church. Are we willing to lose people, money, our ministries and our reputations in order for God's corporate dream of city-wide revival to explode?

Do nothing from selfish ambition or conceit, but in humility count others more significant than yourselves. Philippians 2:3

3. We must repent for being mindful of man ahead of God.

We are to resign our positions as salespeople and again lead with a bold prophetic mantle. As a leader, the primary role is to hear God in prayer and to declare his Word to the people. The body must renounce consumerism in the Church by asking not what our Church can do for us but what we can do for our Church.

But he turned and said to Peter, "Get behind me, Satan! You are a hindrance to me. For you are not setting your mind on the things of God, but on the things of man." Matthew 16:23

4. We must repent for forsaking the house of prayer.

The primary ministry of every church must be prayer. This commitment to intercession is to be modeled and led by senior leadership. The primary purpose of the Church is not teaching, visitor assimilation or fellowship. It is undeniably night and day prayer for the nations. Lengthy prayer should be taught and modeled as the dominant activity of every believer.

...these I will bring to my holy mountain, and make them joyful in my house of prayer; their burnt offerings and their sacrifices will be accepted on my altar; for my house shall be called a house of prayer for all peoples." Isaiah 56:7

5. We must repent of pride.

God resists the proud, and we can't afford for God to move away from us. We must repent, humble ourselves and cry for Jesus to come!

"God opposes the proud, but gives grace to the humble." James 4:6

6. We must repent for quenching the Holy Spirit.

Our cry to the Holy Spirit must be, *"Come as you are and do what you want!"* Services should be marked by significant and earth-shaking supernatural moves of the Holy Spirit.

Do not quench the Spirit. 1 Thessalonians 5:19

7. We must repent for resisting the prophetic.

Now, more than ever, we need to hear the Word of the Lord. We must teach every believer how to hear God, how to steward that Word and how to take responsibility in the fulfillment of that Word.

Do not despise prophecies, 1 Thessalonians 5:20

8. We must repent for canceling services, closing the church doors and lowering the expected commitment.

We have submitted to a deadly and apathetic American culture, and it's time to lead the way and bring reformation to that culture. The Church must dominate our calendars again.

9. We must cry out for the love of God to weigh on His church in the form of both mercy and judgment.

Pray for God's love-fueled judgment to rest on you, the Church and your city so as to ensure wrong things are made right, holiness prevails and God reigns supreme.

For it is time for judgment to begin at the household of God; and if it begins with us, what will be the outcome for those who do not obey the gospel of God? 1 Peter 4:17

10. We must admit there are demons and that they must be dealt with.

Not through programs and projects but through prophetic proclamation. A unified assault on the kingdom of darkness will result in mass deliverance in our city.

Submit yourselves therefore to God. Resist the devil, and he will flee from you. James 4:7

11. We must be available for repositioning and do away with the redundancy that a church on every corner invites.

Many churches in our cities should close. Those pastors would then assume more appropriate positions of service in other churches. Teachers would lead centers of teaching, pastors would lead small groups, and other leaders would serve in a variety of physical locations within the City Church. The goal is one City Church, many departments, unified leadership and individualized roles instead of innumerous, competitive, autonomous organizations.

12. We must again become Holy Spirit sensitive instead of seeker sensitive.

People aren't looking for something worth living for, but rather a cause worth dying for. Show them the cross. The normal New Testament Church experience is one of extreme manifestations of God, death to self, prophetic preaching and an unapologetic invasion into the culture which results in momentous change.

And calling the crowd to him with his disciples, he said to them, "If anyone would come after me, let him deny himself and take up his cross and follow me. For whoever would save his life will lose it, but whoever loses his life for my sake and the gospel's will save it. Mark 8:34-35

13. We must again embrace dreams, visions, praying in the Holy Spirit and extreme encounters with God.

So, my brothers, earnestly desire to prophesy, and do not forbid speaking in tongues. 1 Corinthians 14:39

14. We must repent for presenting a watered down, socially acceptable gospel.

Salvation requires death, surrender and commitment to the plans of God.

And Jesus, looking at him, loved him, and said to him, "You lack one thing: go, sell all that you have and give to the poor, and you will have treasure in heaven; and come, follow me." Disheartened by the saying, he went away sorrowful, for he had great possessions. Mark 10:21-22

15. We must repent for emphasizing what people can get instead of what they are to give.

To enter a church with the expectation of leaving with more than you entered with is to embrace the same spirit the money changers did. We must again, with fear and trembling, enter the House of Prayer with the expectation of making a sacrifice and giving an offering.

And Jesus entered the temple and drove out all who sold and bought in the temple, and he overturned the tables of the money-changers and the seats of those who sold pigeons. He said to them, "It is written, 'My house shall be called a house of prayer,' but you make it a den of robbers." Matthew 21:12-13

16. We must call for the fear of the Lord to return to the Church.

Let not your heart envy sinners, but continue in the fear of the LORD all the day. Surely there is a future, and your hope will not be cut off. Proverbs 23:17-18

17. We must repent for rebellion, self-government, lawlessness and an independent spirit.

This is evidenced through church hopping and by leaving a church without being sent out by the leaders. This results in compromised missions, a divisive spirit and a splintering of the body. Accountability and submission to authority must again return to the Church.

Obey your leaders and submit to them, for they are keeping watch over your souls, as those who will have to give an account. Let them do this with joy and not with groaning, for that would be of no advantage to you. Hebrews 13:17

18. We must repent for embracing a religious spirit.

Religion is man's attempt to use God to get what he wants. It's time to cry out for God to remove our man-made structures and advance his Kingdom in our city!

19. We must repent to the world for misrepresenting America as a significant center of Holy Spirit activity.

It is not. We have wrongly stewarded this responsibility.

20. We must repent for not praying intently for our leaders. Their failure is our failure.

First of all, then, I urge that supplications, prayers, intercessions, and thanksgivings be made for all people, for kings and all who are in high positions, that we may lead a peaceful and quiet life, godly and dignified in every way. 1 Timothy 2:1-2

As we pray, unify, preach the cross, love God and the people of our city with passion and embrace the present Word of the Lord, the Church will be a propellant for revival around the world.

Do we trust God?

I often find myself wondering, *"Do I really trust God?"*

When honestly analyzing God's call for reformation and change, is it possible that we can think that our lives are going to get worse? Is our first thought one of dread instead of celebration?

Of course, the current church is the way it is largely because mankind has set it up this way. It's easy to dismiss what God knows to be best for something less costly yet appearing quite spiritual. The altars and images that we set up are there because of fear, selfishness, insecurity or unbelief.

But, what if we truly trusted God? When his call for reform is sounded, what would happen if the current Church joyfully gave way for the coming Church?

Radical trust of a zealous, loving Father is what today's Church needs so desperately! God is a very good God! His plans are to give us a future and a hope! Sure, the process and the cost is difficult and extreme at times, but do we truly understand the exchange that God is asking us to make?

I pray that there's a yearning for the love, life and wisdom of God coming to the Church again! He is trustworthy!

His love is indescribable! He has plans to prosper us! Do we trust that truth? Do we read the promises in Scripture and rejoice or recoil in doubt?

One second in God's love-saturated presence is worth billions of dollars, all of our free time, our personal security blankets, our energy and everything else we may hold dear.

He is wooing us. He is drawing us. The passion of the lover of our souls is a white hot passion. It will sear us in the very deepest places of our hearts if we only let him, if we only trust him.

The Church needs reformation not because of our badness, but because of God's goodness! He wants everything that hinders love to be fully removed, and wants us to be calibrated to his heart!

The coming Church will burn with love that none of us could ever imagine.

~ Ten ~

Carry Like Mary

The Coming Church will consist of carriers of God.

God suddenly woke me up one night and deposited an urgent mandate in my spirit. He said, *"John, tell everyone you can that it's time to carry like Mary."*

The revelation was hot and clear, and I was suddenly burning with a mandate that I couldn't wait to communicate.

One of the key focuses of our ministry is to awaken sleepers and to call people's destinies out of them. It's shocking how many Christians in today's Church are hindered by a spirit of insignificance that convinces them they have little value and will have little impact in ministry.

The coming Church will be marked by bold, Holy Spirit-filled prayer warriors who burn night and day. They will be an explo-

sive people who carry and release the fire of God into the cities of the Earth. There will be a regular tremble and a continual burn on them as they live in the supernatural realm in historic fashion.

The coming invasion from Heaven will shock the Church and will finally break many Christians free from feeling rejected and abused as victims and puppets of the enemy. There is a holy rage and unmistakable authority that will emerge in the camp of God.

Have you ever sung the old song, Enemy's Camp?

Well, I went to the enemy's camp and
I took back what he stole from me,
I took back what he stole from me,
I took back what he stole from me
I went to the enemy's camp and
I took back what he stole from me

You know
He's under my feet,
He's under my feet,
He's under my feet,
Satan is under my feet

I remember singing that song and dancing at the altar many times. Boy, does it have a ring of victory to it!

As I was considering the superpowers we have as Christians, as carriers of God, a question arose. Just why did the enemy take my stuff? Where is this camp I've heard so much about? Why do I have to take time out of my day to go there and retrieve my stuff?

Of course, the answer is obvious. He's a thief and he steals. However, the only way he has any confidence at all to get close to us so he can steal what is rightfully ours is that we don't have confidence that we can defeat him!

Have you noticed that Christians seem to always be playing catch up, trying to regain what was lost, trying to convince themselves of their victory? This is an identity issue. It's a revelation issue.

Satan discerns our lack of faith and revelation of who we are in Christ, and even more importantly, who Christ is in us!

If you saw the raging, churning, burning crater that I did in my vision, you'd know that the enemy would be a fool to approach such a fearful place. The coming Church is going to be a place, a people, who have the fear of the Lord coursing through their veins like fire—and the corporate expression of that will be felt around the world.

Carriers

> *Now I rejoice in my sufferings for your sake, and in my flesh I am filling up what is lacking in Christ's afflictions for the sake of his body, that is, the church, of which I became a minister according to the stewardship from God that was given to me for you, to make the word of God fully known, the mystery hidden for ages and generations but now revealed to his saints.*
>
> *To them God chose to make known how great among the Gentiles are the riches of the glory of this mystery, which is Christ in you, the hope of glory. Colossians 1:24-27*

In the above passage, Paul wanted you to know the mystery that was hidden for ages and generations, but is now revealed! What is this mystery? The depth of his glory which is Christ in you! In YOU!

He said the same thing to the Ephesians:

> *For this reason I bow my knees before the Father, from whom every family in heaven and on earth is named, that according to the riches of his glory he may grant you to be strengthened with power through his Spirit in your inner being, o that Christ may dwell in your hearts through faith—that you, be-*

> *ing rooted and grounded in love, may have strength to comprehend with all the saints what is the breadth and length and height and depth, and to know the love of Christ that surpasses knowledge, that you may be filled with all the fullness of God. Ephesians 3:14-19*

> *Blessed be the God and Father of our Lord Jesus Christ, who has blessed us in Christ with every spiritual blessing in the heavenly places, Ephesians 1:3*

And the Romans:

> *I know that when I come to you I will come in the fullness of the blessing of Christ. Romans 15:29*

So, it sure looks like there is something to the "Christ in you" concept. Mary certainly thought so. So did Elizabeth. Let's check out their stories, stories about history shaking carriers of God that turned the world upside down.

> *"Behold, I will send you Elijah the prophet before the great and awesome day of the LORD comes. And he will turn the hearts of fathers to their children and the hearts of children to their fathers, lest I come and strike the land with a decree of utter destruction." Malachi 4:5-6*

This prophecy was about John the Baptist who would arrive in the spirit and the power of Elijah. His goal? To turn the hearts of the fathers to their children and the hearts of the children to their fathers. This is a significant end-time Scripture! We will see, as the story continues, how God is preparing the generations to converge.

Now, at this point John the Baptist was not yet on the Earth. How would he arrive? Well, it's quite simple. He would have to arrive the same way every other human ever had—he would be conceived, carried and then delivered. But, of course, there's a bit of a problem with this scenario. Elizabeth, John's future mom, was barren.

> *In the days of Herod, king of Judea, there was a priest named Zechariah, of the division of Abijah. And he had a wife from the daughters of Aaron, and her name was Elizabeth. And they were both righteous before God, walking blamelessly in all the commandments and statutes of the Lord. But they had no child, because Elizabeth was barren, and both were advanced in years. Luke 1:5-7*

So, Elizabeth had what was in her control taken care of. She and her husband both were righteous and blameless. They embraced holiness in the fear of the Lord. That set them up for quite a story. What was not in her control was the fact that she was barren. She was physically impaired. She could not conceive.

The coming Church will be identified by those who fear God and who walk uprightly—and who become conduits of God's supernatural power.

As we continue in the story, consider Elizabeth's predicament this way: *she was old and barren.*

> *Now while he was serving as priest before God when his division was on duty, according to the custom of the priesthood, he was chosen by lot to enter the temple of the Lord and burn incense. And the whole multitude of the people were praying outside at the hour of incense. And there appeared to him an angel of the Lord standing on the right side of the altar of incense.*
>
> *And Zechariah was troubled when he saw him, and fear fell upon him. But the angel said to him, "Do not be afraid, Zechariah, for your prayer has been heard, and your wife Elizabeth will bear you a son, and you shall call his name John. Luke 1:8-13*

In the midst of a prayer-fueled church, there was angelic activity. The coming Church will be a prayer meeting first and foremost, and the supernatural, angelic activity will increase markedly.

Now, check this out:

> *...and he will be filled with the Holy Spirit, even from his mother's womb. And he will turn many of the children of Israel to the Lord their God, and he will go before him in the spirit and power of Elijah, to turn the hearts of the fathers to the children, and the disobedient to the wisdom of the just, to make ready for the Lord a people prepared." Luke 1:15-17*

Now, that is the way to carry a baby! Elizabeth would be carrying baby John the Baptist who, in turn, would be carrying God! This mighty prophet of God, this carrier of the Holy Spirit, would be birthed from the elder generation. Now let's look at Mary, the younger generation.

> *In the sixth month the angel Gabriel was sent from God to a city of Galilee named Nazareth, to a virgin betrothed to a man whose name was Joseph, of the house of David. And the virgin's name was Mary. And he came to her and said, "Greetings, O favored one, the Lord is with you!" But she was greatly troubled at the saying, and tried to discern what sort of greeting this might be.*
>
> *And the angel said to her, "Do not be afraid, Mary, for you have found favor with God. And behold, you will conceive in your womb and bear a son, and you shall call his name Jesus. He will be great and will be called the Son of the Most High. And the Lord God will give to him the throne of his father David, and he will reign over the house of Jacob forever, and of his kingdom there will be no end." Luke 1:26-33*

Elizabeth was old and barren.
Mary was young and a virgin.

And Mary said to the angel, "How will this be, since I am a virgin?" And the angel answered her, "The Holy Spirit will come upon you, and the power of the Most High will overshadow you; therefore the child to be born will be called holy—the Son of God. And behold, your relative Elizabeth in her old age has also conceived a son, and this is the sixth month with her who was called barren. For nothing will be impossible with God." And Mary said, "Behold, I am the servant of the Lord; let it be to me according to your word." And the angel departed from her. Luke 1:34-38

Elizabeth was old and barren.

Mary was young and a virgin.

Another impossible situation, another angelic encounter and another entrance by the Holy Spirit. Like Elizabeth, Mary was called to be a carrier of God.

If that wasn't powerful enough for you, look at what happens next. Do you remember the prophetic promise in Malachi? The generations would again come together through the ministry of John the Baptist. This happened quicker than you might think.

In those days Mary arose and went with haste into the hill country, to a town in Judah, and she entered the house of Zechariah and greeted Elizabeth. And when Elizabeth heard the greeting of Mary, the baby leaped in her womb. And Elizabeth was filled with the Holy Spirit, and she exclaimed with a loud cry, "Blessed are you among women, and blessed is the fruit of your womb! And why is this granted to me that the mother of my Lord should come to me? For behold, when the sound of your greeting came to my ears, the baby in my womb leaped for joy. And blessed is she who believed that there would be a fulfillment of what was spoken to her from the Lord." Luke 1:39-45

When the older and younger generations met, both carrying God (Elizabeth carrying John who was carrying the Holy Spirit and Mary carrying Jesus), there was a leaping of the baby and a greater infilling of the Holy Spirit!

Being a willing participant as God searches our hearts is a very good idea! Repenting is critical!

In this end-time generation, we are called to carry like Mary! There will be a leaping and a rejoicing and a great manifestation of the Holy Spirit when the carriers of God unite in faith and mission.

The burning fiery love of God in the coming crater of his presence will overtake end-time carriers who will impact regions all around the world.

Christ in Us

Now, this revelation causes everything to change. Christ, in fullness, is in you and me! That sounds impossible if you think about it. God, who created the universe fits inside of us fully! This should radically change the way we think and live.

Think of it this way. God knows everything. He lives in you. This means that every answer in the world is within you, correct? God knows the cure for cancer. I'm not talking about God miraculously healing someone of cancer, but rather, he knows the scientific resolution to this plague. He could email a cancer researcher with the scientific blueprint that would once and for all end cancer on the Earth.

Do you understand what this means? The scientific cure for cancer is within you! The cure for cancer is in God, and God is in you. Of course, that knowledge hasn't been activated and revealed, but the point is that the fullness of God is in us!

The powerful truth is this: We aren't God ourselves by any means. We are weak and broken humans. However, that makes the truth so much more remarkable! We as weak, fallible people are carriers of an omnipotent God! This certainly opens up a lot of opportunities for God's end-time army in the coming Church!

~ *Eleven* ~

The Salvation Equation

The Coming Church will affirm the realities of Hell, repentance and the cross.

Regarding the focus of this chapter, I want to make my point very clear right up front. The reason I feel it's mandatory for us to start focusing on the issue of false grace (some call it hyper grace or distorted grace) is because of the eternal implications. My angle is not mostly earthly focused, how our lives are impacted in the here and now, though our short experience on Earth will certainly be impacted as we react rightly to this message (on Earth as it is in Heaven). The coming Church will bring calibration to the teaching of Scripture, and the false grace doctrine is most probably the most deadly teaching in the Church today. I say that without any exaggeration whatsoever. The coming Church will affirm many truths that are either refuted or minimized by false grace teachers. These truths

include repentance, holiness, the fear of the Lord, brokenness and living a fasted lifestyle.

My angle is this: A false grace doctrine is a drug—a poisonous sleeping pill that feels freeing, relaxing and euphoric. Yet the false grace overdose that's occurring in churches all over the world is resulting in people's careless, self-focused slumber that they will, one day, fail to awaken from.

Many in the false grace movement have already been shocked on the day of their death to find themselves escorted not into the presence of God by glorious angels, but rather by the most horrific demonic creatures into their new, eternal residence in Hell. It happens every day. I'm grieved and broken.

The Apostle Paul accurately predicted,

> *For the time is coming when people will not endure sound teaching, but having itching ears they will accumulate for themselves teachers to suit their own passions, and will turn away from listening to the truth and wander off into myths. 2 Timothy 4:3-4*

The good news is that God loves us. Period. It's settled. We don't have to feel it. We don't have to experience it. He loves us. No amount of work or activity will cause him to love us more. The question isn't his love of us, it's our love of him. He already responded to our condition—by his true grace. Now, we have to respond to his condition. He is a holy and fearful God.

I'll make it very clear: We are righteous because of Jesus, not because of our works. Our works are an evidence of his righteousness applied in our lives. Our repentance comes when there is a collision between the reality of our righteousness in Christ and our choice to sin. The two can't mix. If we do repent, righteousness remains. If we don't repent, it does not. It's as simple (though not always easy) as living a life that's alive in Christ and quick to repent as his wonderful Holy Spirit convicts us. It's when we presume sin and holiness can coexist that eternity is provoked. There is a true-grace message that is more powerful, freeing and desirable than anything the false grace message promises.

> *Look: I, Paul, say to you that if you accept circumcision, Christ will be of no advantage to you. I testify again to every man who accepts circumcision that he is obligated to keep the whole law. You are severed from Christ, you who would be justified by the law; you have fallen away from grace. For through the Spirit, by faith, we ourselves eagerly wait for the hope of righteousness. For in Christ Jesus neither circumcision nor uncircumcision counts for anything, but only faith working through love. Galatians 5:2-6*

Our works apart from the cross are meaningless. Filthy rags. Even deadly. But in response to the cross of Christ, our obedience is beautiful indeed! If we believe, we will respond to his instructions out of the fear and love of the Lord. Yet, if we are not truly in Christ, we do have reason for concern.

> *that whoever believes in him may have eternal life. "For God so loved the world, that he gave his only Son, that whoever believes in him should not perish but have eternal life. For God did not send his Son into the world to condemn the world, but in order that the world might be saved through him. John 3:15-17*

One of the key indicators that someone is at least at risk of falling into a false grace mindset is when they are mostly focused on their personal condition. When I have discussions about false grace, the regular, immediate reaction is very often, *"I don't have to do anything to convince God to love me."*

I always respond by saying something like, *"Why are you bringing up an unrelated topic of discussion? We aren't talking about causing God to love us. We are talking about a lifestyle that's obedient and biblical. I suppose if love were to enter the conversation, it would be from*

the opposing direction. There's no question God loves us, but do we truly love him?"

God loves with a depth we'll spend eternity discovering, yet that doesn't mean people won't go to Hell. The issue isn't whether God loves us, it's whether we love him.

"If you love me, you will keep my commandments. John 14:15

Five Marks of the False Grace Movement

With the possibility of such a permanent and terrifying destiny before us, eternal damnation, we must analyze our theologies. What we believe absolutely can affect where we will live forever. How can we know we have been influenced by this heretical teaching of false grace? It's not hard.

ONE: We believe in a theology of exemption.

A theology of exemption states that since we are saved, we are exempt from the penalties of sin and that there are parts of the Bible that no longer apply to us. Yes, it's a heresy. False grace removes Bible-based responsibilities to respond to God in holiness.

Of course, if we live a repentant life, then by all means the penalties of sin are eradicated. However, if we don't repent and respond rightly to Scripture, we can't presume to be free.

The number of people who subconsciously or unwittingly embrace a theology of exemption is far greater than those who explicitly pronounce their agreement with this doctrine. Many subscribe to false grace doctrines without realizing their deception.

Many have been lulled into a false sense of security while actually existing in an unsaved state. They are confident they'd enter Heaven if they died, yet the reality is that they would not. They have come to believe they are exempt from certain parts of the Word of

God that requires response. They are following Jesus in an unsaved condition.

> *but as he who called you is holy, you also be holy in all your conduct, since it is written, "You shall be holy, for I am holy." And if you call on him as Father who judges impartially according to each one's deeds, conduct yourselves with fear throughout the time of your exile, 1 Peter 1:15-17*

Be holy. God judges according to one's deeds. Those who hold to a theology of exemption don't believe they are subject to what this verse is communicating. The command to be holy is to them a great goal but not a mandate. A principle not a command.

Our name can actually be removed from the book of life—and that is determined by our obedience, our holiness. Sin can still separate a follower of Christ from him. The Rich Young Ruler saw that this was the case. He wanted to follow Jesus but could not. He was not exempt from judgment even though he wanted to follow Jesus. Could he have returned to Jesus at a later date? Yes. Absolutely. But, in this story, he had yet to do so.

Our name can actually be removed from the book of life—and that is determined by our obedience, our holiness.

> *Yet you have still a few names in Sardis, people who have not soiled their garments, and they will walk with me in white, for they are worthy. The one who conquers will be clothed thus in white garments, and I will never blot his name out of the book of life. I will confess his name before my Father and before his angels. He who has an ear, let him hear what the Spirit says to the churches.' Revelation 3:4-6*

The argument of grace is actually quite revealing. People in the false grace movement would say, *"It's not possible to be holy, or to avoid sin, so thank God for his grace that covers those sins. In fact we are automatically holy… innocent by association!"*

Grace isn't meant to cover up or hide sin, grace is power! Those who walk in true grace would never say that we, as Christians, are predisposed to sin! True grace enables us to do the impossible! False grace confesses that we cannot. Because of the cross and the resurrection of Jesus, we now have something they didn't have in the Old Covenant—we have the power to obey! We can do this!

It infuriates me when people presume inability to obey Scripture and to live holy. That mindset is an offense to the cross of Christ! The blood of Jesus is powerful enough to empower us to live a holy life! We are mandated to do so.

In fact, not only are we not exempt from obedience in the New Covenant, the call to obedience is even more humanly impossible than in the Old!

> *You have heard that it was said to those of old, 'You shall not murder; and whoever murders will be liable to judgment.' But I say to you that everyone who is angry with his brother will be liable to judgment; whoever insults his brother will be liable to the council; and whoever says, 'You fool!' will be liable to the hell of fire. Matthew 5:21-22 "*

We as Christians are not exempt from judgment or from the repercussions of sin. If we are in Christ, there is no condemnation, but if we are deceived by false theology into thinking we are in Christ, while actually living in disobedience, we are in trouble. We are not in Christ and there is condemnation. No salvation. The wrath of God remains on us. False grace doctrine is eternally deadly. As I said before, tragically there are many people going to church, reading their Bibles, lifting their hands in worship and paying their tithes all while following Jesus today in an unsaved condition. Someone must sound the alarm.

In my book *The Terror of Hell,* I share the story when I was dragged toward Hell. Coming out of the horrifying experience, God said, *"Many in the church will be shocked to find themselves in Hell one day."* I was wrecked.

> *The Father loves the Son and has given all things into his hand. Whoever believes in the Son has eternal life; whoever does not obey the Son shall not see life, but the wrath of God remains on him. John 3:35-36*

> *Whoever believes in him is not condemned, but whoever does not believe is condemned already, because he has not believed in the name of the only Son of God. And this is the judgment: the light has come into the world, and people loved the darkness rather than the light because their works were evil. John 3:18-19*

Deeds. Fruit. Works. They are evidences of our position in Christ.

Yes, it's hard to get saved, hard to stay saved, but if we walk in humility, grace and in the Spirit, eternity with Jesus is our inheritance!

TWO: Sin is treated as temporally troubling but eternally benign.

> *For if we go on sinning deliberately after receiving the knowledge of the truth, there no longer remains a sacrifice for sins, but a fearful expectation of judgment, and a fury of fire that will consume the adversaries. Hebrews 10:26-27*

That verse stands on its own. The false grace teachers emphasize that our sin may cause problems in the here and now, but there is no risk of Hell. This has to be one of the most troubling positions those in the false grace movement take.

Universalism is creeping into the Church very subtly. False grace teaches that Hell is not a concern for Christians and Christian Universalism teaches that there is no Hell. Different twists on the same false doctrine. I've even come across theologies that state sinners will go to Hell for 1000 years, but will then be rescued and welcomed into Heaven. It's absolutely unbelievable.

Yes, sin does result in trauma here on the Earth. But, it doesn't end there. If we embrace a lifestyle of sin, we are not saved, even if we've previously been saved. We won't go to Heaven. The day of judgment will be a day of horror.

The false grace/semi universalist position is one that would adhere to the "once saved, always saved" position. My belief is actually quite the opposite—once saved, rarely saved. The road is not wide. It's narrow, and it's rare to find people on it…and people who decide to stay on it.

> *The one who conquers will be clothed thus in white garments, and I will never blot his name out of the book of life. I will confess his name before my Father and before his angels. He who has an ear, let him hear what the Spirit says to the churches.' Revelation 3:5-6*

If we don't conquer, don't work out our salvation with fear and trembling, our name is blotted out of the book of life.

> *But I say, walk by the Spirit, and you will not gratify the desires of the flesh. For the desires of the flesh are against the Spirit, and the desires of the Spirit are against the flesh, for these are opposed to each other, to keep you from doing the things you want to do. But if you are led by the Spirit, you are not under the law. Now the works of the flesh are evident: sexual immorality, impurity,*

> *sensuality, idolatry, sorcery, enmity, strife, jealousy, fits of anger, rivalries, dissensions, divisions, envy, drunkenness, orgies, and things like these. I warn you, as I warned you before, that those who do such things will not inherit the kingdom of God. Galatians 5:16-21*

If we walk in the Spirit, our flesh is subdued. However, if we aren't walking in the Spirit, we are under the law, because Christ's sacrifice has been made of no effect. Therefore, even though we may have said the sinner's prayer, paid tithes and lived a good life, that salvation is nullified for us. The above Scripture reveals the clear evidence to look for when analyzing our position in Christ.

I've heard of pastors who boast that they no longer preach on the cross, sin or Hell because we are in the age of grace. My God! The cross must be central to our churches! A church that doesn't preach the cross and the blood is not a Christian Church. Period. It is heretical. The coming Church will have the cross of Christ front and center.

There can be pastors who preach powerfully, pray in tongues and lead large, growing churches who won't inherit the kingdom of God. If they are driven by jealousy of other pastors or embrace division, the Bible is clear. If they don't repent, Hell is in their future. Do you have any idea how much of the fear of the Lord I'm feeling right now? I tremble continually. False grace provides temporal security in exchange for eternal torment. The enemy is more than happy to make this exchange.

THREE: Repentance and confession of sin is not necessary after we have been saved.

False grace teachers proclaim that our sins are forgiven past, present and future. This is simply not true. If we repent, yes, we are forgiven. If we retain our sins they are retained. The provision for forgiveness has been made, and true grace has been given to us to respond.

The Lord's Prayer itself makes it clear that we must both ask for forgiveness and forgive!

> *and forgive us our debts, as we also have forgiven our debtors. Matthew 6:12*
>
> *If we confess our sins, he is faithful and just to forgive us our sins and to cleanse us from all unrighteousness. 1 John 1:9*
>
> *If we say we have fellowship with him while we walk in darkness, we lie and do not practice the truth. 1 John 1:6*

The false grace theology commonly teaches that we, as humans in a fallen world, are expected to sin and that it's the focus on sin, not sin itself, that puts us into bondage. The reality is that people are becoming affirmed in a sinful state with no fear of the Lord or fear of damnation to be found. Of course, false grace teachers don't encourage a lifestyle of sin, but they also don't sound the alarm communicating any sort of eternal threat. To them, there is no eternal risk whatsoever.

A friend of mine shared this:

> *Amy Smith: Misrepresented grace has caused us to respond to the command to be holy with an elbow bump and a wink, wink. "Ok God, we know what you mean. You're not really asking us to be holy, you're just telling us to make sure we're under your grace. We know that You're overlooking those little sins we're not dealing with. In fact, your grace allows us to also overlook some things, such as all the Scripture verses that call for standards that are higher than we can achieve."*

Another friend shared this:

> *Ed Hull: When we die, it will not be what we believed about our identity in Christ that will save us. It will be whether the concept of our identity produced good fruit, the fruit of righteousness.*

Simply put, repentance and confession are absolutely critical to our position in Christ after salvation. Most are unclear on their identity. They presume themselves to be "in Christ" though they very well may not be. If we are 'in Christ', there is no condemnation, but if we analyze our position wrongly, presuming to be "in Christ" when in fact we are not, we are still condemned.

Repentance is actually a very wonderful, joyful, fulfilling lifestyle! The closer I get to God, the deeper into my heart I allow him to peer, the more repentance comes flowing out. I love to repent! Even if it's grieving, my heart comes alive as I realign with the lover of my soul! The more I turn, the deeper into God I go! Ignoring sin, unbelief and other barriers to intimacy just can't be our strategy! Presuming they aren't there when they are just doesn't work. Repent continually, and enjoy an indescribable journey into intimacy with Jesus!

FOUR. A biblical works message is renounced as legalism.

It's striking to me how often I hear that a focus on holiness and obedience equates to legalism. How far from orthodox Christianity has the Church fallen?

The only point at which it's legalism is if we were to reject the cross and resurrection of Christ by attempting to work our way into Heaven. But, if we agree that Jesus is the only one who could have paid for our sins, yet we also refuse to work, our salvation is a myth.

Legalism is our attempt to get to Heaven by bypassing the cross of Jesus. Holiness and works are our response to the cross of Jesus.

> *"Why do you call me 'Lord, Lord,' and not do what I tell you? Luke 6:46*

> *But he answered them, "My mother and my brothers are those who hear the word of God and do it." Luke 8:21*

But he said, "Blessed rather are those who hear the word of God and keep it!" Luke 11:28

Truly, truly, I say to you, if anyone keeps my word, he will never see death." John 8:51

"If you love me, you will keep my commandments. John 14:15

If you keep my commandments, you will abide in my love, just as I have kept my Father's commandments and abide in his love. John 15:10

You are my friends if you do what I command you. John 15:14

Therefore, my beloved, as you have always obeyed, so now, not only as in my presence but much more in my absence, work out your own salvation with fear and trembling, for it is God who works in you, both to will and to work for his good pleasure. Philippians 2:12-13

His master said to him, 'Well done, good and faithful servant. You have been faithful over a little; I will set you over much. Enter into the joy of your master.' He also who had received the one talent came forward, saying, 'Master, I knew you to be a hard man, reaping where you did not sow, and gathering where you scattered no seed, so I was afraid, and I went and hid your talent in the ground. Here you have what is yours.'

But his master answered him, 'You wicked and slothful servant! You knew that I reap where I have not sown and gather where I scattered no seed? Then you ought to have invested my money with the bankers, and at my coming I should have received what was my own with interest. So take the talent from him and give it to him who has the ten talents. For to everyone who has will more be given, and he will have an abundance. But from the one who has not, even what he has will be taken away. And cast the worthless servant into the outer darkness. In that place there will be weeping and gnashing of teeth.' Matthew 25:23-30

Throughout the New Testament it's proven over and over again that obedience, works and production (fruit) is mandatory if we are to be—and stay—saved.

FIVE. Salvation is depicted as easy and/or permanent.

Jesus didn't die on the cross to make it easy for us to get saved. He died so it would be possible for us to get saved.

There is a temptation to withdraw from the pressures of persecution, the call to holiness, surrender and the cross, and a false grace message is the perfect solution to that problem. It offers an escape from an urgent and fervent focus on obedience by disjoining it from our position in Christ. The false grace doctrine teaches that our eternity and our relationship with Jesus is already settled, and we can simply relax and enjoy God. Our obedience is in no way joined to our relationship with Jesus or our eternal destiny.

Additionally, there is a misunderstanding of the process of salvation. Those impacted by the false grace movement tend to believe that they play no part in salvation other than believing that Jesus was the Son of God. Anything other than that would scream of works, and false grace teaching has convinced them to have an averse reaction to anything that feels like human effort.

The Scripture that most often comes to mind is Ephesians 2:8-9:

> *For by grace you have been saved through faith. And this is not your own doing; it is the gift of God, not a result of works, so that no one may boast. Ephesians 2:8-9*

First, this Scripture is quite often misunderstood. It is NOT saying that works don't play a part in salvation. It IS saying that works ALONE can't save us. Basically, we can't say, *"Thanks Jesus for dying on the cross for me, and rising from the dead. Great job! But, you know, I'm not really interested in your version of salvation. So, I reject the cross and*

the resurrection... it's just too narrow for me. Instead, I will give $1 million to a local church and will buy my way into Heaven. I'll pay the price myself."

We can't pay the price. We can't substitute Jesus' payment for our own.

But, that doesn't mean we don't work in RESPONSE to and in ACCORDANCE with the price that only Jesus could pay. We love Ephesians 2:8-9, but usually leave off verse 10:

> *For we are his workmanship, created in Christ Jesus for good works, which God prepared beforehand, that we should walk in them. Ephesians 2:10*

It's shocking to me how sharply resistant Christians can be when the doctrine of salvation is discussed.

We were created for good works. Paul reveals that we receive the Spirit via hearing by faith and not of works, yet that does not communicate to us that works are not to be expected. First faith, then works and not the other way around.

> *What good is it, my brothers, if someone says he has faith but does not have works? Can that faith save him? James 2:14*

It's a rhetorical question. The answer, of course, is no. Faith without works cannot save us. This means, if we have faith in Jesus, worship him, pray to him, honor him... but don't obey, we cannot presume to be saved. False grace theology would not agree with this.

> *But someone will say, "You have faith and I have works." Show me your faith apart from your works, and I will show you my faith by my works. You believe that God is one; you do well. Even the demons believe—and shudder! Do you want to be shown, you foolish person, that faith apart from works is useless? James 2:18-20*

The false grace movement is shouting, *"Show me your faith apart from works!"* The question must be, *"Are we like demons who have faith (believe), or do we also work in response to the mandates of God?"*

It's easy and common to be falsely saved, but to truly be saved requires an extreme price—both on the part of Jesus and on our part. We can't do his part, and he can't do ours—and this does have eternal implications. The false grace message that minimizes obedience and works absolutely does result in people being cast into eternal fire.

A Deeper Look at False Grace

The chapter up to this point has been short and concise. Such an important topic requires a deeper look.

Some may wonder why I am so passionate about this issue of grace, and why I continue to sound the same alarm again and again.

It's simple—this is my life message. Silence on this issue will result in tragedy beyond comprehension.

My burning passion is to see the Church shaken out of slumber into a deep, intimate encounter with Jesus. Out of complacency and any false assurance of salvation into zealous devotion to follow our all consuming leader. This is all about eternity.

It's shocking to me how sharply resistant Christians can be when the doctrine of salvation is discussed. Many have been lulled into a state of false comfort through incredibly dangerous and fast-spreading theologies—anything that would threaten their confidence is reacted to fiercely. A pastor once told me that the most violent

reaction from Christians against him comes when he deals with false grace.

> *For the grace of God has appeared, bringing salvation for all people, training us to renounce ungodliness and worldly passions, and to live self-controlled, upright, and godly lives in the present age, waiting for our blessed hope, the appearing of the glory of our great God and Savior Jesus Christ, who gave himself for us to redeem us from all lawlessness and to purify for himself a people for his own possession who are zealous for good works. Declare these things; exhort and rebuke with all authority. Let no one disregard you. Titus 2:11-15*

My life message is to awaken the comfortable, sleeping Church and declare the true, empowering grace of God.

It's not a message that I chose. In the natural, that would be insanity as my fervent attention to it has brought trouble and grief not only to me but to my family. We've lost friends and awakened enemies we didn't know we had.

Here's an email from our great friend Julia Palermo:

> *Hi John! I wanted to let you know that the Lord has really put you, Detroit Revival Church and the city of Detroit on my heart the past few weeks. I've been following your posts and just carrying you all in my heart. I feel like you are very much in need of extra prayer coverage as you are stepping out very boldly in some areas of proclamation of the truth. Just wanted you to know that I am going to be praying for you and for the church. Would love to talk some time and hear what the Lord is doing. Though I think this bold stand may cost you in some sense, I truly feel that for the remnant who receives these messages and signs up to pursue Him in holiness, He is going to come with His fire and His presence. I believe you are going to experience some times of such a weight of his holiness and nearness in the room that people will only be able to weep on the floor and won't move for hours. You have not seen before what He is about to do in you and in the church. Be encouraged! He is with you! Julia*

Thankfully, it's a teaching that has resulted in continual messages from people sharing how their life has been powerfully impacted by it.

> *Shortly after hearing a teaching that God forgives all sin, past, present and future, I was ignorantly relieved of the struggles I was having with particular sins and then went so far away from truth, deep into more self justified sin, self deception, coldness, distance from God, family, etc. .... Now I've been hearing teaching from John Burton and others against sin and this false doctrine (false grace teaching) and now for the first time since I became a Christian almost 10 years ago, I have been free from the power of habitual sin and no longer live a life of torment ... All Glory to GOD!!! God needs more TRUTH Ministers. ~Nick*

It's a message that, by design, urgently and aggressively provokes those who are personally comfortable yet eternally vulnerable.

The Terror of Hell

It's a message that was hand-delivered to me, by God, over twenty years ago, in a dream where I was dragged toward Hell by a demon that, strangely, had full authority to do so. In a split second, in my nighttime encounter, I went from wonderful comfort and complete confidence in my position in Christ to maddening terror as I was slowly, methodically dragged toward Hell. The confusion that gripped me was met by the truth that I was indeed going to spend the rest of eternity—multiplied trillions of years consisting of innumerable hours that feel like decades—being tormented in Hell.

I thought, *"It's impossible! I can't be going to Hell!"*

After all, I'm a Christian!

After I came out of this deeply disturbing experience, God spoke clearly to me: John, in your dream you represented the many in the Church who will be shocked to find themselves in Hell one day.

I knew my life assignment was now to humbly yet boldly—and expediently—warn everybody I can. According to Mike Bickle, his opinion is that the number one, most dangerous threat in America today is the distorted grace message… Even a greater threat than abortion. Greater than 55 million murdered babies! Why is it a greater threat? Because as sickening and horrifying as abortion is, there are 55 million babies in Heaven today. False grace results in millions of casual Christians ending up in Hell.

Christians in Hell?

Leonard Ravenhill states that he doubts that 5% of professing American Christians are actually saved!

I have to be perfectly clear at this point:

Yes, it is my conviction that many in the Church, many in even the most fiery, vibrant and alive churches in the world, are convinced they are saved while living in an unsaved state. False theologies have been so widely embraced that the thought of them being false seem absolutely ridiculous.

Additionally, I am quite comfortable with differing Christian streams emphasizing different biblical principles and even respectfully disagreeing over them—if they don't threaten eternity. We can disagree over tongues, prophecy, gifts, the timing of the rapture and a myriad of other doctrines—but, the issue of false grace is different. Eternity is at stake, and many worshiping, Bible reading, tithing, professing Christians have been deceived and Hell is being made ready for them.

I will share a lot of Scripture in this lengthy chapter to support my position.

How do works fit into the salvation equation?

For by grace you have been saved through faith. And this is not your own doing; it is the gift of God, not a result of works, so that no one may boast. Ephesians 2:8-9

False grace teachers are vigilant in their attempts to invalidate any measure of works for the Christian—at least as they relate to salvation. In fact, the logical end to the false grace theology is actually universalism. We do nothing, God did everything, everybody is saved.

Of course, it would be said that we have to believe to be saved. Well, first, that is a work. It takes participation on our behalf. Second, even the demons believe. Even the Rich Young Ruler believed. He was rejected, because he was unwilling to do his part. The true motive of his heart was revealed, yet in today's churches it would be offensive to turn such a man away at an altar call! The common reaction is to give someone assurance of their salvation, all while they may not actually be saved at all. This is a serious indictment on the Church to say the least! How many people are going to Hell because a pastor told them they are eternally secure if they simply repeat a prayer after them? I believe the sinner's prayer may actually be sending more people to Hell than to Heaven!

Leonard Ravenhill states that he doubts that 5% of professing American Christians are actually saved!

The above Scripture in Ephesians 2 is actually quite easy to understand. It's NOT saying that we don't have to participate in the salvation process. The truth is that we have to be radically involved. The salvation equation includes us!

What the passage is saying is that we cannot bypass Jesus. We can't give a million dollars to a charity and volunteer at Habitat for Humanity every weekend in order to work our way into Heaven. We can't decide that the call to serve Jesus is not appealing to us, so we opt instead for option two or three. We can't create our own salvation

plan and then boast about our own abilities. There is only one way, and Jesus is it. And, obedience is very much a part of the equation.

> *Therefore put away all filthiness and rampant wickedness and receive with meekness the implanted word, which is able to save your souls. But be doers of the word, and not hearers only, deceiving yourselves. James 1:21-22*

> *Works minus Jesus equals no salvation.*
> *Jesus minus works equals false salvation.*
> *Jesus plus works equals evidence of true salvation.*

The cross of Christ doesn't eliminate our responsibility, it redefines our responsibility. He did what only he could do, and we must do what he will not do.

When he said, *"It is finished,"* he meant it. His job is done—and ours begins. He emphasized this again in Acts 1. The disciples wanted Jesus to do more work (establish his Kingdom), but Jesus made it clear that his job was indeed complete. However, he let them know that their work was just beginning. They must walk in obedience to Jesus.

> *And being made perfect, he became the source of eternal salvation to all who obey him… Hebrews 5:9*

We can have "intimacy" with Jesus without works, and death is the result. We can also have works without intimacy, and the result is also death.

Being intimate with Jesus doesn't automatically mean we'll do good works, and doing good works doesn't automatically mean we'll be close to God. Attention must be given to both endeavors. In Matthew, being known by God intimately AND doing God's will are required. We can't call him Lord without doing his will, and we can't do works without also knowing him:

"Not everyone who says to me, 'Lord, Lord,' will enter the kingdom of heaven, but the one who does the will of my Father who is in heaven. On that day many will say to me, 'Lord, Lord, did we not prophesy in your name, and cast out demons in your name, and do many mighty works in your name?' And then will I declare to them, 'I never knew you; depart from me, you workers of lawlessness.' Matthew 7:21-23

Additionally, we see God dealing with the churches in the book of Revelation. Repeatedly he said, *"I know your works."* And, their position in Christ absolutely did hinge on what they did or did not do.

Interestingly, as I said previously, when I talk about biblical works, the most common response goes something like this, *"John, we don't have to perform for God to love us."* Hmmm, why is the issue of God's love introduced into a discussion about an entirely different topic? I didn't mention God's love. I didn't say that we had to do stuff to convince God to love us, but that is the most immediate reaction I receive. Is it possible that we are living in a "me-centered" generation where personal satisfaction and experience are the goal? The issue isn't God's love of us; it's our love of God.

We see this play out all throughout the Church. Prayer meetings, conferences and other events are full when the focus is on personal blessing, encounter, healing, prosperity and other bonuses. But, when the call is to die, to intercede for the nations, to carry our cross, to do the work of fervent prayer, to lay down our lives to impact the world, the crowds disperse.

"And to the angel of the church in Sardis write: 'The words of him who has the seven spirits of God and the seven stars. "'I know your works. You have the reputation of being alive, but you are dead. Wake up, and strengthen what remains and is about to die, for I have not found your works complete in the sight of my God. Revelation 3:1-2

Remember, then, what you received and heard. Keep it, and repent. If you will not wake up, I will come like a thief, and you will not know at what hour I will come against you. Yet you have still a few names in Sardis, people who have not soiled their garments, and they will walk with me in white, for they are worthy. The one who conquers will be clothed thus in white garments, and I will never blot his name out of the book of life. I will confess his name before my Father and before his angels. He who has an ear, let him hear what the Spirit says to the churches.' Revelation 3:3-6

Incomplete works can result in names being blotted out of the book of life.

The ESV Study Bible gives clarity to what is being said in Revelation 3:3-6:

Hope for revival is in the fact that a few names—alert and unstained disciples—can still be found in this church. Their unsoiled garments symbolize consistent obedience and courageous faith. Christ promises them the conqueror's reward: communion with himself (walk with me) and the white raiment of victory. Their name is secure in his book of life, and he will confess their name before the Father, since they have confessed Jesus in hostile circumstances (Matt. 10:32).

Both obedience and faith make up the salvation equation.

From the AMG Bible Commentary on the same verses:

Believers must wake up, change their ways, and determine to follow the teaching of the gospel they first believed. If not, swift judgment will fall upon them.

From Dake:

Here Christ promises not to blot the name out of the book of life of any man who will obey the commands of Rev. 3:2-3. If some refused to obey these commands, would their names not be blotted out? If we say such is impossible we accuse God of

> *using vain threats on His people. He definitely promised Moses, "Whosoever hath sinned against Me, him will I blot out of my book" (Ex. 32:32-33).*

Again, we see obedience, works, directly involved in the salvation equation.

The call to wake up and strengthen is a call to works! If that work is not done, that person will in fact one day be cast into Hell.

> *What good is it, my brothers, if someone says he has faith but does not have works? Can that faith save him? James 2:14*

Life Application Commentary on James 2:14:

> *Faith not accompanied by deeds has no saving value.*

Dake:

> *Christianity demands of its followers good works to all men (Mt. 5:16; 16:27; Eph. 2:10; 1Tim. 6:18; 2Tim. 3:17; Tit. 1:16; 2:7,14; 3:8). One is not justified by works (Rom. 3:25-31; 4:1-6; 9:11; 11:6; Gal. 2:16; Eph. 2:8-9; Tit. 3:5), but justified ones must do them to prove their Christian consecration (vv. 14-18,20-26).*

> *Faith without works is dead; works without faith is dead (vv. 17,20,26). Neither is complete in itself.*

False Grace is closely related to the false teaching of Antinomianism.

Wikipedia:

> *Antinomianism in Christianity is the belief that under the gospel dispensation of grace, moral law is of no use or obligation because faith alone is necessary to salvation.*

Regarding Antinomianism, Steve Hill wrote:

Purveyors of this poisonous teaching fail to realize that Jesus calls us beyond the requirements of the law in His teaching, stating, for example, that adultery refers to adultery of the heart and not just the physical act (Matt. 5:27-28).

Are our sins forgiven past, present and future?

False grace teachers turn a deaf ear to scriptural truths that reveal that we as Christians absolutely have to deal with sin. Again, Jesus told us that his job is finished. He died, and rose and that was sufficient to cover every sin, past, present and future.

However, that does not mean our future sin is automatically resolved. We have a part to play.

Are our sins forgiven past, present and future?

PAST: Yes.

PRESENT: Why are you sinning right now?

FUTURE: It's conditional.

No? Jesus did his part, but we must do ours. We can absolutely lose our salvation due to a decision to sin. The blood of Jesus didn't grant us immunity from future repercussions of sin. The blood of Jesus granted us power and authority over sin, power to live holy.

We've understated the power of the blood while overstating the role of the blood. The blood has enough power to eradicate every sin ever committed throughout history and into the future. However, the role is ours, not God's to embrace the cross, repent and work out our salvation with fear and trembling. The blood must be applied.

> *For if we go on sinning deliberately after receiving the knowledge of the truth, there no longer remains a sacrifice for sins, but a fearful expectation of judgment, and a fury of fire that will consume the adversaries. Hebrews 10:26-27*

The sacrifice that was fully sufficient for the believer at the time of his conversion to Christ can be invalidated based on our behavior.

Additionally, this Scripture clearly reveals that Jesus paid the price for our past sins:

> *for all have sinned and fall short of the glory of God, and are justified by his grace as a gift, through the redemption that is in Christ Jesus, whom God put forward as a propitiation by his blood, to be received by faith. This was to show God's righteousness, because in his divine forbearance he had passed over former sins. Romans 3:23-25*

Leonard Ravenhill said:

> *"I've heard people say "Jesus died for your sins past, present and future." Imagine a judge tell a thief "you are forgiven of all the purses you stole in the past, the ones you stole today, and the all of the ones you'll …steal in the future." If that's insane in real life it's just as insane in so called doctrine."*

The historic Church has always taught that Christ died potentially for all sins; in other words provision has been made for all sins. But that provision has to be applied.

The presumption is that Christians are exempt from, and can ignore, certain biblical standards and warnings. For example, the following verse would be ignored:

> *…but if you do not forgive others their trespasses, neither will your Father forgive your trespasses. Matthew 6:15*

If we believe in a theology of exemption, we'll rewrite this verse to say, *"If we don't forgive others, we are still forgiven."*

If we believe we are saved while still living in sin, we cast off and even mock what the Bible reveals. The Word deals with the conditions and requirements of salvation that cannot be ignored.

Jesus told five of the churches in Revelation that they were lost! They were on their way to Hell!

There is no single instance, no single prayer that can lead to unconditional, future salvation. We are called to endure to the end. We are to grow in grace. We can't lean on a past experience in God and presume today or tomorrow is covered.

Do we need to confess our sins as believers? Should we be sin conscious?

Yes and yes.

False grace teachers would say that it's not necessary to confess sins because there is no sin in us. God's grace has eradicated it.

Folks, let me be very, very clear: that is a heretical teaching that absolutely puts people at risk of Hell.

> *If we say we have no sin, we deceive ourselves, and the truth is not in us. If we confess our sins, he is faithful and just to forgive us our sins and to cleanse us from all unrighteousness. 1 John 1:8-9*

Life Application Bible notes:

> *Being God's people does not mean denying sin (1:8), but confessing it. Because all people are sinners, Jesus had to die. Because sin is not completely eradicated from the lives of those who believe in Jesus, God graciously gave his followers provision for the problem of sin.*

It's not only critical, but it's wonderful to live in a state of continual repentance! God's love for us is so amazing that running away from sin and to him is awe inspiring!

As we daily allow God to search our hearts and reveal issues that are barriers to his love fully impacting us, the freedom and resulting life is amazing!

I often hear people say that Christians shouldn't be sin conscious. Not only is that not biblical, it does us a disservice. Ignoring sin doesn't disarm it, it empowers it! Allow God to reveal the darkness and set us free!

I often hear people say that Christians shouldn't be sin conscious. Not only is that not biblical, it does us a disservice. Ignoring sin doesn't disarm it, It empowers it!

> *Since we have these promises, beloved, let us cleanse ourselves from every defilement of body and spirit, bringing holiness to completion in the fear of God. 2 Corinthians 7:1*

We must remain diligent regarding sin. As we grow in grace and knowledge, we will have the strength to remain stable.

> *Therefore, beloved, since you are waiting for these, be diligent to be found by him without spot or blemish, and at peace. 2 Peter 3:14*

> *You therefore, beloved, knowing this beforehand, take care that you are not carried away with the error of lawless people and lose your own stability. But grow in the grace and knowledge of our Lord and Savior Jesus Christ. To him be the glory both now and to the day of eternity. Amen. 2 Peter 3:17-18*

The idea that we don't have to confess sins because the penalties of sin are no longer an issue is radically unbiblical. It's a clear heresy.

> *Watch yourselves, so that you may not lose what we have worked for, but may win a full reward. Everyone who goes on ahead and does not abide in the teaching of Christ, does not have God. Whoever abides in the teaching has both the Father and the Son. 2 John 1:8-9*
>
> *For if, after they have escaped the defilements of the world through the knowledge of our Lord and Savior Jesus Christ, they are again entangled in them and overcome, the last state has become worse for them than the first. For it would have been better for them never to have known the way of righteousness than after knowing it to turn back from the holy commandment delivered to them. 2 Peter 2:20-21*

If we don't live in a state of glorious repentance, the sins can overcome us, and the result would be worse than if we had never been saved! Many have had revelations of Hell where they see special attention given to those who walked in the truth and then fell away. This is special attention that nobody would ever want. Additionally, pastors and leaders who don't reveal this truth are in danger as well!

It's true that, after we are saved, choosing to sin can disqualify us. Our position in Christ can be put at risk. It can result in us being unholy and spiritually dead.

But isn't it true that God can't see the sin of a Christian since he's washed in the blood of Jesus? No, it isn't true.

Read through the New Testament. Check out the warnings to the seven churches. God saw their sins. Sins that are not repented of are not covered by the blood of Jesus. Willful sinning results in us being removed from right standing in God.

> *Take care, brothers, lest there be in any of you an evil, unbelieving heart, leading you to fall away from the living God. But exhort one another every day, as long as it is called "today," that none of you may be hardened by the deceitfulness of sin. Hebrews 3:12-13*

Again, if our future sins are forgiven, and there's no need to repent or confess, why does this verse in Hebrews, written to believers (brothers), reveal that sin can cause them to fall away from God?

False grace teachers will say that the Holy Spirit doesn't convict Christians of sin. Whoa. This is an extremely dangerous and UNWANTED concept! We want conviction! We are actively involved in the salvation process. Salvation is NOT a one-time occurrence, but it's a life-long life-changing process. We need conviction. We need God to search our hearts!

Additionally, we have a lot to do to ensure we remain saved!

> *His divine power has granted to us all things that pertain to life and godliness, through the knowledge of him who called us to his own glory and excellence, by which he has granted to us his precious and very great promises, so that through them you may become partakers of the divine nature, having escaped from the corruption that is in the world because of sinful desire.*
>
> *For this very reason, make every effort to supplement your faith with virtue, and virtue with knowledge, and knowledge with self-control, and self-control with steadfastness, and steadfastness with godliness, and godliness with brotherly affection, and brotherly affection with love. For if these qualities are yours and are increasing, they keep you from being ineffective or unfruitful in the knowledge of our Lord Jesus Christ.*
>
> *For whoever lacks these qualities is so nearsighted that he is blind, having forgotten that he was cleansed from his former sins. Therefore, brothers, be all the more diligent to confirm your calling and election, for if you practice these qualities you will never fall. For in this way there will be richly provided for you an entrance into the eternal kingdom of our Lord and Savior Jesus Christ. 2 Peter 1:3-11*

We must know our heart! Let God search it out!

> *The heart is deceitful above all things, and desperately sick; who can understand it? "I the LORD search the heart and test the mind, to give every man according to his ways, according to the fruit of his deeds." Jeremiah 17:9-10*

If you don't believe this is true, spend hours in prayer and ask God to reveal every thought, every motive, every sin, every issue in your heart—and he will do it! In love! What's our reaction? Life! Rejoicing! Repentance! Confession! An encounter in the love and forgiveness of Jesus! There is nothing like it!

But, if we do not repent, what God finds in our hearts will condemn us! This is serious!

So many in the false grace movement say that God is always in a good mood. This is ridiculous. In fact, it would make God quite deranged if this were true! What would you think of a God who was happy and laughing and in a good mood when he cast people he loves into Hell? No, though judgment will certainly come from God, his love precludes him from being happy about the devastation that it will bring.

> *'I know your works, your love and faith and service and patient endurance, and that your latter works exceed the first. But I have this against you, that you tolerate that woman Jezebel, who calls herself a prophetess and is teaching and seducing my servants to practice sexual immorality and to eat food sacrificed to idols. I gave her time to repent, but she refuses to repent of her sexual immorality.*
>
> *Behold, I will throw her onto a sickbed, and those who commit adultery with her I will throw into great tribulation, unless they repent of her works, and I will strike her children dead. And all the churches will know that I am he who searches mind and heart, and I will give to each of you according to your works. Revelation 2:19-23*

Being a willing participant as God searches our hearts is a very good idea! Repenting is critical! Confession is mandatory! To teach a gospel that relieves people of the need to repent and confess can lead them right into fearful judgment at the hands of God!

We even see the results of a non-repentant Christian in the passage about holy communion:

> *Whoever, therefore, eats the bread or drinks the cup of the Lord in an unworthy manner will be guilty concerning the body and blood of the Lord. Let a person examine himself, then, and so eat of the bread and drink of the cup. For anyone who eats and drinks without discerning the body eats and drinks judgment on himself. That is why many of you are weak and ill, and some have died. But if we judged ourselves truly, we would not be judged. But when we are judged by the Lord, we are disciplined so that we may not be condemned along with the world.*
> *1 Corinthians 11:27-32*

What About the Law?

I've often heard Christians say that the Old Testament does not apply to us anymore. That to call Christians to obedience is to put them into bondage under the law. What? This is clear evidence of biblical ignorance.

Some Christians mistakenly think we no longer have to obey any of the basic laws and commandments set out by God the Father in the Old Testament since we are now operating under a new covenant with Jesus. But this view is wrong. Jesus Himself says that He did not come to do away with the law, but to fulfill it.

> *Do not think that I have come to abolish the Law or the Prophets; I have not come to abolish them but to fulfill them. For truly, I say to you, until heaven and earth pass away, not an iota, not a dot, will pass from the Law until all is accomplished.*
> *Matthew 5:17-18*

> *There is therefore now no condemnation for those who are in Christ Jesus. For the law of the Spirit of life has set you free in Christ Jesus from the law of sin and death. Romans 8:1-2*

> *What then shall we say? That the law is sin? By no means! Yet if it had not been for the law, I would not have known sin. For I would not have known what it is to covet if the law had not said, "You shall not covet." Romans 7:7*

There are three kinds of laws in the Old Covenant:

Ceremonial laws

These are related to the priesthood, sacrifices, the temple, and cleanliness. These are now fulfilled in Jesus (for example, nearly the entire book of Hebrews addresses this issue for Jews who struggled with the Old Testament laws once they were saved). These laws are no longer binding on us, because Jesus is our Priest, Sacrifice, Temple, and Cleanser.

Civil laws

These refer to the governing of Israel as a nation ruled by God. Since we are no longer a theocracy, these laws, while insightful, are not directly binding on us. As Romans 13 says, we must now obey our pagan government, because God will work through it, too.

Moral laws

Moral laws prohibit such things as stealing, murdering, and lying. These laws are still binding on us even though Jesus fulfilled their requirements through His sinless life. Jesus Himself repeats and reinforces the Ten Commandments.

First we need to understand that the law and works are not the same thing! We are still called to good works… while the law refers to a specific set of commands found in the Old Testament.

Adherence to the law is not a part of salvation. Works, however, is. Faith alone can't save us.

> *What good is it, my brothers, if someone says he has faith but does not have works? Can that faith save him? James 2:14*

Check this out… there is a certain type of works that does no good:

> *For we hold that one is justified by faith apart from works of the law. Romans 3:28*

…of the law. In the Old Testament it was the Mosaic law that was their only hope. In the New Testament, faith in Jesus that's evidenced through New Covenant obedience and works is what saves us.

> *Or is God the God of Jews only? Is he not the God of Gentiles also? Yes, of Gentiles also, since God is one—who will justify the circumcised by faith and the uncircumcised through faith. Romans 3:29-30*

We don't have to be circumcised, but we do still have to obey, to respond to God's New Testament commands.

> *"Teacher, which is the great commandment in the Law?" And he said to him, "You shall love the Lord your God with all your heart and with all your soul and with all your mind. This is the great and first commandment. And a second is like it: You shall love your neighbor as yourself. On these two commandments depend all the Law and the Prophets." Matthew 22:36-40*

The power of that Scripture is that God's attributes are affirmed. Loving God and others covers a lot of ground!

In the Old Testament obedience was required and in the New Testament obedience is required. The difference? Jesus often told people to obey God, but Moses is not the standard by which obedience is now measured.

Jesus told his disciples to preach the gospel throughout the world. This gospel focuses on the message of repentance and forgiveness of sins through faith in Jesus Christ.

We don't take the cross lightly, but we realize how profoundly it obligates us to obey the One who gave himself for us.

Matthew 28:20 tells us that Christians should be taught to obey their Lord and Savior in addition to believing in him.

> *Go therefore and make disciples of all nations, baptizing them in the name of the Father and of the Son and of the Holy Spirit, teaching them to observe all that I have commanded you. And behold, I am with you always, to the end of the age." Matthew 28:19-20*

Wake up, Church!

The *happy Christianity* movement that is focused on personal experience and self-serving is not scriptural! When we become Christians, we sign up to die—we embrace martyrdom! It's not all about experiencing happiness and blessing!

Of course, there is significant blessing, joy and life in Jesus, but the focus is not on feeling good about life, it's about taking up our cross and following Jesus in fear and trembling! This may seem like a contradiction to previous chapters that heavily affirmed encounter, but, believe me, it is not. The true experience and encounter of God will result in something much different than personal highs! The call to death, to being living martyrs, will result in a raging fire that burns us deeply.

Taking up our cross doesn't mean to wear it around our necks! It's the same thing as saying today, *"put your head on the guillotine,"* or *"sit in the electric chair."*

Following Jesus isn't easy. It's not about our happiness. It's about him! It's falling in love with the lover of our souls and responding to his leadership!

I'd strongly recommend reading my book *The Terror of Hell.* In it I discuss the connection between intimacy with Jesus and salvation. We want to be known by God in a place of deep, intimate encounter and full devotion. We want to avoid God ever saying, *"Depart from me, I never knew you."*

~ TWELVE ~

REGIONAL IMPACT

The Coming Church will have dramatic impact on the region.

You will remember in the vision of the crater, the coming Church will have regional impact. The fire will hit areas near and far, and it's fully appropriate for us to have this in mind when we consider how to function.

Today, most churches are extremely local in their focus, and most of their energy is spent developing the small, local expression of the Church. This will give way for a church that functions as a ministry of intercession, standing in the gap for the city and region it is in.

Many, many local churches that are outside of the plans of God in this new wineskin Church will find themselves closed. Others will have Ichabod hung over their doorposts. We are about to enter a very serious season.

The coming Church will be known by the region it is in, as it was in early Church history. The one Church of Detroit will emerge. There will still be distinctions, but it will be unified around the core values of revival, intercession and the leadership of the Holy Spirit.

Read my book *20 Elements of Revival* if you want a clear, comprehensive explanation of what this regional Church will look like.

I am going to share a remarkable story that will give you a very clear understanding on how the Church must have regional impact. But, please, brace yourself. The story does not have a mostly happy ending.

Manitou Springs, Colorado

> We had a regional vision, a regional mandate and we prayed continually.

My wife, kids and I were called to plant a church, a house of prayer (they are one in the same if we understand Scripture!), and to contend for extreme revival in the Pikes Peak region. Manitou Springs sits at the base of America's Mountain, Pikes Peak, and is well known as a haven for witchcraft, the New Age and other occult religions.

It's rumored that Anton LaVey wrote at least some of the Satanic Bible from his home in Manitou Springs. Christianity, especially Spirit-filled Christianity, is rejected and resisted with great force in Manitou.

It would have been nice to know this before we decided to plant our first church there! What a wild ride we were in for! The stories about our journey there would make this book much longer than it is intended to be. We learned in the heat of battle how to engage in dramatic spiritual warfare, and the resulting supernatural experiences were eye-popping enough to warrant Hollywood offering to make a movie or two about them.

Why was so much regional activity and disturbance taking place? It's easy. We had a regional vision, a regional mandate and we prayed continually. That's it. The coming Church is a regional Church, and when it has that understanding, and the unity to advance in prayer, the atmosphere responds. Angels and demons engage, demonic systems are troubled and God prepares the land for Kingdom advance.

At the end of this chapter, I am going to share a stunning story from earlier this year that will simply astound you—and it will make it clear just how important and powerful churches that pray are. But first I want to communicate some of the unusual experiences we had in that city of destiny. It will help you more easily see why the final story I will share is as sobering and mind-boggling as it truly is.

Broadway in Colorado

Well into our tenure in Manitou Springs, after countless spiritual experiences and otherworldly encounters, we had shifted our ministry into a highly focused, night and day prayer center. Our atmosphere was exciting and quite intense as we prayed and groaned in the Holy Spirit several nights a week. It was during this season that I received an email from a Broadway theater company.

I responded to the email and then connected in person with the leadership of this organization. They explained that they were in Colorado Springs to do research for an upcoming live docudrama about the various social, political and religious expressions in the Pikes Peak region. They requested an opportunity to interview me and some of our team and to sit in on some of our events.

Now, understand, this was a non-Christian theater company from New York. You can imagine how interesting it might be to have researchers from such a place sitting in a bizarre, loud, expressive and maybe even a little unsettling environment like we had at Revolution House of Prayer!

I explained what they would be getting themselves into and asked if that was OK. They were absolutely OK with it and were eager to join us in some services. Though non-Christian, their team was amazing and quite impressive. It was an honor to connect with them.

Remember, their goal was to collect as much data as they could from interviews, research and live events so they could present an intriguing production. Boy, did we give them some stuff to write about!

The docudrama would consist of scene after scene of various Colorado groups that were represented by the actors. The actors studied mannerisms of the people they were researching and the culture of the groups they were a part of. They also recorded everything that was said and that resulted in their script for the production. They added nothing. What was depicted on stage was taken word-for-word from their research.

So, what does this mean? It means that an actor playing me, on stages in cities across the nation, was speaking word-for-word prophecies, testimonies and the truth of Scripture to mostly secular audiences!

A dramatic healing that I experienced in the cave was played out on stage. So was a whiteboard session where I explained another journey into the cave with seasoned intercessors from across the state. This prayer journey resulted in the only dealing I've ever had with an actual principality, and the liberating truth from that encounter was proclaimed in, literally, dramatic fashion!

The reason why this story is an important one is this—we had a regional focus in Manitou Springs that would impact the nation. God had made it clear that we were to pray from this perspective. So, we would always intercede for Manitou Springs to be a catalyst of revival in the nation. This unusual experience with Broadway was a sign, a manifestation, of our focus and efforts.

This is how the coming Church will function governmentally. As we focus on the region and the greater mission, we will be in step with God's passion for the nations. Grace and favor will follow. Unusual interventions by God will become common.

This is such an important point, especially with the state of today's Church in mind. We no longer can sweat, bleed and burn out by trying to build our own local ministries. The vision absolutely must be a regional one as we give ourselves to true city unity, intercession for revival and Kingdom advance. This doesn't mean all local churches will close (though many will), but it does mean that they will no longer be at the pinnacle of the priority list. Local church leaders will mostly give their attention to corporate advance regionally with the Church of the city instead of to local issues.

Shaking in the Church

> *For it is time for judgment to begin at the household of God; and if it begins with us, what will be the outcome for those who do not obey the gospel of God? And "If the righteous is scarcely saved, what will become of the ungodly and the sinner?"*
> *1 Peter 4:17-18*

The coming Church won't be a perfect Church because, of course, it's made up of humans like you and me. However, it will be a holy Church. It must be.

I have learned over the years to actually embrace the fearful yet loving judgment of God. I have found that God is our defense, and God is most capable of making wrong things right.

I was troubled in my spirit on one specific day at Revolution Church in Manitou Springs. I had my staff with me as it was a staff prayer day. I felt a strong spirit of witchcraft coming against the church, though I didn't know where it was coming from. As a church with a regional focus, it was very common to stir up various hornet's nests in the spirit realm, and there are many stories of strategic attack against us. This was nothing new.

As I tried to pray through it, I felt myself getting weaker, which was disconcerting. Then, God spoke to me, *"John, the way you have to combat the spirit of witchcraft by approaching from the opposite direction. Witchcraft is rebellion. You must attack from a place of unity."*

I then called my staff together and explained what was going on. Everybody was agreed, except, it appeared, one person. Our newest staff member just didn't appear to be connected at all. I felt a slight measure of resistance from him. He was clearly uncomfortable, though he tried to hide it. I had the slightest check in my spirit when we hired him, and, believe me, I have learned to listen to those small checks of God!

Everybody (possibly with the exception of my new staff member) prayed with power. I was specifically declaring, *"God, bring a shaking! Shake our church!"* Though it didn't seem to be related to the feeling of witchcraft I was dealing with, it's what my spirit shouted over and over again. Strength was evident, and it didn't take long before I felt it snap in the spirit. It was just as if a strong cord was pulled on so strongly that it just broke.

I was in the church a day or so later with my children's pastor, her husband and their baby in a stroller. We were sitting in the sanctuary, which was in a 100 year old wood building. There was a false ceiling above us, and above that were giant, heavy wooden beams high up at the roof line.

All of a sudden, my prayer in the spirit for shaking to come to our church manifested in the natural. The entire building started violently shaking as if an earthquake had come.

Then, we heard a snapping and crashing sound as a massive wooden beam fell through the false ceiling and landed next to the baby in the stroller. Shaking had come to our church—but it was only beginning.

We cleaned up the mess, removed the false ceiling and ultimately replaced the beam, but the shaking was about to continue. God will prune, and though it's hard, it will bring greater unity to the church. Do you remember how my new staff member was struggling, and clearly not unified as we prayed against a spirit of witchcraft?

Well, it became clear that he was wrestling through some things that resulted in a resistance to the ministry.

Shortly after the beam came crashing down as shaking hit our physical church, I received an email. It was from this man and his wife. They simply stated that he was done, and that he resigned his position. I was shocked (thought in hindsight, I shouldn't have been). I emailed him back requesting a meeting, letting him know I was surprised at his decision. He refused a meeting, and I've never seen him again.

He took about one fourth of our church with him, started his own church, and then let it collapse about a month later. He and his wife moved back to Florida where they were originally from.

The end result for our ministry was a strengthening and greater unity, even though the shaking was difficult. God will allow shaking, and we've seen it more than once on a local level. He will shake a region, and he is about to do so quite dramatically.

The Earth is Groaning

> *For we know that the whole creation has been groaning together in the pains of childbirth until now. Romans 8:22*

> *For nation will rise against nation, and kingdom against kingdom, and there will be famines and earthquakes in various places. All these are but the beginning of the birth pains. Matthew 24:7-8*

I could share many additional stories about shaking and regional impact, but it's time to drive this home.

After my wife and I moved to Kansas City from Colorado, we passed the leadership to our great friends and giants in the faith Miles and Jodi Anderson. They led the ministry with great passion and extreme focus day after day. Prayer was continual and very strategic.

Their impact was phenomenal, as we'll soon see, but it wasn't always visibly discernable.

Though there were some powerful manifestations of their impact, such as occult shops closing and a general feeling that the Kingdom was advancing, their true impact was not yet visible.

Early in 2013 Miles called me, which was not uncommon. What was uncommon is what he wanted to talk about. Miles is, without question, the most faithful person God has ever put in my life (though he has some competition with my current team here in Detroit!). His heart was to steward the ministry I birthed and to ensure he wasn't a burden to me (which he never was).

But, this time, he needed some help. Things were changing at Revolution House of Prayer (formerly Revolution Church), and he was seeking after guidance. He admitted that his heart was changing as God was putting fresh ministry burdens on him, though the Manitou Springs vision was the most important for him. He also shared that the number of people who were connecting there was diminishing and, as a result, the finances were disappearing. They were literally down to a handful of people with dwindling revenues.

I immediately determined that I needed to head to Manitou Springs, and I decided to take a team with me. I rented a van and loaded it up with several from my team, and headed to Kansas City to pick up two additional warriors from IHOP.

We arrived at IHOP that evening, and we had about 45 minutes to enjoy the prayer room before we had to move on. I hadn't been back to IHOP since we moved from there to Detroit five years prior. I was looking around for people I might know, and saw none. I casually prayed a prayer as I stood in the back of the prayer room, *"God, this is a really prophetic place. Would you give me a sign that we are on the right track, and that there is a connection between my vision for Manitou Springs and Detroit?"*

I then walked into the foyer, and heard from behind me someone say, *"John Burton!"* It was someone I knew—from Detroit! We connected briefly, and then I went back into the prayer room. Just before I was to leave, someone I knew walked through the door—someone from Colorado Springs!

This friend prayed over me, and then I left.

God then revealed, *"You are on the right track, and, yes, your mission in Colorado and your mission in Detroit are connected, and they are connected by the prayer movement."*

That sealed it. We were on our way to Colorado with great passion.

We had a conference planned, and the goal was to cast the vision for Manitou Springs and, prayerfully, gather some new intercessors.

The conference was extremely unique and supernaturally charged. The warfare was intense and the breakthrough was powerful. People gave financially, which helped with all of the bills that were due, and lives truly were transformed.

When we returned to Detroit, the news from Manitou was not encouraging. The crowds remained small and it was clear the issue was not resolved.

We had talked about returning to Colorado again, and this news solidified that plan. We planned another conference, but from the beginning of planning all the way through to the actual conference, there were trials. The unction wasn't there. The response was limited. It was obvious to all of us that transition was coming.

We returned one more time, but did not hold a conference. We simply flew into town and prayed. We met with Miles and Jodi. We discussed vision. It was a wonderful though sad trip as much was discussed but, when all was said and done, we made the decision to close Revolution House of Prayer.

Miles agreed that, though difficult, and though everything didn't make sense, this was the right move. In fact, it really was the only possible move as the finances weren't there to even come close to sustaining the ministry, and no signs, wonders or miracles were causing us to believe the money and support were coming.

It was a difficult decision, as that ministry was my baby. I started it twelve years prior, and there are so many memories attached to it. But the greatest difficulty was not the memories—it was the future. The vision for massive revival that would impact the nations was (and is) still alive in me.

Miles and Jodi requested that I, as their apostolic covering, would pray over them and release them from their assignment. So, after dinner at a nice restaurant we sat in the van and prayed. I honored them for their faithfulness and released them from their assignment. I also understood that the active intercession covering over Manitou Springs was being lifted. I knew in my spirit that this was not good, but God was in control. I released Manitou Springs fully into God's hands as we all moved on from this very special assignment.

I believe closing RHOP was Plan B, not Plan A. We see throughout history how a lack of response can put a mission at risk, and this is, in my opinion, what happened in Manitou Springs. Moses and the masses under his leadership didn't enter the Promised Land due to fear of some giants. I believe similar fear keeps people out of Manitou, and that has delayed the fulfilled mission.

We are praying for a Joshua company to rise up, of which I may or may not be a part, and advance into Manitou Springs and take it for the Kingdom.

With RHOP closing, there was a lot of work to do. We decided to move most of their chairs, musical instruments, artwork and other items out of that 27,000 square foot church and into a moving truck that we would drive back to Detroit.

The night before we were to load up the truck, my father-in-law had a dream. In the dream, I was loading up the moving truck as it was parked outside of RHOP. The church sits over a slow moving, shallow creek. My father-in-law started urgently warning me to get out because a flood was coming. He was frantic and said, *"John, your time here is done. It's time to go!"*

I threw a few last things into the truck and drove off.

That night at the dinner table I said, "*Wow, wouldn't it be crazy if 24 hours after intercession was lifted off of this city that a flood really came?*"

Crazy happened.

As I was driving the moving truck the next day on my way to Detroit, well away from Colorado, I received information of a sudden catastrophic flood in Manitou Springs. It really happened. The creek that ran under the church was usually no more than six inches deep, but that day it was over nine feet!

The water actually hit the foundation of what used to be Revolution House of Prayer! The story of the flood hit the national news. I never saw anything remotely like that in all of my years there. The earth was groaning.

Crazy happened.

Have you noticed a bizarre increase in the number of sink holes emerging all around the world? The earth is groaning. Nature is reacting to the governmental authority of the Church—or the lack of it.

If that wasn't enough to get our attention, shortly after the floods hit, a whirlwind did as well. A tornado was sighted on the top of America's mountain, Pikes Peak. In fact, it was the highest (in terms of elevation) recorded tornado in American history! Pikes Peak is situated right at Manitou Springs. In fact, one day we took the Cog Railway to the top of Pikes Peak on a prayer journey, and then that night went into the belly of the earth for prayer in a cave.

Governmental, regionally focused intercession like that absolutely has impact, as does the lack of it. During our years in Manitou Springs, we experienced many supernatural and natural events that demonstrated our prayers were impacting the spiritual realm. The flood that hit as we completed our assignment for that season indicates to me that our prayers were effective in holding back tides of wickedness. God is faithful to raise up another ministry of intercession in the region if we will offer him our willing hearts.

The coming Church will be a praying Church that understands its authority and responsibility in the region.

Terrors overtake him like a flood; in the night a whirlwind carries him off. Job 27:20

~ *THIRTEEN* ~

THE SCATTERING MOVEMENT

The Coming Church is a unified Church.

Get ready. The reformation has begun, and the messengers are beginning to relay information about the soon coming Church, about the shocks and shifts that are coming to the world.

What is so saddening to my spirit is that so much of what was written about in this book will be received as negative instead of positive by those who are hoping for pixie dust in the next chapter of their fairy tale religious journey. The holy remnant will feel the force of the threat just like everybody will, yet they will joyfully welcome it instead of fearfully resist it. Many will scatter due to an offended heart while others gather together in humility and the fear of the Lord.

It's easy to read something like this, even for a remnant believer, and shout and cheer from the sidelines. It's common, even today, for people to get excited about a supposed fresh arrival of the Holy Spirit. However, what is usually the case is that the excitement is premature, based on only the potential benefits to their life. When the true cost is revealed, and the call to action is presented, you discover the remnant is truly small. Many will sadly scatter. Will you?

My challenge to you is simple—sign up. Embrace holiness. Prepare the way for the return of the Lord. Reorder your life. Pray like you never have. Be in the Word. Die daily. Humble yourself.

The Scattering Movement

Before we can discuss the coming Joshua Generation model of Church advance, we have to briefly deal with something that is causing great damage to the Church. To say that I'm concerned would be a gross understatement.

There is a *scattering movement* in the nation that's causing deep harm to the mission of the church.

This scattering of believers is so widespread that we are seeing theologies and philosophies emerging that support the idea that it's actually healthy to disband and withdraw.

It's becoming common to hear people say things like, *"The church isn't a building,"* or, *"I am the church, so I don't have to go 'to church.'"*

The idea is that people have become so wounded or dissatisfied with their local church experience that they have decided that it's not only better but actually biblically acceptable to minimize participation in an organized church setting.

This mindset is threatening the corporate mission to a terrifying degree. The coming Church will not be scattered. Quite the contrary, it will be led by bold, apostolic and prophetic leaders, such as Joshua, who call for precision and great unity around the mission.

You Are Not The Church

If we understand the meaning of the word 'church' we could never presume that we alone can be identified as *the church*. That idea doesn't match up with the definition and origin of the word (ekklesia, meaning "assembly"). In fact, that word has secular origins. It literally means an assembly of people who have been called together by an authority in the city or region. Wow! That sheds a lot of light on what the church is.

Church (ekklesia): an assembly of people who have been called together by an authority in the city or region

The church is an assembly of people organized under defined, human governmental leadership who are under the ultimate leadership of Christ. It's a regular gathering of people who are deeply agreed and in pursuit of mission advance under God's apostles, prophets and other governmental leaders.

Further, the pure definition of the word more clearly identifies the regional gathering of believers than the global company of believers. (It's hard for a global body to gather together.) We certainly can identify with the global Church, but we can't unite and advance as a single unit. This is why it's important to stay locked in to a regional church body. There are city-level missions that are awaiting the awakening of the city Church.

The definition reveals that in order to function in the ekklesia, the Church, we have to identify the regional leadership, and we need clarity on what our role is. We can't be a part of the Church if we aren't gathered together with other parts of the Church, on site. Church is corporate.

And I tell you, you are Peter, and on this rock I will build my church [assembly], and the gates of hell shall not prevail against it. I will give you the keys of the kingdom of heaven, and whatever you bind on earth shall be bound in heaven, and whatever you loose on earth shall be loosed in heaven." Matthew 16:18-19

So the church [assembly] throughout all Judea and Galilee and Samaria had peace and was being built up. And walking in the fear of the Lord and in the comfort of the Holy Spirit, it multiplied. Acts 9:31

And he is the head of the body, the church [assembly]. He is the beginning, the firstborn from the dead, that in everything he might be preeminent. Colossians 1:18

There is authority (Matthew 16:18-19) that is reserved for the assembly, for those who are gathered together under apostolic leadership.

Additionally, the church is a locally assembled people who fellowship, pray and respond together to apostolic teaching. That can't happen in a more nebulous scattered context. It won't work if believers are on their own in their homes.

The church has inherent in its core call the expectation of assembly and a corporate response so as to ensure the regional mission is fulfilled. Again, a fulfilled mission can't be realized without this type of intentional and faithful participation at a local/regional level where communication and commonality are clearly defined.

What About Church Online?

I agree that there is much to enjoy and gain from this amazing technological world. We can watch church services online (I was watching one myself just tonight), listen to worship, meet Christians in forums and on Facebook, pray for one another and involve ourselves in Kingdom business in very unique ways.

However, if this is the limit of one's involvement, there are some key issues that arise. Online ministry is great for personal growth but not for corporate missions. Limiting our involvement to conferences, personal study or online resources presents the following problems:

It's devoid of Apostolic Leadership: There is most probably (with exceptions) no clearly defined apostolic leadership involved in online communities. We have to know who we're called to serve with and who our leaders are. There is a corporate message that we must hear together so we can respond together. What's God calling our leaders to focus on? How are we to participate? What are the goals? What steps must we take to prepare ourselves to see this come to pass? If we are only connected online, we can't usually respond in a corporate way to the instructions.

Lack of Strategic Corporate Intercession: While not impossible, it's very hard to involve ourselves in the number one purpose of the church—corporate intercession. We absolutely have to be together often to pray with unity and consistency if we are to have the sufficient strength to see significant impact.

No Accountability: Accountability and discipline are nearly non-existent outside of the context of the local church. Many who flock from the church and into alternative spiritual activities do so to avoid conflict, accountability and correction from leadership. We have to understand that this is a critical part of the refining process. We must be receptive and humble and ready to be challenged—even if the leaders God established for us are exceptionally flawed and out of touch with our needs.

Promotes Misunderstanding of the Purpose of the Church: Limiting our spiritual involvement to online opportunities can quite easily reinforce a wrong understanding of the purpose of the church. I would say this is the most serious issue. The prevailing thought these days is that the church is to be there for us. Whatever needs we have, we can get many of them met in

the church. So, we attend if we are ministered to. Or, we may determine that we can get what we're looking for without regular church attendance. So, the church becomes unnecessary to us, and we can glean our spiritual food from online sources. Friend, this concept is a defilement of the Church. I can't say it any less striking than that. We are called to gather together with other believers primarily to intercede for the nations. We are there to give, to leave offerings, to serve, to minister, to pray, to grow. The Church isn't primarily there for us, we are to be there for the mission of the church. We may say that we don't need the church but have we considered that the Church needs us?

I believe the scattering movement is one of the enemy's most urgent assaults in these end-times. He knows the power of unified togetherness. He used that very strategy when attempting to build a tower to Heaven. God himself said that Satan's plan of unity would actually succeed if scattering didn't happen!

> *Now the whole earth had one language and the same words.*
> *Genesis 11:1*

The enemy had gathered the people and unified them.

> *Then they said, "Come, let us build ourselves a city and a tower with its top in the heavens, and let us make a name for ourselves, lest we be dispersed over the face of the whole earth."*
> *Genesis 11:4*

It was a spiritual endeavor, an attempt to reach God, but also to make a name for themselves. They were self-focused and they were spiritualizing it.

> *And the LORD came down to see the city and the tower, which the children of man had built. And the LORD said, "Behold, they are one people, and they have all one language, and this is only the beginning of what they will do. And nothing that they propose to do will now be impossible for them. Genesis 11:5-6*

This is one of the most remarkable statements in Scripture. God said that, due to their unity, that nothing would be possible for them! The strength of unity, whether evil or holy, is immeasurable!

> *Come, let us go down and there confuse their language, so that they may not understand one another's speech." So the LORD dispersed them from there over the face of all the earth, and they left off building the city. Therefore its name was called Babel, because there the LORD confused the language of all the earth. And from there the LORD dispersed them over the face of all the earth. Genesis 11:7-9*

So, God scattered those who were unified against him. I can imagine how this infuriated Satan. God's strategy now is for his Church to be together working on divine projects with great, holy unity. Satan is now attempting to use God's Babel strategy against him by bringing confusion and offense that results in scattering. His goal is for God's Church, his people, to abandon the "building of the city," the advance of the Kingdom.

Today, in the end times, when the church must be together continually as we advance against the kingdom of darkness, Satan has every intention of pulling people out of that mission. The scattering and loose commitment to God's method of prayer-driven Kingdom advance is resulting in a weak and impotent army.

In a day when less than two services a month equates to *normal* church attendance, I believe we must see the 24/7 church advance in strength, unity, commitment and power. Instead of two services a month, in the coming Church I believe we'll see it become normal to be in church twenty or more times a month as we pray together, receive apostolic instruction, move out in ministry and take the fire of the Holy Spirit to the world—together.

Five Insufficient Reasons to Leave a Church

I'm fully aware that a book like this where I talk about a new Church paradigm can be prematurely celebrated by the millions who are wounded and mad at the current Church. I'll be as clear as I can: it is not appropriate to abdicate our responsibilities to serve within the context of the current Church as we prepare to help usher in the new. This is an *all-hands-on-deck* season.

> I find it disturbing when rejection causes people to leave a church when rejection is what propelled Jesus to die and launch the church!

The mission is critical, now more than ever, and fleeing the very governmental organism that can foster change would be a tragic misstep. Everybody must be in position, gathered together with other believers under apostolic leadership involved in fervent intercession and ministry.

Unity around the mission of the church is something Satan cannot risk. The moment people lock arms, take their positions and unify with the Great Commission in front of them, it's over. He's done.

Unity is so powerful that Satan used it as his primary weapon to build his kingdom on the Earth as we saw in the story of the Tower of Babel.

The unity-driven plan—as impossible as it seemed, was on track to succeed—so God dealt a blow to what? Unity. It worked. The people scattered.

Now, in an attempt to turn the tables on God as he is building his Kingdom through unified people, Satan is attempting to scatter the church. It's working. The church is at risk.

A spirit of independence is convincing Christians that it's time to take control of their lives and forsake the call to gather under leaders within the structure of the church. We must repent, and we must return to position and get ready to move as the alarm sounds.

While there are (rare) times to move from one church to another, I want to share five reasons NOT to leave.

ONE: When you don't fit in

My three sons and two daughters would never leave the Burton family if they struggled to fit in, if they were misunderstood or if they were having a bad season of life. My wife wouldn't either, nor would I. If we see the church as a part of the service industry like McDonald's or Wal-Mart, we will end up leaving if we don't feel welcomed or served. However, God plants us in a covenant family, not a shopping center.

What most people really mean when they say, *"I don't fit in at this church,"* is that they aren't enjoying themselves. Possibly, they feel rejected. I find it disturbing when rejection causes people to leave a church when rejection is what propelled Jesus to die and launch the church! Remember, the church isn't to be there for us as much as we are to be there for the church. The mission of the church is demanding and not always enjoyable and we must be in position and ready to work. I guarantee anybody who approaches leadership and offers to serve in the nursery or by cleaning the church would absolutely fit in. Their serving heart makes a place for them.

> *This Jesus is the stone that was rejected by you, the builders, which has become the cornerstone. Acts 4:11*

> *But first he must suffer many things and be rejected by this generation. Luke 17:25*

TWO: When it's easier for you to connect with God elsewhere

I know this may be a shock, but the primary purpose of the church isn't to make it easy for you to connect with God. If we understand this, a million arguments against staying at your church will instantly disappear. It's our job, individually, to develop intimacy with Jesus. If we are dependent on a pastor, worship leader or others to nurture our relationship with Jesus, we're in big trouble.

We should never arrive at church empty. We should be full of God and ready to pour out. If it's easier for us to encounter God in our home or with a small group of friends, then great! That's the way it should be! Then, take the fire that you've cultivated to the critical corporate gathering and burn hot. Serve well. Get into position, lock arms, serve the leaders and advance the mission.

If we focus on personal edification and connecting with God as the primary purpose of the church, we can quickly forget the many additional needs that we have: discipleship, challenge, discipline, accountability, maturing, giving, serving, and on and on.

Remember, you are not the Church. You can't leave the corporate gathering and be a functional part of the Church. The Church only exists when we gather under the call of leadership.

> *When they had preached the gospel to that city and had made many disciples, they returned to Lystra and to Iconium and to Antioch, strengthening the souls of the disciples, encouraging them to continue in the faith, and saying that through many tribulations we must enter the kingdom of God. Acts 14:21-22*

THREE: The leaders aren't doing things the way most people think they should.

Many people believe leaders should make it easy for people to follow them. I disagree. Church leaders are mandated to lead people into some of the most challenging, risky and costly missions the world has ever known. People should actually make it easy for church leaders to lead them.

People made it hard for Moses to lead them into the Promised Land and they died. They made it easy for Joshua to do the same, and they dominated.

The demand of the people can be so strong sometimes that pastors and leaders forsake their mission. They end up pleasing the people instead of God.

Check this out. Jesus had just identified Peter as *the Church,* and he made it clear that the gates of Hell would not prevail.

> *And I tell you, you are Peter, and on this rock I will build my church, and the gates of hell shall not prevail against it. Matthew 16:18*

Then immediately after this, Peter, the church, unwittingly renounced the cross. He removed the cost, the surrender, the sacrifice. Watch what Jesus did:

> *From that time Jesus began to show his disciples that he must go to Jerusalem and suffer many things from the elders and chief priests and scribes, and be killed, and on the third day be raised. And Peter took him aside and began to rebuke him, saying, "Far be it from you, Lord! This shall never happen to you." But he turned and said to Peter, "Get behind me, Satan! You are a hindrance to me. For you are not setting your mind on the things of God, but on the things of man." Matthew 16:21-23*

Peter (the Church) was mindful of the things of man, not the things of God. Wow! The pressure of the people to steer the church in a certain direction can result in heeding their demands instead of the inconvenient and extreme mandates of the mission. Don't be one of those people.

> *Obey your leaders and submit to them, for they are keeping watch over your souls, as those who will have to give an account. Let them do this with joy and not with groaning, for that would be of no advantage to you. Hebrews 13:17*

FOUR: When another church has better programs for you and your family

We should never choose a church based on what we can get out of it. We are actually assigned by God himself to serve and build it.

As stated earlier, my definition of religion is: man's attempt to use God to get what he wants.

When we expect to gain from the church ahead of sacrifice, we are embracing the same spirit that killed Jesus. The spirit of religion wanted to use Jesus for personal gain.

Consider the money changers. Right after the crowds were "worshiping" Jesus by shouting Hosanna (which actually means, "save us now,") Jesus dealt with that spirit. The crowds wanted Jesus to save them, to focus on them, to give them what they demanded. Then, the money changers, driven by the same spirit of religion attempted to use the church for personal gain.

> *And Jesus entered the temple and drove out all who sold and bought in the temple, and he overturned the tables of the money-changers and the seats of those who sold pigeons. He said to them, "It is written, 'My house shall be called a house of prayer,' but you make it a den of robbers." Matthew 21:12-13*

The sin of the money changers? They expected to leave the temple (the church) with more than they entered with. The used the temple for personal gain. We see this same spirit in churches around the world. The expectation is to leave the temple with less than we enter with. We bring a sacrifice. An offering. We serve. We give. We place no demands on the place of sacrifice, but instead honor God through the sacrifice of intercession for the nations. Prayer is the primary purpose of the church, and the church needs you to join in that mission.

FIVE: When God tells you to

OK, I'm sure you are awake now! Have you ever played the God card? As a leader I've heard many times, usually through the grapevine, that, *"God told so and so to move to another church."* Really? That's odd. I was entrusted as their leader, which is a very serious position, and God just forgot to tell me about this? He left me out of the loop? Maybe Hebrews 13:17 isn't what we think it is? The church I'm leading isn't important enough for people to honor the mission?

I hope you are getting the point.

We are called to submit to authority—even ungodly authority like judges, elected officials and our bosses at work. Certainly it makes sense that God would include our godly authority in a decision-making process as important as leaving one family and one mission for another.

The point is this—God wouldn't just tell you to leave without your leader being involved in the process. In fact, can I just be blunt? It's extremely disrespectful, presumptuous, rude and self-serving to abdicate your responsibility in your current church by leaving without honoring the authority in your life. Your pastor has every right to participate with you in your process. If you want more information on how to handle difficult situations like leaving a church and honoring authority, read my book *Covens in the Church.*

> *We ask you, brothers, to respect those who labor among you and are over you in the Lord and admonish you, and to esteem them very highly in love because of their work. Be at peace among yourselves. 1 Thessalonians 5:12-13*

Three Modern Churches

Though we are to stay connected in the Church, we have to also understand that the rock from Heaven is about to crush faulty, self-serving religious systems. The reason we need to stay is so we can serve in the process of reformation—and the reformation will be quite severe. The church is both broken and in need of laborers. What a season this is!

The coming Church will be a pure Church. While there are several compromised structures that will soon feel the impact of a heavenly asteroid, there are three I'd like to draw your attention to. These three ministry models are rampant today, and they must repent and calibrate to God's plans.

The Money Changers Church

The story of the money changers occurs in Scripture just after the Triumphal Entry. We'll look at the Triumphal Entry church model next.

I previously mentioned the money changer's church. Lets look at it a little further.

> *And Jesus entered the temple and drove out all who sold and bought in the temple, and he overturned the tables of the money-changers and the seats of those who sold pigeons. He said to them, "It is written, 'My house shall be called a house of prayer,' but you make it a den of robbers." Matthew 21:12-13*

Jesus made it clear: they were using the church for the wrong purpose. Jesus was about to go to the cross to establish with finality what he revealed here. The Church is to be a House of Prayer, a place of giving, not a place of selfish, personal benefit.

Did you notice how violent Jesus was? Interestingly, he was equally as sharp with Peter when he rebuked him as we saw above. Jesus is jealous of the Church!

Today, prayer is nearly dead in the church. Additionally, even in churches that support prayer, if every service was cancelled and replaced with prayer meetings, there would be a mass exodus of disappointed people who aren't getting their desires met. People want to attend churches that result in personal gain.

Pastors have fallen for the deception often in today's consumer culture. Instead of raising the bar to match the demands of Scripture, the bar is lowered to match the demands of the people. Churches are marketed in an attempt to draw in the consumers (the tithes) by promising perks and benefits.

Most conferences today are promoted by focusing on what the people can expect to get instead of what they are to give. I often wonder what would happen if we held a "come and die" conference. Would people choose that one over the others that are selling hopes of healing, prosperity and success?

The Triumphal Entry Church

Now this is church! This is a church growth model that is very appealing. Simply announce that Jesus is in the house and watch the people flood in!

The celebration began and people were ready to receive their new king. However, the focus of the people at the Triumphal Entry was similar to the focuses in the other churches we are discussing. They wanted their lives to be better. Blessing and personal gain were their motives.

As previously stated, the word *Hosanna* literally means, "save us now." The people wanted a king who would give them life in a kingdom that would be personally fulfilling. There's nothing inherently wrong with that desire—unless that's the extent of the desire.

> *Most of the crowd spread their cloaks on the road, and others cut branches from the trees and spread them on the road. And the crowds that went before him and that followed him were shouting, "Hosanna to the Son of David! Blessed is he who comes in the name of the Lord! Hosanna in the highest!" And when he entered Jerusalem, the whole city was stirred up, saying, "Who is this?" And the crowds said, "This is the prophet Jesus, from Nazareth of Galilee." Matthew 21:8-11*

Hosanna! Most pastors and worship leaders would absolutely love such an environment! This was a blow-out celebration of Jesus! People were not only happy, they were jubilant! It was a revival atmosphere! If possible, Christian television would have covered this event. It was a historic moment!

Many local churches today have this as a key goal—to create a worship environment that's electric and full of supposed "life." Of course, the desire to have a true worship environment that affirms the abundant life that Jesus provides is appropriate. I love environments like this! I can imagine a Spirit-filled environment with people at the altar dancing, laughing and worshiping. I've seen that happen in churches I've led many times, and it's great! Many churches are growing with this very positive, happy focus—but, the growth is, in my opinion, often (not always, of course) driven by people who will not stay the course if the cross is preached with boldness. They embrace anything that promises personal gain, but the call to daily death is resisted.

In my own ministry I had to make a hard decision—I could focus mostly on a satisfying, dynamic, happy culture that affirms the supernatural while minimizing the cross and the cost. Or, I could focus mostly on a culture that mostly affirms the cross and the call to die, repent and surrender, while expecting a supernatural outflow to come from it.

The first option would require compromise and bigger crowds. We chose the second option that has literally resulted in a diminished (pruned) crowd of like-minded firebrands who die daily and take up their crosses. We affirm that the cost of discipleship is so extreme, that few will respond. At Revival Church and the Detroit Prayer Furnace we are moving in unity with a small group of forerunners who are more interested in the cross and resurrection than in the Triumphal Entry. We chose dozens instead of hundreds, and it's this group will burn in the night and change the world.

This crowd of energetic worshipers switched quickly to energetic crucifiers.

You will notice in this historic story of the Triumphal Entry that the people were willing to make a measured sacrifice, to pay a limited price, to experience what they hoped to. They gave their cloaks. They got to work and cut down palm branches. They were exuberant in their worship. However, we'll soon see that their offerings had strings attached.

The word hosanna literally means "save us now." The crowd was unified in their cry for their personal situation to improve, and Jesus was the man of the hour who they felt could pull that off.

Don't forget the definition of religion: *man's attempt to use God to get what he wants.* It was a spirit of religion that was disguising itself in a vibrant worship service.

See, Jesus was willing to *save them now*. However, his methods were nowhere near satisfactory for a crowd of people who were looking for safety, prosperity and life, not death. Jesus chose the cross as the means to answer their prayers. This crowd of energetic worshipers switched quickly to energetic crucifiers.

I'm all for wild, fervent worship. I am a proponent of continual joy. We should dance and smile a lot. However, we can't dismiss the burden of the cross and the call to die.

Don't presume a church is alive just because there's an electric atmosphere. Human energy and desire can create quite an environ-

ment. Wait and see who remains when the call to surrender is high, and the alarms of intercession are sounded.

The Rich Young Ruler Church

Like the Money Changer's church and the Triumphal Entry church, the Rich Young Ruler church affirms the motive of personal gain.

The Rich Young Ruler, however, possessed a sincere desire to follow Jesus. Notice how Jesus reveals this story is all about salvation:

> *And behold, a man came up to him, saying, "Teacher, what good deed must I do to have eternal life?" And he said to him, "Why do you ask me about what is good? There is only one who is good. If you would enter life, keep the commandments." He said to him, "Which ones?" And Jesus said, "You shall not murder, You shall not commit adultery, You shall not steal, You shall not bear false witness, Honor your father and mother, and, You shall love your neighbor as yourself." The young man said to him, "All these I have kept. What do I still lack?" Jesus said to him, "If you would be perfect, go, sell what you possess and give to the poor, and you will have treasure in heaven; and come, follow me." When the young man heard this he went away sorrowful, for he had great possessions. And Jesus said to his disciples, "Truly, I say to you, only with difficulty will a rich person enter the kingdom of heaven. Again I tell you, it is easier for a camel to go through the eye of a needle than for a rich person to enter the kingdom of God." When the disciples heard this, they were greatly astonished, saying, "Who then can be saved?" Matthew 19:16-25*

I am convinced there are millions of people following Jesus in an unsaved condition. Pastors have affirmed people's commitment to Christ and, in turn, their eternal security, all while, in many of those cases Jesus knew the deeper truth—they were not willing to surrender all. I believe the sinner's prayer has probably led more people to Hell than to Heaven. Handled wrongly it gives people false confidence in their position in Christ.

How many go to church each week, raise their hands in worship, pay their tithes and "follow Jesus" in a very public way, the same way the Rich Young Ruler wanted to—but are actually not saved?

If you are struggling with this and the truth of your own salvation, that's good! That's healthy! I don't know where it started being negative for us to wrestle with that. Today leaders don't want to upset people with messages like this out of fear of accusation and ridicule. We must work out our salvation with fear and trembling! The disciples in the above passage wrestled with it, and so should we. Let's see what Jesus says next:

> *But Jesus looked at them and said, "With man this is impossible, but with God all things are possible." Then Peter said in reply, "See, we have left everything and followed you. What then will we have?" Jesus said to them, "Truly, I say to you, in the new world, when the Son of Man will sit on his glorious throne, you who have followed me will also sit on twelve thrones, judging the twelve tribes of Israel. And everyone who has left houses or brothers or sisters or father or mother or children or lands, for my name's sake, will receive a hundredfold and will inherit eternal life. Matthew 19:26-29*

Is there any part of the Rich Young Ruler in me? Is it possible that I could fall away? I talk to Jesus about this on a regular basis, and it's a very positive, wonderful discussion. It's necessary. It would be arrogant for me to presume that I'm exempt from the great falling away. I wrestle with Jesus and with my own heart—and I love that process.

Again, it's healthy and necessary to work that out day by day. And, we need pastors and leaders who won't skirt that tough topic out of fear of losing people who would rather be coddled. It's possible that the best giver and most vibrant member of your church is on a track that leads to Hell. We can't stay silent on this issue.

When you understand how deeply God loves you, it's wonderful to wrestle with the difficult topics. It's invigorating! It's critical! So many will be shocked to enter Hell. We see this proven in Scripture:

> *"Not everyone who says to me, 'Lord, Lord,' will enter the kingdom of heaven, but the one who does the will of my Father who is in heaven. On that day many will say to me, 'Lord, Lord, did we not prophesy in your name, and cast out demons in your name, and do many mighty works in your name?' And then will I declare to them, 'I never knew you; depart from me, you workers of lawlessness.' Matthew 7:21-23*

Certainly there are many other parallels that we could make between events in Scripture and today's modern church. Of course, we could spend a lot of time talking about the churches in Revelation as they provide a very clear understanding of this issue. I'll let you study that out for yourself. Now it's time to finish up by looking at a key prophetic mandate that's on the Church today.

Let's look at a military-level strategy of Church advance where we all have urgency in our hearts and end-time roles to step into. The coming Church will not tolerate false, self-centered movements that are driven by a spirit of religion. It also won't tolerate a spirit of independence that drives us out of the gathering. The call to all is to get into position, lay down our opinions, complaints and our very lives as we prepare for divine instructions that will bring a holy, end-time shock to Planet Earth.

~ *Fourteen* ~

False Human Rights

The Coming Church is a sacrificial Church.

Does a moment go by that we don't hear about some group or movement making demands for their supposed human rights?

> *My fellow Americans, ask not what your country can do for you, ask what you can do for your country. John F. Kennedy*

What happened to this? What happened to America? What happened to the church?

> *Greater love has no one than this, that someone lay down his life for his friends. John 15:13*

Today we are absolutely overwhelmed by the constant, self-centered shouts of those who demand that their country—or their church—gives them what they believe is rightfully theirs.

It's a false human rights movement.

The RIGHT to abortion. The RIGHT for same sex marriage. The RIGHT to be equal. The RIGHT to be heard.

It's a sickening, selfish focus that is driven by human desire instead of a willingness to take up our cross and die. How often have people left churches because their supposed rights weren't addressed? How much dissention is in the workplace because people are looked over in favor of another?

I've said it before—today, when people's self-centered pursuits are rejected, they abandon relationships, leave churches and cause division, but when Jesus was rejected, he didn't abandon people. He didn't forsake the church.

He let people kill him so they might be saved. He died so the church could thrive.

My point isn't to address specific issues as much as it is to deal with a deadly demonic spirit that is extremely advanced in its progress in the destruction of the church, and thus, the nation.

A Spirit of Entitlement

This spirit is pervasive in our nation, and, unfortunately it has infiltrated the church to such a degree that it has altered its identity. Today people attend church with expectations of how they should be treated instead of with the intent to lay down their lives for the sake of the mission—a mission that will result in either the populations of Heaven or Hell expanding. There is a predetermined checklist of items that they presume they are rightfully entitled to. If those demands aren't met, then trouble is initiated—just as the enemy planned.

This spirit of entitlement convinces us to look inward and fight for our perceived rights. It's fueled by pride that results in the pursuit of personal attention, gain and satisfaction.

> *"How you are fallen from heaven, O Day Star, son of Dawn! How you are cut down to the ground, you who laid the nations low! You said in your heart, 'I will ascend to heaven; above the stars of God I will set my throne on high; I will sit on the mount of assembly in the far reaches of the north; I will ascend above the heights of the clouds; I will make myself like the Most High.' But you are brought down to Sheol, to the far reaches of the pit.*
> *Isaiah 14:12-15*

Lucifer was focused on self—entitlement. This pride resulted in destruction beyond anything we could measure. He fell and weakened the nations simply because he was focused on self!

America, are you listening?

Because of Lucifer's attitude, millions of people have been destroyed, the Holocaust terrorized a generation, an ancient flood destroyed the masses, 55 million American babies have been murdered and Hell is growing in size to hold the increasing number of people who will live there for eternity.

Yes, a spirit of entitlement destroys.

> *Pride goes before destruction, and a haughty spirit before a fall.*
> *Proverbs 16:18*

When pride comes, then comes disgrace, but with the humble is wisdom. Proverbs 11:2

Before destruction a man's heart is haughty, but humility comes before honor. Proverbs 18:12

Taking on Offense

When entitled people gather together, you have a union. Here in Detroit, this is understood well. There are certain expectations that must be fulfilled by leadership, or those in union will threaten harm to them or the organization. This concept isn't hard to understand. Often on the news we hear of school teachers or bus drivers who are in a union, and when their demands aren't met, they strike.

When an entitlement isn't met, offense is the result—and when people are in union with another who has been offended, they very quickly take on that offense—and, again, it is deadly.

We see this happen in churches all the time. Offended people have friends, who unify with them and come into agreement with their arguments. In the coming Church, schisms and inappropriate unions won't survive as the burning love of his presence trumps human endeavors.

Of course, it would be very easy right now to start considering all of the secular benefits to actual unions. We could discuss how the playing field is evened and the way leadership treats the working class is improved by holding them accountable.

But, I'll say this very clearly—this spirit of false unity, entitlement and offense has no place in the church. Our nation would begin down the road of healing and strengthening if we all stopped making demands and started serving, loving and following Jesus and the principles of Scripture.

An offended people will destroy a nation. A surrendered people will build a nation.

As an example, the spirits of entitlement and offense drive the abortion industry. False compassion, demonic in nature, is one of the tools that is used to gain sympathy and support for that movement. The threat is that we will come across as unloving, uncaring people if we oppose that movement. The same is true with the homosexual agenda. False love results in accusations of homophobia and hatred for those who don't support their movement.

As Christians, we are handcuffed as we are forced into a position of affirming our love of these people, and if we don't, they win the debate.

Our only weak, predictable response seems to be, *"We love the sinner and hate the sin."*

Boldness!

We as prophetic voices in the church must break off intimidation and fear of man! Keep in mind we are wrestling against demons, not humans. Admittedly it is difficult when humans embrace the lies of the demons. When we attack the spirits, it can appear that we are attacking those people. So, many Christians avoid any appearance of conflict at all.

Listen closely: people are going to enter into Hell today! If we don't have bold prophetic messengers rise up in the spirit of John the Baptist, in the spirit of David and other historic Godly warriors, millions upon millions of people will actually, literally go to Hell! If it's rare to make it to Heaven, and common to enter Hell, how can we sit back and avoid a violent conflict with those forces of Hell? We cannot!

> *From the days of John the Baptist until now the kingdom of heaven has suffered violence, and the violent take it by force. Matthew 11:12*

Check out this commentary on the above Scripture:

> *Greek: biazo (GSN-<G971>), to use force, to force one's way into a thing. The idea here is that before John the kingdom could only be viewed in the light of prophecy; but now that it was preached, men were pressing into it with ardor resembling violence or desperation. They appeared as if they would seize it by force (Mt. 11:12; Lk. 16:16). It expresses the earnestness that men must have in getting rid of sin, all satanic powers, the world, and in standing true when relatives oppose them (Mt. 10:34-39). Dake's Annotated Reference Bible: Containing the Old and New Testaments of the Authorized or King James Version Text.*

This is where we are now! Let the fire-branded, love-driven warrior bride arise!

When David killed Goliath, it's true that he killed a human, but he was actually fighting against a demon that was manifesting through a human. David didn't sit down in a coffee shop to passively, casually discuss the dispute with Goliath. He was ready for a violent assault against the kingdom of darkness.

He made clear what the situation was and what was to be done! How easy it would be for David to be accused of not loving Goliath! But, the truth is that David loved God first (Luke 10:27) and was fully invested in partnering with him. Human arguments would have to meet the fierce decrees of the child of God! Fear-driven false humility was not an option for David. David was on a mission of salvation—the salvation of God's people.

> *And David said to the men who stood by him, "What shall be done for the man who kills this Philistine and takes away the reproach from Israel? For who is this uncircumcised Philistine, that he should defy the armies of the living God?" 1 Samuel 17:26*

David was bold! Who is this uncircumcised Philistine? He was calling out Goliath's immorality and his lack of consecration to the Lord.

Come on Church! Quit cowering in false humility and rise up in the greatest love this nation has ever known! It's time to declare the word of the Lord to the uncircumcised enemies of the Lord in America!

But, beware, many in your sphere, in the camp of the Lord, will also be intimidated by your love-driven boldness. The prophetic, apostolic anointing often results in jealousy and accusation against the one advancing fearlessly. Accusations of pride will always accompany those who are willing to live radically by laying down their lives for the Lord.

> *Now Eliab his eldest brother heard when he spoke to the men. And Eliab's anger was kindled against David, and he said, "Why have you come down? And with whom have you left those few sheep in the wilderness? I know your presumption and the evil of your heart, for you have come down to see the battle." And David said, "What have I done now? Was it not but a word?" 1 Samuel 17:28-29*

His brother attacked him! I'm sure he felt conviction as little brother David was going to do what every other person should have done—deal with the uncircumcised Philistine with expediency!

Will you raise your anointed, prophetic voice, or will you seek a false sense of peace? Remember we are to be peacemakers not peace-keepers! We cannot keep peace where there is no peace!

We have no obligation to passively form our words in such a way that we will be heard. It's time to bring a shaking to this nation—before it is literally destroyed!

And the Philistine moved forward and came near to David, with his shield-bearer in front of him. And when the Philistine looked and saw David, he disdained him, for he was but a youth, ruddy and handsome in appearance. And the Philistine said to David, "Am I a dog, that you come to me with sticks?" And the Philistine cursed David by his gods. The Philistine said to David, "Come to me, and I will give your flesh to the birds of the air and to the beasts of the field." Then David said to the Philistine, "You come to me with a sword and with a spear and with a javelin, but I come to you in the name of the LORD of hosts, the God of the armies of Israel, whom you have defied. This day the LORD will deliver you into my hand, and I will strike you down and cut off your head. And I will give the dead bodies of the host of the Philistines this day to the birds of the air and to the wild beasts of the earth, that all the earth may know that there is a God in Israel, 1 Samuel 17:41-46

It's time that we go after the anti-Christ spirits that are overtaking our nation! We can no longer use human arguments. It's time that we are anointed in the boldness and power of the Holy Spirit! We aren't to prove our love, we are to love—and true love brings true problems in the pursuit of liberty for a nation! We see this cover to cover in Scripture.

I Deeply Love You—But I Do Not Care

I will say it very, very clearly. I RADICALLY love those who are advancing humanistic agendas, even though you may not believe me. That's your battle, not mine.

Jesus loved people though he would not bend to their demands. He cared about their emotions, their hearts, their eternities—but he didn't defend himself. He let his accusers kill him. Who was the one who cared and loved when he was lifted up on a cross that day?

In an attempt to break the church out of a passive, false-love-driven debate over holiness and morality I will say this very clearly:

I DO NOT CARE ENOUGH, young woman, about your career, your comfort, your supposed right to independence or the crisis and cost a new baby will bring to your life to affirm your plan to kill your baby. You are not entitled to comfort. You are not promised happiness. I challenge you to lay down your life for a baby— a precious life that God entrusted to your care. He valued you that much!

When you wave a coat hanger in the air during an abortion rights protest, you are declaring that you have more compassion for one who would intentionally harm someone than one who is being harmed. The answer to losing access to "safe abortions" (how is intentional murder safe?) is not to head out to the back alley to abort the baby yourself with a hanger—it is to have the baby and love it with selfless passion! The answer is so simple!

I DO NOT CARE about a supposed right to sexual freedom, gay or straight, that results in a devastating lifestyle that is bringing destruction on our nation. Decrees of holiness must return to our churches and nation again!

I DO NOT CARE about equality in our nation if it results in climbing over people who are in our way or forcing them to affirm our self-centered position. It's time that we lay down our demands, surrender our agendas and quit manipulating systems in a selfish pursuit of personal gain. It's time for humility to reign in America again!

Christian leaders I honor you deeply and pray for you and I do understand the pressures you are under. However, I DO NOT CARE about personal agendas, self-centered ministry projects, your self-assigned titles or ego-driven programs and will not unite with those who embrace them. Your legacy and history in the city is meaningless unless it results in a future of Holy Spirit freedom for desperate people. I will expend energy, time and money to run with you if you are humble and passionate about the plans of God in the region. Let's slow the flow to Hell together.

Let each of you look not only to his own interests, but also to the interests of others. Have this mind among yourselves, which is yours in Christ Jesus, who, though he was in the form of God, did not count equality with God a thing to be grasped, but emptied himself, by taking the form of a servant, being born in the likeness of men. And being found in human form, he humbled himself by becoming obedient to the point of death, even death on a cross. Philippians 2:4-8

I CARE ABOUT THE HEART OF GOD and his overwhelming love for people—and the fact that Hell is swallowing millions of them. I care about the clear truths of Scripture. I trust in God's wisdom and I refuse to allow humanism to gain the upper hand in the debate. I care about bold prophetic messengers who will lay down their lives and open their mouths and shout truth from the rooftops.

Today, not tomorrow, it's time to die to self and run to the battle as the spirit of Goliath is threatening to destroy us. It's time for the circumcised, consecrated lovers of God to take back America.

~ *FIFTEEN* ~

THE SPIRIT OF ABORTION

The Coming Church will steward their mandate.

I'd like to start this chapter with an important explanation. The title and the content are both provocative to say the least. It can be easy to shrink back in offense or with premature judgment, and I do understand that tendency.

What I am about to present is quite simple—the enemy is using similar methods to impact both the Church and the world. A common spirit can manifest itself in different ways depending on the environment it is in.

For example, in the world a spirit of witchcraft may very well manifest in a coven meeting with witches. In a Christian, it may manifest as rebellion to authority (1 Samuel 15:23). It's the same spirit with different manifestations.

I addressed a similar issue earlier in the book when I wrote about the root causes of homosexuality—causes that manifest differently in the Church.

The spirit of the age is overwhelming the church in ways we may not have considered.

As is necessary when addressing an ultra-sensitive issue, I will make some qualifications on the front end:

God is without question—and I will declare without apology— passionately interested in blessing his children. It is fully appropriate to give a measure of attention to the wondrous process of discovery of God's abundant life, overwhelming benefits and blessings.

That being said, I now must move on to offering some analysis on a hidden tragedy.

The Spirit of Abortion—in the Church?

As a prophetic messenger, a primary driving force of my daily life is to reveal and help destroy any barriers to Kingdom advance and the revelation of the cross and resurrection of Christ. In fact, we all must have our eyes wide open to this disturbing movement that is overtaking the church and stand in unity against its advance.

Now, of course, the thought of the spirit of abortion in the church is potentially offensive and certainly provocative. It's a bold statement to say the least.

It's important at this point to understand our discussion isn't about all of those other Christians or all of those other churches that just don't get it. We must look inward. Yes, we have to boldly and humbly ask ourselves the question, *"God, are the same spirits that drive the abortion movement also driving me?"*

Check out this quote which highlights the issue quite well. Notice how this person affirms eliminating threats to other more desirable endeavors:

> *Abortion is not the lesser of two evils. Abortion is pro-family, pro-life, moral, and good. For many millions of women, abortion has meant getting on with their lives and continuing to meet their responsibilities to themselves, their families, and society. PATRICIA W. LUNNEBORG, Abortion: A Positive Decision*

Is it possible that we in the church are also more focused on getting on with our lives at the expense of God, the church, our mission, the Word and other people?

It's shocking to me how Little League, school, family vacations and rest and relaxation are not looked at as threats to our personal freedoms, but a call to the prayer room is.

With that in mind, here's another qualifying statement: the demonic abortion strategy is multi-faceted. It includes spirits of murder, violence, hatred and many others. While we as Christians may not be driven by those spirits, there is one spirit that has a foundational, comprehensive assignment. This spirit is what has infiltrated the church, and it's, in my opinion, a key reason why we haven't had the authority to eradicate it from its assignment of murdering babies.

This spirit has one key focus, one goal as it ministers to the minds and hearts of people: personal experience.

People are focused primarily on their personal experience.

You could also call it selfish ambition.

Check out this passage of Scripture:

> *Who is wise and understanding among you? By his good conduct let him show his works in the meekness of wisdom. But if you have bitter jealousy and selfish ambition in your hearts, do not boast and be false to the truth. This is not the wisdom that*

comes down from above, but is earthly, unspiritual, demonic. For where jealousy and selfish ambition exist, there will be disorder and every vile practice. James 3:13-16

Selfish ambition is demonic. Jealousy, which results when we focus on our own personal experience, is also vile, earthly and demonic.

When a woman is carrying an unwanted baby, her focus immediately shifts to her own personal experience. Her ambition. Her dreams.

The call to lay down her life for another, to make a great sacrifice, to change her priorities and to embrace a life of struggle and inconvenience for another person all fall on deaf ears. After all, it's her body and she can do what she wants with it, right?

One method of destroying a concept is by diluting its meaning. Observe that by ascribing rights to the unborn, i.e., the non-living, the anti-abortionists obliterate the rights of the living. AYN RAND, The Ayn Rand Lexicon

The unwilling mother has rights! It's her life. It's her time. It's her dreams. It's her decision, and in the case of abortion, she makes the decision for self instead of for another. Her personal experience was instrumental in her decision.

Do nothing from selfish ambition or conceit, but in humility count others more significant than yourselves. Let each of you look not only to his own interests, but also to the interests of others. Philippians 2:3-4

What's in it for me?

So, how does this affect the Church? This issue is impacting the Church and Christians in very deep, disturbing ways. It's not a minor issue that's affecting a few. It's a major problem that's a primary driver in the very fabric of Western Christianity.

We have to understand that so much of preaching today has been fashioned to appease people looking for a positive personal experience. This must end.

> *For the time is coming when people will not endure sound teaching, but having itching ears they will accumulate for themselves teachers to suit their own passions, and will turn away from listening to the truth and wander off into myths.*
> *2 Timothy 4:3-4*

Do you know how difficult it is to find churches that preach the cross? Cost? Death? Surrender? The personal experience must be positive and without much cost if we hope to fill the pews. The same thing happened at the cross. The place where Jesus died was empty except for those killing him and those closest to him. Where were the crowds who were looking for a message to satisfy their itching ears? They left when the message included death. When you preach the cross the masses will run and you will be left with those who are the closest to you and those who are out to kill you.

> *"If Jesus had preached the same message that ministers preach today, He would never have been crucified."*
> *-Leonard Ravenhill*

> *"The early church was married to poverty, prisons and persecutions. Today, the church is married to prosperity, personality, and popularity." -Leonard Ravenhill*

> *"I believe that there are too many accommodating preachers, and too many practitioners in the church who are not believers. Jesus Christ did not say, 'Go into all the world and tell the world that it is quite right.' The gospel is something completely different. In fact, it is directly opposed to the world." -C. S. Lewis*

What should send us to our knees is that it's the very gospel of Jesus that is being rejected for the sake of the pursuit of personal blessing and benefit! There are preachers in churches with crosses on their steeples who refuse to call people to the cross at the altars! A minimized cross results in Christians that are only artificially vibrant as they pursue blessing, but are dead and dying inside—and this has eternal implications!

It's time for us to respond positively to what many have called negative messages; these piercing, demanding, shocking negative messages of death at the cross were born through God himself and delivered to us in the form of Jesus.

Just like the woman who wants to remove the threat of a baby for the sake of her own personal experience, we in the church are all too often looking for relief and blessing instead of carrying a heavy cross for the sake of others! The refusal to sacrifice time, money, energy and our very lives on a daily basis results in a prayerless, self-centered, quasi-Christian that's driven by the question, *"What's in it for me?"*

Have you noticed that the biggest offerings tend to come when the emphasis is on what we can expect in return? The biggest conferences tend to be those that highlight personal breakthrough. The most appreciated sermons are those that reveal the blessings we can expect as Christians. I often wonder what would happen if we held a conference titled, *"Come and die."*

We live in a day when we unwittingly embrace a deadly, self-centered spirit of religion.

Again, religion is: Man's attempt to use God to get what he wants.

When we don't get what we want out of God or the church, we have an opportunity to accuse, to get angry, to place demands and to flee. When Jesus was here, the spirit of religion killed him because they didn't get out of Jesus what they wanted.

Jesus didn't give them what they wanted in the way they wanted it. So that spirit of abortion, of murder, took care of business.

Theocentric simply means we exist for God rather than He for us. Egocentric praying is our attempt at managing and directing God to accomplish our will instead of His. If "covetousness is idolatry" then attempting to harness the power of God to the priorities of self-centeredness is SIN! - *Harold Vaughn*

The emphasis today seems to be on God alleviating our struggles instead of joining in on the great end-time struggle!

"If a Christian is not having tribulation in the world, there's something wrong!" - *Leonard Ravenhill*

Again, God loves to bless his children, but we must discuss the approach:

I absolutely love to give my kids presents. I come alive! My son Jet's birthday was yesterday and I had so much fun watching his face beam as we opened presents, and as the famous mouse at Chuck-E-Cheese led out in singing happy birthday. I also couldn't wait to get him home, after he thought all of the presents had already been given, and see his face as he opened the shed to ride his bike...only to see his brand new bike sitting there! What a moment! Later that night we were laying on the hammock under the stars together, and he very casually and thoughtfully said, *"Yep, this was about the best birthday ever...the best Chuck-E-Cheese birthday ever."*

Now, compare that to other days when I take the kids for a routine shopping trip to Walmart. From the moment they hit the door their sad, frustrated faces reveal what's coming next. *"Dad, please, can I have..."*

No. No. NO! Over and over again. The tears come. The sadness increases. Their carnal nature is showing in radiant brilliance! Their consideration is not for mom and dad, our focus on saving money or anything else. It's on self! You see, I often bring my kids

with me when I go out just because I want to be with them, and to their credit, my wonderful children often want to be with me too! We love being together. But, something happens when the focus turns to self. What's in it for me?

Troubled

When threats to your dreams or your time or your personal endeavors come, how do you react? When preaching cuts instead of satisfies, how do you respond? The answer to these questions can go a long way in revealing what spirit you are driven by.

When the threats came to Jesus, he didn't resist—he died. He surrendered for the sake of the world.

However, when the threat of a new King being born was discovered by Herod, he was troubled. The threat to his own personal experience, his reign as king, resulted in the spirit of abortion entering him.

> *Now when they had departed, behold, an angel of the Lord appeared to Joseph in a dream and said, "Rise, take the child and his mother, and flee to Egypt, and remain there until I tell you, for Herod is about to search for the child, to destroy him." Matthew 2:13*

> *Then Herod, when he saw that he had been tricked by the wise men, became furious, and he sent and killed all the male children in Bethlehem and in all that region who were two years old or under, according to the time that he had ascertained from the wise men. Matthew 2:16*

We see this pattern repeating itself throughout history. Massive resistance comes when a threat to personal experience arrives. It emerged, for example, when the African-Americans threatened a segment of society's idea of racial purity. That resulted in the Ku Klux Klan and the horrific murders of many innocent people.

We saw it during the holocaust as Hitler was threatened by the Jews and other groups. Again, millions of innocent people died for the sake of one demented person's overzealous aim to ensure his personal life experience was protected.

Today, terrorism is on the rise and murder is the strategy of choice for many who refuse to allow their life experiences to be threatened by other cultures.

This demonic spirit is incredibly crafty. The call of Christianity is to die for others and the call of this demonic spirit is for others to die for us.

Angry People

Of course, the act of murder isn't the strategy of choice for those who are threatened in the church—or is it?

> *"You have heard that it was said to those of old, 'You shall not murder; and whoever murders will be liable to judgment.' But I say to you that everyone who is angry with his brother will be liable to judgment; whoever insults his brother will be liable to the council; and whoever says, 'You fool!' will be liable to the hell of fire. Matthew 5:21-22*

Jesus equates anger to murder. In the church the manifestation of anger usually results in gossip, which is a deeply destructive spirit. Gossip results in dark hearts manifesting outwardly against those who threaten them. The same accusation that the abortionists hurl are used by the uncrucified, angry Christians— *"You are threatening my freedom and my rights!"*

> *No woman can call herself free who does not own and control her body. No woman can call herself free until she can choose consciously whether she will or will not be a mother. MARGARET SANGER, Woman and the New Race*

When we become Christians we gain freedom but we lose our freedoms.

> *There are six things that the LORD hates, seven that are an abomination to him: haughty eyes, a lying tongue, and hands that shed innocent blood, a heart that devises wicked plans, feet that make haste to run to evil, a false witness who breathes out lies, and one who sows discord among brothers. Proverbs 6:16-19*

It's also possible to take on the offense of others. We have to be very careful! If we allow others who have had their own personal experiences threatened to lure us into an inappropriately merciful, sympathetic position, we are at great risk of taking on their offense and embracing anger against the threatening person. We saw Absalom do this as he took on the offense of others who didn't get what they wanted out of King David.

Again, we are to expect a sharp sword, a high bar, a challenging life and a call to die to everything, including our own opinions, for the sake of others.

The spirit of abortion fights for personal rights no matter the cost to others. It resists the preaching of the cross with a vengeance. The cross threatens our very life!

Repentance

Repentance must hit our churches. We have to return to the cross and refuse to buy into the demand for messages that tickle our ears. It's time to once again be OK with deep inspection of the Lord into our hearts.

It's this type of life that is a manifestation of deep, selfless love. This love will result in a great authority against the mission of murder against the millions of precious babies.

If we embrace the same self-centered spirit that drives the abortionists while at the same time crying out against them, we will be powerless. But if we die to self we will have the authority to defeat the spirit of abortion, murder and death that has overrun our nation.

> *Men tell us in these days that sin is what you think it is. Well, it is not. Sin is what God thinks it is. You may think according to your own conscience. God thinks according to His. –John G. Lake*

> *People do not drift toward Holiness. Apart from grace-driven effort, people do not gravitate toward godliness, prayer, obedience to Scripture, faith, and delight in the Lord. We drift toward compromise and call it tolerance; we drift toward disobedience and call it freedom; we drift toward superstition and call it faith. We cherish the indiscipline of lost self-control and call it relaxation; we slouch toward prayerlessness and delude ourselves into thinking we have escaped legalism; we slide toward godlessness and convince ourselves we have been liberated. –D.A. Carson*

> *It is perilously easy to have amazing sympathy with God's truth and remain in sin.– Oswald Chambers*

~ SIXTEEN ~

A REMNANT MOVEMENT

The Coming Church will reveal the remnant.

You might be surprised at the danger that exists in the worship movement in the current Church.

I had a prophetic dream that is extremely simple to understand—the prophetic warnings are being drowned out by casual spirits and, yes, even by today's worship movement.

> *The word of the LORD came to me: "Son of man, prophesy against the prophets of Israel, who are prophesying, and say to those who prophesy from their own hearts: 'Hear the word of the LORD!' Thus says the Lord GOD, Woe to the foolish prophets who follow their own spirit, and have seen nothing!*
> *Ezekiel 13:1-3*

They have seen false visions and lying divinations. They say, 'Declares the LORD,' when the LORD has not sent them, and yet they expect him to fulfill their word. Have you not seen a false vision and uttered a lying divination, whenever you have said, 'Declares the LORD,' although I have not spoken?" Therefore thus says the Lord GOD: "Because you have uttered falsehood and seen lying visions, therefore behold, I am against you, declares the Lord GOD. My hand will be against the prophets who see false visions and who give lying divinations. They shall not be in the council of my people, nor be enrolled in the register of the house of Israel, nor shall they enter the land of Israel. And you shall know that I am the Lord GOD. Ezekiel 13:6-9

There is a rapidly increasing movement of people who are shutting their ears to any prophetic words that have any measure of alarm to them. The warnings are not wanted as they threaten the current structures of comfort and ease.

These people are at risk of a catastrophe that will mercilessly hit them and those who have been influenced by their messages of peace and safety.

There are true voices that must emerge and declare the word of the Lord in its pure form.

If we EVER temper a message in the pulpit, online or one-on-one in the hopes of maintaining an audience, we've become a 2 Tim 4:3-4 false teacher.

For the time is coming when people will not endure sound teaching, but having itching ears they will accumulate for themselves teachers to suit their own passions, and will turn away from listening to the truth and wander off into myths. 2 Timothy 4:3-4

Revival always includes the conviction of sin on the part of the Church. What a spell the devil seems to cast over the Church today! -Billy Sunday

The Dream

I was the guest speaker at a church, and I was burning with an extreme prophetic message that I knew every single person must hear. Not only must they hear it, but they had to allow God to break and wreck them so they could become carriers of that burning message. God needed them to proclaim the word with boldness and brokenness.

It was time to begin the service, and I was on the platform feeling troubled and confused. I had about eight friends with me, people who were absolutely given to the message and who were standing very close to me.

Other than my friends, literally nobody was listening. Even the leadership was absent. People were dressed in shorts and flip flops and casual clothing and were just slowly walking around talking to friends.

My disturbance kept intensifying.

To my right there were a couple of large garage doors that were both open. People were moving out of the building and out onto the grass. It was a beautiful, sunny day.

As people kept leaving the building, someone walked close to the stage. He began singing a worship song in an attempt to drown out the message even while I was preaching with unction and urgency. It was a brilliant tactic. After all, it's good to sing songs of worship in the church, right?

When he finished singing, the building was nearly empty. In my desperation to get the message relayed, I too went outside.

My friends and I left the building and stood on a small slab of concrete outside. I continued to preach, but it was as if I was nearly invisible and inaudible. From time to time people would wave and wink to me as an indicator that they are "with me" and to thank me for my ministry. I didn't want their thanks. I wanted their hearts.

My friends pressed very close to me…so close that we were all squashed together as a single unit as I kept preaching truth.

The people kept playing while we kept trembling.

I then noticed that some chose to climb a tree. When they decided to come back down, one of them fell just a couple of feet and those around them were alarmed and looked right me. They demanded that I leave my place and come over to help. I was grieved.

I did leave the concrete and tended to the person who had an extremely minor injury.

Distraction and a casual, playful, self-centered spirit overpowered the prophetic word of the Lord.

I then woke up.

The Interpretation

We live in a day when churches promote comfort and self-satisfaction. Coffee, personal ministry, blessing, programs and other lesser things are overshadowing the call to the cross. The alarm of the hour is not a welcome sound.

Casual spirits are driving the culture. The problem? The message of the cross is not a casual message.

The bottom line is this: A casual spirit will always reject a prophetic warning if it threatens their comfort. A prophetic spirit will always threaten something.

> *A.W. Tozer: I want the prophetic spirit upon me or I want to die.*

In the dream it was significant that even the leaders were absent. The pastors of that church should have been on their faces in deep repentance as they led their people into brokenness!

Nobody in that church had any concern about their own salvation (they should have), the condition of their city or the message of God. All was well. Peace and safety were the cries of their hearts.

My friends who were very close to me represented the remnant—those who are broken and surrendered and devoted to the call. They counted the cost and said, *"yes."*

Please keep this in mind—the remnant is an extremely small percentage of people in the church. Don't presume that you have signed up as an end-time remnant Christian just because you go to church, love God and want revival. True remnant people aren't only interested in revival, they are invested in it. To find a remnant Christian is actually quite rare, though every Christian has been extended that invitation.

Worship

Possibly the most interesting part of the dream had to do with the person who walked up to me and started singing a worship song.

I believe we are in a place of both great hope and great danger in regard to worship in the church.

True worship is going to return to the church. That's the hope. There is a great movement of groan and intercession-driven worship and adoration to Jesus that's coming. It's not here yet, but soon can be.

The present danger is great, however.

The worship service can easily become the lazy man's intercession. Please consider this point carefully! The church is to be a house of prayer for all nations!

I've been in ministry for over 22 years and it has grieved me time and again when people would come and go based on the skill, style and feel of the worship team, but are indifferent regarding the

prayer focus. In fact, when the call to worship is sounded, people flock, but when the call to prayer is sounded people flee.

This is disturbing and it's an indictment on the church!

We don't attend a church based on it's ability to appeal to our desires! My God! How far have we fallen?

At Revival Church we recently made a bold decision for our current season—when our worship leader moved on, I decided it was time to bring intercession back to first place.

Instead of sitting back or lightly engaging as someone else leads in worship, we are calling the entire body to pray with us boldly for an hour prior to the teaching. Fervent prayer has replaced musical worship! The experience of worship or any other thing can no longer trump the call to pray and to deliver the prophetic messages of God.

In fact, I'm confident that biblical worship will emerge from this platform of prayer and no longer will we casually connect to God when the music plays. Musical worship has taken a back seat to the word of the Lord and it will again be calibrated to God's heart.

If you want to gauge the spiritual maturity of your team, call a prayer meeting. Develop a prayer culture. Bring prayer front and center where nobody can hide. It may be offensive, but it's simply true that only the broken, hungry and maturing will remain. It shocks me that people can lead worship, pastor a church or function in ministry without a vibrant, all-consuming life of prayer! It is actually rare to find praying church leadership in America!

> *There are individuals who have never done anything for Jesus Christ, and I have no doubt there are preachers as well, who have never done anything for the God Almighty. —Billy Sunday*

> *"If we do not praise we shall grow sad in our conflict; and if we do not fight we shall become presumptuous in our song." —Charles Spurgeon*

Worship leaders who don't burn night and day in intercession need to take a critical break to rediscover the God of their songs. A fearful tremble and awe must return to worship.

Pavement People

In the dream, I moved to a concrete slab outside of the building as the people were scattering and playing. I have been crying out for the last several months for the pavement people to emerge! These are people in the remnant who are not looking for personal comfort, affirmation or anything other than hitting the pavement in true worship.

> *When all the people of Israel saw the fire come down and the glory of the LORD on the temple, they bowed down with their faces to the ground on the pavement and worshiped and gave thanks to the LORD, saying, "For he is good, for his steadfast love endures forever." 2 Chronicles 7:3*

I was on the pavement with my friends who were staying very close to me. I continued to preach in desperation as people were in the vicinity, but who were not at all provoked by the message. They were certainly not responsive, and, of course, they were in no place to become carriers of that fiery word for the nations.

Again, my grief escalated.

Distractions

The types of distractions that the enemy will attempt to force on us are extremely hard to counteract.

First, it can seem strange and wrong to label worship as a disturbance or distraction. The enemy is often using worship, as I shared

above, to provide people with a false sense of intimacy with Jesus, or at least a radically minimized encounter with him. If the music is good and even slightly anointed, and it feels peaceful or invigorating, then our job of honoring God seems to be done. We don't have to go any deeper in Jesus. We are satisfied. It's time to move to other things.

Additionally, the person that fell out of the tree was wounded, ever so slightly, and all eyes were on me to stop what I was doing and help. So, the corporate prophetic alarm ceased.

The problem? The person should never have been in the tree. They were called to the pavement. Their improper positioning negatively impacted the masses. Their wounding was minor and should not have resulted in a corporate diversion.

When we are close together, there is safety. Risk is minimized. Even when there is an issue, we can all stay together, in position as we serve one another.

Those in the Upper Room in Acts 2 certainly tended to each other as they were all on that holy pavement, that place of coming encounter and intercession for the nations.

Those who are scattering and playing instead of gathering and praying are loosely connected until crisis comes.

It's time that we are "all together in one accord in one place" as they were in Acts 2.

A Resistant Church

As it was in the days of Noah, so it is today. The alarms are resisted.

> *For as were the days of Noah, so will be the coming of the Son of Man. For as in those days before the flood they were eating and drinking, marrying and giving in marriage, until the day when*

Noah entered the ark, and they were unaware until the flood came and swept them all away, so will be the coming of the Son of Man. Matthew 24:37-39

Do we not know that God is raising up prophetic voices to help us? Why would we reject the warnings?

It's time we gather and pray. It's time.

I asked a question on Facebook recently:

If your church cancelled everything for a year...cancelled children's ministry, teaching, programs, pot lucks, small groups... and replaced those activities with prayer meetings, would you stay in your church?

One response rocked me. It encouraged me that the remnant is out there:

That's when I'll return to the church.

Friends, it's time that we embrace a God that loves us enough to keep us from slumber, to shake us with warnings and to prepare us for the tragic and glorious end-time shocks that are coming to the Earth. The coming Church is going to be a very intense place—both refreshing and demanding, and sadly, not many will choose to participate.

~ *Seventeen* ~

Wake Up! Strengthen What Remains!

The Coming Church is a Church on alert.

A Reputation of Being Alive

One of the most terrifying verses in the Bible just may be found at the beginning of Revelation chapter 3:

> *"And to the angel of the church in Sardis write: 'The words of him who has the seven spirits of God and the seven stars. "'I know your works. You have the reputation of being alive, but you are dead. Revelation 3:1*

While I am most certainly a man who is clearly weak and flawed, I can easily say that I am a man on fire, and I have been

burning through seasons of both joy and crisis for over 23 years. A day hasn't gone by when the raging fire of the Holy Spirit hasn't been burning within.

Though I endorse the process of allowing God to search my heart, and I am hungry for every unholy issue to be brought to the surface, what God spoke to me recently wrecked me. He wanted me to personally consider the message in Revelation 3:1.

Is it possible that I have a reputation of being alive and little more? Now, please understand, I'm a fervent lover of Jesus! The fear of the Lord is on me as I grow more intimate with him. However, is it possible that I'm not as fully given to Jesus as my reputation might reveal? I hate to admit it, but, yes, it's possible.

In fact, it brings me great peace to admit that it's possible. I need to stay broken and attune to the true condition of my own heart. Do I love Jesus. Oh, yes! Does he love me? Of course. Am I fully given to him? I can't imagine that being the case. Is anything left undone? Most certainly. So, what can I do to ensure I am responsive to the constant course corrections that God wants to be active in my life? Pray for judgment.

> *But if we judged ourselves truly, we would not be judged. But when we are judged by the Lord, we are disciplined so that we may not be condemned along with the world. 1 Corinthians 11:31-32*

Judge myself, and then, if necessary, be open to the loving, merciful judgment of God.

The Church must do the same. We need to consider the possibility that we, like the church of Sardis, have a reputation of being alive while, in reality, are dead.

A Dream

I had one of the most shocking and personally horrifying dreams of my life recently. My wife and I were in a military grade nuclear submarine following behind a second submarine that contained my Father-in-law and Mother-in-law.

As I stood along the wall inside the submarine, I was analyzing the situation, trying to gain understanding on what exactly we were doing. My wife was enjoying the ride, playfully looking through the periscope. Both submarines were staying at the surface of the water functioning as tour vessels instead of war vessels. The atmosphere was playful and carefree.

After a short time everybody was done playing and we decided to park the submarines alongside a long pier. We climbed up a ladder and out into a beautiful sunny day at the beach. We walked down the pier and onto a boardwalk. There were people everywhere enjoying a happy summer day. The restaurants and shops were full of activity.

We then walked off of the boardwalk and onto the sandy beach which was about one hundred yards through the water from the submarines.

The four of us were standing on the beach taking in the view. As we gazed out over the water, both submarines suddenly began leaving. They headed out toward deeper water.

My in-laws were alarmed and immediately started running into the water giving chase to the submarines. As they did, I was immediately bothered, thinking that it was impossible for them to get anywhere near to the fast moving vessels and I didn't understand why they had tried.

Then, my trouble intensified as my wife ran into the water as well.

What I saw next can't easily be described in a way that is true to the emotion I felt. The sunny day immediately shifted into a fearful, stormy threat to every one of us. The water immediately began erupting as if a powerful hurricane was upon us. I was absolutely terrorized as I frantically tried to devise a plan to help.

What I saw next drained every bit of hope from my being. About fifty yards from the beach, in the midst of the storm, a whirlpool opened up underneath my in-laws and sucked them under. Then, a second whirlpool took my wife.

I was screaming for help. A few people gathered around but could offer no assistance whatsoever. I frantically called 911 and all I heard was this recording, *"We can't send help for an hour. We can't send help for an hour."*

It looped over and over. That was unacceptable! I knew that THIS was the hour. I couldn't wait! The emergency was upon us.

As I stood on the beach, hopeless, the scene suddenly changed again.

I knew that after the scene shifted that only a few days had passed yet instead of a warm sunny day, or even a violent stormy day, it was now bitterly cold and the water had frozen over. There was at least ten feet of snow on top of the ice.

I started moving slowly, though as quickly as I could, through the deep snow in the direction of where the whirlpools were.

When I finally made it to the general location where I lost my family I started digging ferociously and what I saw next will forever be seared in my memory.

It was my wife's face, frozen. She was gone.

I ran back to the boardwalk and into a restaurant. I saw someone who had tried to help previously behind the counter of a sports bar. I remembered that he was a volunteer firefighter in addition to working at the restaurant. I yelled, *"Help! Help! I found her! I found her! Come quickly!"*

He just casually said, *"Sorry man, I'm working."*

What? I couldn't believe what I heard. I said, *"No, you don't understand! I found my wife! I need help!"*

He just said, *"Sorry."* and then looked at a customer and said, *"How can I help you?"*

I ran back to the snow where my wife was buried. I thought that maybe, just maybe, since she was so deeply frozen that there was a chance she could be revived. I've heard of people freezing and their heart beat is slowed to almost nothing before miraculously being brought back. I was hoping for a miracle.

As I was thinking about this I looked down at her, and there was a paper right next to her frozen face.

I picked it up. All it said was, *"Wake up and strengthen what remains and is about to die."*

Then I woke up.

The Interpretation

When I woke up I was shaken to my core.

As I started to pray and analyze the dream, the following is what was highlighted to me.

The submarines:

Vehicles often represent ministry in dreams, and I believe the submarines represented the church. The church is not meant to be casually playing at the surface of the water. It's a military weapon of war designed to move into the deep as it advances toward enemy targets. When the submarines left on their own, that represented the truth that the church will most certainly advance on its mission with or without us. We can be left behind as we continue our focus on entertainment and leisure if we so choose.

My family:

Of course, this was a hard core part of the dream for me personally. My first reaction is to do everything I can to ensure those close to me are doing well and burning hot for Jesus. Beyond that, symbolically I feel they represented familiarity and presumption. It's very easy to presume those who are close to us are most certainly doing well in their relationship with Jesus—and then, a natural reaction is to model our lives after theirs. What happens so often is that we can adopt their pace and their level of passion instead of staying locked in, on alert and advancing in the fire of God. The pressure of maintaining civilities and false unity can result in a marginalized, lukewarm, casual disposition.

This verse best represents what I am communicating:

> *...I know your deeds; you have a reputation of being alive, but you are dead. Revelation 3:1*

We must be careful not to presume that we are alive and that others are alive simply because of the preceding reputations. There are many people with both a legacy in ministry and a name for being zealous who are doing little more than playing—and it's possible that those people may be some of our closest friends, family, pastors and other personal heroes. Don't measure your life by their grid. We must calibrate to the truth in Scripture that will bring light to every issue of our heart.

Then, we can be true awakeners. If we think people who are asleep are already awake, then we will have no need to step into our roles as end-time prophetic messengers.

911:

I was sounding the alarm in a variety of ways including by calling 911. I also ran into the sports bar looking for help. Both rejected the alarm. It's clear that the hour is now for awakening though even those trained as emergency responders won't see it. What was the alarm? Those that have a reputation of being alive are dead! Wake up!

The storm:

It was sudden, violent and completely out of place. It didn't make sense, but it wasn't obligated to explain itself. If we would have been in the submarines AND in the deep, the storm would not have touched us.

> *"No one knows about that day or hour, not even the angels in heaven, nor the Son, but only the Father. As it was in the days of Noah, so it will be at the coming of the Son of Man. For in the days before the flood, people were eating and drinking, marrying and giving in marriage, up to the day Noah entered the ark; Matthew 24:36-38*

The Call

So, what's the call? What should our response be?

It's simple, and it's directed to the church, to those who are to be in the deep:

> *Wake up! Strengthen what remains and is about to die, for I have not found your deeds complete in the sight of my God. Revelation 3:2*

> *Yet you have a few people in Sardis who have not soiled their clothes. They will walk with me, dressed in white, for they are worthy. He who overcomes will, like them, be dressed in white. I will never blot out his name from the book of life, but will acknowledge his name before my Father and his angels. He who has an ear, let him hear what the Spirit says to the churches. Revelation 3:4-6*

God instructed me to wrestle with Revelation 3:1. I've been burning hot for Jesus for over 20 years, yet, is it possible that my devotion is not as deep as I might think? Yes, it is possible.

God didn't accuse me of being dead. He didn't reveal that my passion was false. He simply wanted me to always consider the possibility that my reputation will always be at risk of being more intense than my reality.

> *...I know your deeds; you have a reputation of being alive, but you are dead. Revelation 3:1*

It's time to go deep, to be awake and alert and then to awaken the sleepers...many who may have a reputation of being very much alive...but are not.

It's time for revival. This is the hour.

~ CONCLUSION ~

A JOSHUA COMPANY

The Coming Church is a city taking Church.

We've Never Been This Way Before

I'm going to end this book with the story that began my ministry journey over 22 years ago.

I was young and raw and so alive in Jesus I thought I might explode! I was in my bathroom one night (where, for some reason, God seems to talk very clearly!) and I heard the Lord say, *"John, I've called you to take a city."*

It was a very powerful, unmistakable word, yet I didn't have the first clue as to what I was to do. I lived in Dayton, Ohio at the time, and I was so inexperienced that I wondered if all of the bars and jails would suddenly be closed in the city by the next morning!

Of course, that's not what happened. There's much more to this process, and this book in your hands is one of the steps I'm taking to eventually see the mandate of entire cities taken for Jesus.

I write in my book, *20 Elements of Revival,* that there are over 19,000 cities in America, and not one of them is experiencing revival. Some have pockets of Holy Spirit activity, and certainly there are true moves of God dotted all across the land—but there are no cities that are fully engulfed in revival. No cities have been taken—yet.

Of course, after reading so much about Manitou Springs, Colorado, you understand that the Pikes Peak region is very much on God's radar. So is Detroit. After sharing my vision and mandate to see the entire Detroit region transformed by fire at a pastor's conference at Catch the Fire in Toronto, something interesting happened. Three different key leaders approached me, all independent of one another, and said, *"John, the vision you see of the Detroit region transformed is incomplete. You aren't seeing the fullness of what God is going to do. It's bigger."*

Bigger? I was speechless. After all, the vision I carried was so massive that it includes something that isn't happening anywhere in the nation—full blown revival!

Apparently, it's bigger than that.

After I received the call to take a city in the bathroom of my apartment in Dayton that fateful night, I asked God for a blueprint. I didn't have any idea how to proceed. I opened a Bible randomly, and the page that opened was Joshua 3. I read it, and the fire of God scorched me. That was, and is to this day, my blueprint.

I want to encourage you to study Joshua 3 over and over again. If you have an opportunity, teach it. Cast the vision of city transformation to anybody who will listen. I believe many emerging prophetic voices and apostolic leaders are about to step into the waters of the Jordan.

I'll end this revelation on the coming Church with a teaching on Joshua 3. It's the same one I've used countless times in my own ministry over the last 22 years. You can steal it. Use it. Add your own revelation to it. A Joshua Company will be key as the impact from Heaven arrives.

Joshua Three

A New Government

> *After the death of Moses the servant of the LORD, the LORD said to Joshua the son of Nun, Moses' assistant, "Moses my servant is dead. Now therefore arise, go over this Jordan, you and all this people, into the land that I am giving to them, to the people of Israel. Every place that the sole of your foot will tread upon I have given to you, just as I promised to Moses. Joshua 1:1-3*

One of the greatest men ever to live, Moses, failed in his mission to lead God's people into Promise. It was not God's plan for them to die in the desert, but that is what happened.

There was fear in the camp. There was disorder in the camp. There was rebellion in the camp. Worst, there was Egypt in the camp. They always wanted to return to Egypt, and that spirit continued to drive them. They were looking out for their own interests, and that cost them their lives.

Now, Moses is dead and there's a new leader, a new government. God's promise went with Joshua just as it did with Moses. Where Joshua walked, God would transfer ownership to him.

> *No man shall be able to stand before you all the days of your life. Just as I was with Moses, so I will be with you. I will not leave you or forsake you. Be strong and courageous, for you shall cause this people to inherit the land that I swore to their fathers to give them. Only be strong and very courageous, being careful to do according to all the law that Moses my servant commanded you. Do not turn from it to the right hand or to the left, that you may have good success wherever you go. Joshua 1:5-7*

God's encouragement was with Joshua. The call was for him to avoid turning from the commands of God to the right or left. God was saying that he was ordering his steps, and the places those steps touched would be given. Joshua knew all too well that he couldn't deviate from God's precise mission, no matter how terrifying the battle might be.

> *Then Joshua rose early in the morning and they set out from Shittim. And they came to the Jordan, he and all the people of Israel, and lodged there before they passed over. At the end of three days the officers went through the camp and commanded the people, "As soon as you see the ark of the covenant of the LORD your God being carried by the Levitical priests, then you shall set out from your place and follow it. Joshua 3:1-3*

The fact that Joshua rose early speaks to the urgency of the call. He was fully on task, just as soldiers in the military are awakened before dawn to prepare for training.

Joshua's leadership was working in its early stages. He had all of Israel gathered together (which is more significant than we might realize) and ready to move across an impossible barrier—the Jordan River.

The fact that they were camping out for a few days doesn't speak to recreation but to preparation. God had to make them ready, and it's clear throughout this chapter that Joshua understood this. He wasn't employing a loose, casual plan. He was leading with the precision of a general.

When the three days came to an end, two important things happened:

1. The officers went through the camp.
2. They commanded the people.

The fact that there were officers reveals that Joshua understood governmental order. Today's Church must embrace this as well. God will absolutely be raising up leaders, and they will have important delegated authority to save and set free. These officers were not salesmen. They weren't trying to form their words just right so they could gain buy-in from those under their leadership. They didn't offer options. They commanded. It would do us well in our independent culture to embrace bold leaders who are ordained as commanders of the Lord.

We see another group of people that was very well organized and on the ready. At the command of the officers, the Levitical priests carried the ark of the covenant—the very presence of God! God is identifying an army of priests, people who are carriers! They carry like Mary! This holy army will know God intimately and will respond to the command of God to move out.

This is a very important phase as it is bringing correction to what ultimately caused the millions under Moses' leadership to die.

> *Yet there shall be a distance between you and it, about 2,000 cubits in length. Do not come near it, in order that you may know the way you shall go, for you have not passed this way before." Joshua 3:4*

Joshua 3:4 is one of the key verses in this chapter. The priests under the direction of Joshua, who's under the direction of God, carried God's presence ahead of the people, and the people were instructed to watch closely. They have never been where they were called to go.

They knew how to wander in the desert, but they had not yet learned how to do what God had planned all along—possess a new land and conquer cities.

In America, we have a lot of people who are wondering and complaining, fearful of the unknown and upset that they aren't cared

for the way they want to be. Joshua level leaders will be emerging to lead them back into calibration with God's plan for their lives.

> *Then Joshua said to the people, "Consecrate yourselves, for tomorrow the LORD will do wonders among you." Joshua 3:5*

Joshua 3:5 is the key verse. The command is simple yet threatening. It's easy to understand, yet difficult to respond to. However, this is our only option. Consecration comes before the wonders. Surrender, holiness and humility come before supernatural breakthrough. The coming Church will absolutely be a consecrated Church. There is no other option.

> *And Joshua said to the priests, "Take up the ark of the covenant and pass on before the people." So they took up the ark of the covenant and went before the people. Joshua 3:6*

The time for action came, and everybody responded without bickering, questioning or waiting back. It's common today for people to take a wait and see approach regarding Kingdom work. They hold back to see if there is traction, and if there is, they put their toe in the water. This approach is a violation of order, and it puts the mission at risk. I can't imagine how many potential moves of God have been thwarted by Christians who were waiting around for something to happen before they responded to the battle.

> *The LORD said to Joshua, "Today I will begin to exalt you in the sight of all Israel, that they may know that, as I was with Moses, so I will be with you. Joshua 3:7*

Again we see God's promise to them. As they stepped, God revealed his plans to make his name known through Joshua and those under his command. One generation's ultimate failure was not the next generation's failure. That generational curse wouldn't land on Joshua. He would succeed.

> *And as for you, command the priests who bear the ark of the covenant, 'When you come to the brink of the waters of the Jordan, you shall stand still in the Jordan.'" Joshua 3:8*

Obedience will often require very difficult and ridiculous steps. It made no sense whatsoever to carry the ark into a raging river, but they didn't question the command. They were getting ready to walk.

> *And Joshua said to the people of Israel, "Come here and listen to the words of the LORD your God." Joshua 3:9*

The coming Church will consist of prophetic voices that will gather the people together to hear the word of the Lord and to prepare to respond. This is the instruction I was referring to in an earlier chapter. Joshua wasn't teaching them biblical principles. He was conveying God's message and instructing them how to respond.

> *And Joshua said, "Here is how you shall know that the living God is among you and that he will without fail drive out from before you the Canaanites, the Hittites, the Hivites, the Perizzites, the Girgashites, the Amorites, and the Jebusites. Behold, the ark of the covenant of the Lord of all the earth is passing over before you into the Jordan.*
>
> *Now therefore take twelve men from the tribes of Israel, from each tribe a man. And when the soles of the feet of the priests bearing the ark of the LORD, the Lord of all the earth, shall rest in the waters of the Jordan, the waters of the Jordan shall be cut off from flowing, and the waters coming down from above shall stand in one heap." Joshua 3:10-13*

Now Joshua was getting serious. The call was immediate, and the promise was big. I can imagine how nervous everybody must have been, but turning back was not an option. It was either time to die in the desert like mom and dad or to embrace their destiny, and cross an impossible river.

> *So when the people set out from their tents to pass over the Jordan with the priests bearing the ark of the covenant before the people, and as soon as those bearing the ark had come as far as the Jordan, and the feet of the priests bearing the ark were dipped in the brink of the water (now the Jordan overflows all its banks throughout the time of harvest), the waters coming down from above stood and rose up in a heap very far away, at Adam, the city that is beside Zarethan, and those flowing down toward the Sea of the Arabah, the Salt Sea, were completely cut off.*
>
> *And the people passed over opposite Jericho. Now the priests bearing the ark of the covenant of the LORD stood firmly on dry ground in the midst of the Jordan, and all Israel was passing over on dry ground until all the nation finished passing over the Jordan. Joshua 3:14-17*

The Jordan was at flood stage. It was harvest time! They stepped into this river and cut off the flow into the Salt Sea, or the Dead Sea! It stood up in a heap back to Adam! Are you seeing this?

The victory against death was theirs, and now it is finally time to step into the destiny that was given to them the day they left Egypt. It's time to possess the land. It's time to take a city.

Just as the Exodus from Egypt wasn't initially about entering the Promised Land (it was about entering into the wilderness of encounter!), moving into the Promised Land isn't about relaxation. It's about taking dominion. It's about advancing the Kingdom of God, battling the enemy and taking cities and regions.

The coming Church is coming soon, and God is identifying many who are ready to proclaim its arrival with humility and boldness. Cities are about to be impacted and walls will truly fall.

> *...Joshua said to the people, "Shout, for the LORD has given you the city. Joshua 6:16*

The coming Church is a city-taking Church—and now is the time to shout.

RESOURCES

USB Drive Master Collection

ALL of John's books PLUS MUCH MORE!
OVER **120** RESOURCES!

ORDER TODAY!

JOHNBURTON.NET/USB

BOOKS in printed and ebook format

ORDER TODAY!

JOHNBURTON.NET/RESOURCES

John has written several books that will result in an awakened spirit, passion for revival and a determination to fulfill your calling!

You are sure to be marked by the fire of God as you read!

You can stay connected to the ministry by subscribing to his email updates.JOHNBURTON.NET/SUBSCRIBE.

Invite John to minister on the topics of his books or other key messages by visiting JOHNBURTON.NET/BOOKING.

Made in the USA
Middletown, DE
01 April 2016